Southern Sudan:
Regionalism & Religion

SELECTED ESSAYS

edited by
Mohamed Omer Beshir

GRADUATE COLLEGE PUBLICATIONS
NO 10
UNIVERSITY OF KHARTOUM

First published in 1984 by the Graduate College,
University of Khartoum, PO Box 321
Khartoum Sudan.

General Editor: Mohamed Omer Beshir
Managing Editor: Maureen Makki
Editor of this volume: Mohamed Omer Beshir and
Maureen Makki

Distributed by Ithaca Press 13 Southwark Street London SE
ISBN 0 86372 019 6
Printed & bound in Great Britain by
Biddles Ltd Guildford & King's Lynn

CONTENTS

INTRODUCTION

The seven essays in this volume were originally part
of post-graduate theses submitted for higher degrees in tl
in the University of Khartoum. Each of them was selected
on the basis of relevence to politics, religion and
education in the southern Sudan.

The essay by Rafia Hassan Ahmed deals with the
issues of regionalism, ethnicity and pluralism in
Africa generally with the southern Sudan. Reference is
made to Uganda, Nigeria, the Congo and Ethiopia, in
each of which regional movements have arisen. The process of integration in these and other underdeveloped c
countries has been hindered by various policies and
actions. Colonial policies have been partly responsible for the growth of secessionist movements and policies carried out by national governments after independence have also contributed. Outside intervention,
such as in the case of Nigeria, Congo and southern
Sudan has also payed a part.

The situation in the Sudan which according to this
writer has been:"bedevilled by a very serious north-
south conflict" is a by-product of many factors: geographical, social and cultural. Colonial administrative
policies and the attitudes of national politicians and
parties including the role of the southerners themselves, especially their educated elite!

The resolution of the conflict in the southern
Sudan is the subject of the second essay by Kamal El
Din Osman Salih. The first part of the essay deals with
the Nigeria-Biafra conflict. The way the Biafran

conflict was settled is dealt with in detail. The rigid attitude of the Biafran leadership towards a peaceful settlement is blamed for the prolongation of the war and the many deaths as a result. The prospects of peaceful settlement in the Sudan became real when Nimeiri came to power in May 1969. The regime realized from the beginning that a military solution was not possible. Details of the peace negotiations are given. The consequences of the settlement reached in the case of the southern Sudan bore out of the realization by the two conflicting parties that they could not achieve their goals through military means. The same can not be said about the Nigerians and the Biafrans.

The third and fourth essays by Damazo Dut Majok and Elias Wakoson respectively, deal with the issues of resistance. Majok's essay deals with resistance in the southern Sudan which started in 1902 among the Agar in Bahr al Ghazal. The Agar have been long known for their opposition to encroachment whether from inside or outside. The other group also known for their hostility to foreigners were the Zande. Their resistance to the British started in 1905. The third group who resisted British rule were the Fertit.

Resistance by these and other groups continued in the southern Sudan, especially in Bahr el Ghazal and among the Nuer, for a long time. It went on until after the First World War. This has no doubt affected life in the southern Sudan. Of special interest and significance is the resistance put up in 1920 by Ariathdit - the Malual Dinka. He is described as a man who hated the government - any government - and also a charismatic and popular local leader. He was supported by Muslim traders. Dinka resistance has been dealt with by Lazarus Leek Mawut in his "Dinka Resistance to

Condominium Rule 1902-1932" also published by the
(Graduate College, University of Khartoum).

The other essay by Elias Nymleel Wakoson deals
with the Anya-Nya movement and resistance. The essay
examines the origin and development of the Anya-Nya
movement in the southern Sudan. The Anya-Nya unlike
other similar movements in Africa, had no ideology
except that of liberating the southern Sudan from the
dominance of the north. The organization of the Anya-
Nya, its revolutionary policies and its activities are
dealt with in great detail. I do not know of any other
written reference where the Anya-Nya movement has been
described in this detail. The essay is by no means
a study of the Anya-Nya only. It also deals with the
political parties in both the northern and southern
Sudan and their attitude to the civil war and handling
of the people of the southern Sudan. He makes it clear
that both adopted a position of bargaining. The strategy of the moderate southern parties for example was
"to start from one extreme bargaining position and
then settle for a more moderate one, i.e. to start by
demanding full independence for the South but accepting a federal status". I do not agree that the others
described as extremists stood for separation. They
also bargained. It is true that there were diverse
views but they all stood for a special status for the
south in "one Sudan". It is significant that the
arrangements suggested in 1965 were the same as those
outlined in the Southern Sudan Regional Self-Government Act of 1972.

The northern parties on the other hand stood all
along against a federal status in the classical sense.
They were always against any suggestion which at any
time could lead to separation. Perhaps the main failure

of the northern political leadership was its inability
to recognize the diversity, respect it and suggest
appropriate structures. This failure no doubt was responsible for the acceleration of the war at the time.

The following three essays deal with religion in
the southern Sudan. The first by Philip Chol Biowel.
"The Christian Church in the southern Sudan before 1900"
It is true that the missionaries were unable to penetrate deep in the south before 1871 as a result of the
hostility of local communities and the obstacles aris-
ing from government policies. But these were not the
only reasons. I think the absence of a properly studied
plan based on knowledge of the environment and the communities has been largely responsible for their failure
to achieve what they set out to do. The Catholic missionaries are perhaps an exception to this. The verona
Fathers guided by the education policies set out by
Daniel Comboni were able to do better than the Angli-
cans.

The latter, we should remember were part of the
establishment, the government in Khartoum.

Bahr el-Ghazal, as far as religion was concerned,
presented a special problem from the beginning. As
Damazo Dutt Majok puts it, Islam unlike Christianity
was not a newcomer. Islam has long been there especially among the smaller, numerous non- Nilotic groups. It
was among these groups that the slave traders, agents
of Islamization among other things, were most active.
The Mahdists too contributed to the process of Islamization through the friendly relations they established with the local people, especially the Nilotics. The
British administration was not happy with a situation
in which Islam was spreading at a fast rate. This fear
led the administration not to establish schools.

When the missionaries were allowed to function
they also encountered many difficulties. This time
from local population who were in the final analysis,
hostile to foreigners.

Although the amount of research relevent to ethnicity and cultural diversity and similar topics in the
continent of Africa and the Sudan in particular has
increased significantly during the last few years, the
number of publications by Sudanese in these fields has
been relatively few. Contributions by non-Sudanese
have been relied upon for source material. It is time
that research by indigenous scholars be better known
and appreciated. These essays are a significant contribution towards that objective.

Mohamed Omer Beshir

June 1984

LIST OF CONTRIBUTORS

Mohamed Omer Beshir: Professor of African History,
   Institute of African and Asian Studies, University
   of Khartoum

Rafia Hassan Ahmed: Lecturer, Sudan Academy of Administration.

Kamal El Din Osman Salih: Teaching Assistant, Department of Political Science, Faculty of Economic and
   Social Studies, University of Khartoum.

Damazo Dut Majok: University of Juba.

Elias Wakoson: Lecturer, Department of Political
   Science, Faculty of Economic and Social Studies,
   University of Khartoum.

Philip Chol Biowel: Regional Ministry of Cooperation
   and Rural Development, Juba.

Sir El Khatim Mohamed Sid Ahmed: ex-Editor Sudanow,
   presently working as a journalist in Saudi Arabia.

REGIONALISIM, ETHNIC AND SOCIO–CULTURAL PLURALISM THE CASE OF THE SOUTHERN SUDAN

By Rafia Hassan Ahmed

The term 'region' denotes a geographical area which possesses either particular characteristics that distinguish it from adjacent areas, or which serves as a unit of government, administration or state. These characteristics can be ethnic, cultural, religious, industrial, economic, political, climatic or topographic[1]. Regionalism as an administrative practice, governmental plan, supranational arrangement or political movement always depends upon some or all of these characteristics. As an administrative practice the term reflects the recognition of actual developments in public administration or public planning which occur in a certain region. It may be recognition of the existence of administrative areas such as districts, counties or provinces within a state and the assignment to these areas of powers and functions intermediate between those exercised by the central government and local governing bodies. As a 'governmental plan', regionalism may be a political structure in which the region enjoys functional autonomy within an integrated or a united state.

Supranational or international regionalism refers to units which embrace more than one state for the purpose of serving common interests; it is the grouping together of separated and often adjoining states for

---

1. P.J.O. Self, "Region" in J. Gould and W.L. Kelb (eds) A dictionary of the Social Sciences (London: Tavistock Publications, 1964), pp. 682-3.

concentrated action on specific objectives. Examples
of international regionalism include the Arab League,
the defence union of Arab Republics comprising Egypt,
Lybia and Syria, the former East African Federation
and the former West African Federation and the former
West African Federation of Ghana, Guinea and Mali. Other
examples are also found in larger continental and regional organisations such as the Organization of African
Unity, the European Economic Community, the North Atlant-
ic Treaty Organization, the South East Asian Treaty
Organization and the Warsaw Powers Treaty. Supranational
regionalism offers opportunities for stronger economic,
political or military roles. Even in the colonial era
France established similar groups in French Equatorial
Africa and French West Africa as a device to cope with,
and cater for, financial and economic problems stemming
from administering such vast territories.

Intranational regionalism is of comparatively recent
origin and has not yet acquired a generally accepted and
precise political definition however, it may be defined
generally as a cultural and political movement seeking
to protect and foster indigenous culture and to promote
autonomous political institutions in a particular region.
As a cultural movement it emerges from the cultural,
economic and historical factors to the extent that distinct political consciousness of a separate identity
and the desirability of autonomous planning and administrative freedom develop among the elite of the region.
Carter defines intranational regionalism thus: 'Intranational regionalism refers to those divisions within
a state that are sufficiently self- conscious to command

ious to command local loyalty'.[1]

In view of the fact that significant regional
differences exist in most underdeveloped states,
especially in Africa, because bounderies have been
arbitrarily drawn by the colonial powers intranational
regionalism has been a common phenomenon in these
countries. Conscious national loyalty and political
maturity are still lacking. Most countries are still
in the process of seeking ways and means of minimiz-
ing tribal differences and creating larger national
allegiances. However, political leaders tend to approach
problems of nation-building in a subjective manner
that continue to serve personal aspirations and interests rather than those of the whole society. They tend
to move towards more centralization to secure their
power position and to neglect strong local or regional
loyalties and expectations. Intranational regionalism
in any society is the result of socio-cultural pluralism, whether ethnic, cultural or religious. Unequal
social, economic and political developments in different parts of the same state frequently lead to intranational regionalism.

In the new states of Africa, on the whole, intranational regionalism has tended to reflect the colonial
heritage, although this tendency has been relatively
weak in former French colonies mainly because of the
considerable centralisation of French colonial administration which limited the power and prestige of
traditional chiefs and used them as appointed local
civil servants with very specific responsibilities.

---

2. G.M. Carter, "Introduction" in G. Carter (ed.),
    National Unity and Regionalism in Eight African
    States (Ithaca, New York, Cornell University Press,
    1966), p. 1.

Unlike the French, the British administration depended heavily on an indirect self-rule policy which enhanced tribalism and socio-cultural diversities in their colonies. Thus intranational regionalism became a common post-independence phenomenon in former British colonial territories.

There are two types of intranational regionalism: One seeking self-identification within the framework of an integrated state, and the other seeking complete separation (secession). Even so the two are closely related and interdependent; the first may be a step towards the second. On the other hand, the secession-ist movement may be solved through recognition of self-identification, e.g. regional autonomy or federation, if an agreement between the leaders of a secessionist movement and state authorities can be reached. As a matter of fact most secessionist movements have not ended in complete separation or independence.

The focus of this study is intranational regional-ism, which seeks self-identification within an in-tegrated state. Such a movement, which may be cultural and political, is in most cases supported by military activities. It may reflect secessionist tendencies at a certain stage of its development but ultimately can be solved through political and administrative arrange-ments which may be federation or a form of autonomous self-rule. These characteristics are true of many African intranational regional movements such as the Katanga movement in Congo, the movement of Buganda, Bunyoro and Ankolo in Uganda and the Biafra movement in Nigeria. The case of southern Sudan, which is the concern of this study, is a clear example of intrana-tional regionalism.

Implications for regional government

Intranational regional movements reflect common problems in underdeveloped states, ethnic, religious and socio-cultural pluralism, regional loyalties, lack of national integration and secessionist tendencies being the most common.

Pluralism refers to sharp cleavages between different human groups within the same state. According to Smith, pluralism 'is a social structure characterized by fundamental discontinuities and cleavages and a cultural complex based on systematic institutional diversities'[3] Most societies have the above mentioned characteristics of pluralism in either a mild or a strong form. Pluralism in European societies has been eroded by national consciousness and progressive national integration. The case is different in underdeveloped states where the concept of one national identity has not yet been accepted by different groups occupying the same state. Intranational regional movements are, to a great extent, responsible for the continuity of these diversities in most of the underdeveloped states, despite the fact that the movements themselves are the by-products of these diversities. Uganda, Nigeria, Congo, Chad, Ethiopia and Sudan are African states which continue to exist because of intranational regional movements.

In Uganda ethnic pluralism can be traced back to the period prior to independence. Before the British could establish their colonial administration, the area now known as Uganda had a continuous history of tribal migration, warfare and even diplomatic and com-

---

3.   M.G. Smith, "Introduction" in L. Kuper and M.G. Smith (eds), Pluralism in Africa (Berkeley and Los Angeles, University of California Press, 1969), p.2.

mercial relations with other areas; and came to include
many diverse ethnic and cultural groups. There were
the kingdoms of Buganda, Ankole, Bunyoro and Toro, the
federal territory of Busoga and the districts of Acholi,
Bugisu, Bukedi, Karamoja, Kigozi, Lango, Madi, Sebei,
Toso and West Nile. From 1894 when Buganda became
a British protectorate separation and centralism inter-
acted upon each other continuously till 1962 when the
whole country moved to independence. These kingdoms
and districts included many tribes and different
groups. The population of each of them consisted mainly of one tribe or closely related tribes with some
European and Asian minorities. A number of Bantu tribes
which live in southern Uganda are separated by Lakes
Albert and Kyoga from the Nilotic, Nilo-Hamitic and
Sudanic tribes of the northern area. Language, Physical appearence and social organization mark the major
distinctions between the ethnic and linguistic groups
occupying Uganda. Buganda has a population twice that
of any of the others.

Religious pluralism is also prevalent in Uganda.
About 34% of the population are Catholic, 28% Protestant, 5% Muslim and the rest pagan. Among the Buganda
the number of Catholics and Protestants are almost
equal. However, many other tribes have preponderantly
adopted one religion or another. Muslims constitute
a significant minority in Busoga, West Nile and the
Buganda tribes. Tribal traditions, norms, values,
religion, language and education give different tribes
distinct cultural modes which in turn have created
a general socio-cultural pluralism all over Uganda.
Political and cultural regional movements in Buganda
as early as 1900 and in the regions of Ankolo, Bunyoro,
Toro and Busoga enhanced and aggravated ethnic,

religious and socio-cultural pluralism.

Nigeria is another example of ethnic and socio-cultural pluralism. There are 8 major ethnic groups accounting for more than 72% of the total population of Nigeria. The Hausa, Ibo and Yoruba, which are the biggest and most influential, account together for about 50% of the total population, and each dominates a certain geographical region. The Hausa occupy the northern half of Nigeria and, with a total number of over ten million persons, is the single largest ethnic group. The basic social unit is the extended family; descent is invariably patrilocal. Inheritance is mainly through the male and is based on the principle that family property must be maintained at the highest possible level. The Ibos, on the other hand, are the most numerous ethnic group in the south eastern forested zone of the country. They are generally homogeneous in language , culture and social structure. Their basic social unit, descent and marriage are similar to those of the Hausa. The Yoruba, who occupy south-western Nigeria, the third major ethnic group, consist of loosely related chiefdoms which claim common descent and a common centre of dispersion. Their principal social unit is the extended family. There are complex kinship relations and territorial groupings.

There is deep social and cultural pluralism among these three major ethnic groups. Although in Nigeria nearly 250 distinct languages are spoken, there are three large linguistic groups, namely Hausa, Ibo and Yoruba which correspond with basic variations in culture, traditions and customs, religious affiliation and social organisation.

The Hausa are predominantly Muslim and Islamic teaching, values and norms dominate social life and

culture. Through the Arabic language they are culturally linked to North Africa. The Ibos were formerly largely
pagan, but recently Christianity has made numerous converts among them. The Yoruba are the least homogeneous in
terms of religious belief, while there is a strong sub-
stratum of pagans, most Yoruba are either Muslim or
Christian, with a large body of adherents belonging to
all denominations and sects.

The first government of independent Nigeria, which
came to power in December 1959, was a coalition of the
three major regional parties, namely the Northern People's
Congress (N.P.C.) dominated by the Fulani-Hausa tribes,
the National Council of Nigeria and the Cameroons (N.C.
N.C.) dominated by the Ibo tribe in eastern Nigeria and
Action Group Party of western Nigeria under the control
of the Yoruba. This indicates that ethnic, religious and
socio-cultural pluralism among the major Nigerian tribes
has developed into an intranational regional movement,
which in turn, is the result of pluralism.

The Congo is a further example of pluralism in underdeveloped states. The earliest distinct racial group in
the Congo are the Pygmies. The rest of the Congo people
are Bantu who occupy lower and middle Congo, Katanga,
Kasei, Kankuru and Lake Leopold II. Besides the Pygmies
and the Bantu, there are the Nilotics, a mixture of
Negroid and Caucasian ancestry.

The tribal groupings of the Congo exhibit great
variations in modes of life and culture. the pygmies
depend on food-gathering and hunting while the Bantu
combine crop cultivation, hunting, fishing and animal
husbandry. According to the anthropological concept of
culture clusters, the Congolese can be classified into
many different cultural groups. They formed ancient

kingdoms and each of them inhabited a certain area and included a number of tribes. This shows the historic depth of diversity in culture and traditional ethnic organizations.

Linguistic diversity also exists in the Congo which can be divided into two major linguistic regions. The Bantu languages of the south, which Joseph Greenberg calls Niger-Congo and the non-Bantu languages of the north, which he terms Macro-Sudanic. To solve the problem of linguistic diversity, all Congolese speak four trade languages as second languages; Kiswahili in the east, Kikongo in the west, Cliluba in the south and Liugala in the north.

The pre-independence Congo was heavily missionized especially by Catholic missions. The country was divided into thirty-four ecclesiastic territories with a high representative, an Apostolic delegate, who resided in Leopoldville, about thirty different missionary orders of Catholic and about forty-seven European and American protestant denominations, of which all but four were non-Belgian.

The Katanga region of southern Congo is the richest part of A f r i c a in mineral wealth. There the Conakat party was formed in 1959 under the leadership of Tshombe of the Lunda tribe. This party led the intranational political movement which ultimately led to Katangan secession on 11th July 1960, only two weeks after the Congo had achieved independence. The Katanga regional movement was an expression of indigenous nationalist sentiment. Secession was designed to preserve the wealth of the region and to advance the interests of Tshombe and his political supporters. No doubt the intranational regional movement of Katanga had great adverse implications on the unity and pros-

perity of the Congo. It encouraged ethnic superiority
and distinction in the Lunda tribe in both the region
and the country at large. Socio-cultural pluralism was
also increased by other political disturbances and
uprisings.[4]

In the case of Ethiopia, the situation is rather
different because it was the annexation of Eritrea by
the Ethiopian Empire that created an intranational
regional movement. The people of Ethiopia are believed
to be an intermixture of the Hamitic people of the
highlands and Semitic immigrants from Arabia. The
present twenty-five million Ethiopian population is
divided into many groups and tribes, the most influential of which, though not the most numerous ethnic group,
is the Amhara of the central highlands. North of them
are the Tigre, while southern Ethiopia is occupied by
the Gallas who constitute the most numerous group in
Ethiopia. There are also the nomadic Danakili who
regularly move across the border between the Ethiopian
Ogaden Province and the Somali Republic. Most of the
people of the Eritrian region are either Tigre or
Danakili. Religiously, Ethiopia is also a plural society with Christians, Muslims and pagans.

There are also socio-cultural collectivities
which make Ethiopia even more pluralistic. The major
linguistic groups are Semitic, Cushitic or Hamitic and
Nilotic. The most important semitic language is Amharic,
because it is spoken by from 35-50% of the population
although the Amhara account for about 25%. Tigrinya is
perhaps as important as Amharic because it is not only
spoken by the Tigre of Ethiopia but also by a great

---

4. K. Nkrumah, Challenge of the Congo, (London: Thomas
   and Sons Ltd., 1967), pp.66-8.

number of other Ethiopians as well as the Tigre in the
highlands of Eritrea. The Cushitic group comprises those
who speak the Galla, Somali and Sidamo languages. The
majority of Muslims who live along the Red Sea are not
Arabic speakers but retain their own languages such as
Tigrainya or Danakili. Even so Arabic is widely spoken
and used in commerce.

Besides all these discrepancies, the federation of
Eritrea with Ethiopia in 1952 accentuated pluralism in
all fields, especially politics. In 1962 after continuous pressure from the Ethiopian Government, the Eritrean
Assembly accepted the termination of Eritrea's autonomy
and eventually Eritrea became the fourteenth province of
Ethiopia. In fact Eritrea had sufficient political power
to make concessions by the federal government necessary.
The authorities in Addis Ababa were well aware that if
allowed continued autonomy Eritrea could pose a serious
threat to the set-up of the entire country, since other
important minorities such as the Gallas and the Somalis
might demand similar rights. Ironically enough, it was
in the closing year of the federation that a political
regional movement started to grow in Eritrea, partly
because of Addis Ababa's efforts to crush the federation
and partly because of workers' discontent with the deter-
iorating economic situation. The Eritrea Liberation Front
came into being to lead the intranational regional movement. Opposition to the Addis Ababa government was particularly strong among Muslims of western Eritrea where the
ELF. gained its first recruits and secured its initial
success. The Muslims were markedly hostile to the idea
of a Christian dominated government. These examples show
that intranational regional movements stem from ethnic,
religious and socio-cultural pluralism.

Another problem facing the newly developing states,
included in our four examples is a lack of national
integration and national unity. The concept of 'national
integration' is of recent use in politics, proposed
mainly by those who are interested in the phenomena of
'socio-cultural pluralism' and regionalism. The term
is used interchangeably with the term 'nation building'.
The process of national integration involves a continued cohesive national consciousness and attitudes,
shared national values and common national loyalties,
all of which would lead to real and concrete national
unity. Mazrui envisages the process of national integration as:

> ...partialization of group identities as the
> tribes of communities lose their coherence as
> a distinct system of life. But the process
> of national integration is not only the part-
> ialization of the old affiliations, but of
> course it is also a quest for a new kind of
> total identity. Success comes when partially
> evolved group-personalities coalesce to form
> a new national entity.[5]

So Mazrui thinks that through solving conflicts between
coherent tribal groups, the integrative process moves
from a stage of ethnic distinctiveness to strong
national unity. It is the cumulative experience of
conflict solution which increases the degree of integration in a given society. Conversely, unsolved conflicts create a situation of potential disintegration.
So one can argue that internal conflict within a country
is inherently disintegrative, yet, paradoxically, no
national integration is possible without internal

---

5. A. A. Mazrui, "Pluralism and National Integration",
    in L. Kuper and M.G. Smith (eds.), op. cit., p.335.

conflict. The paradox arises because while conflict itself has a propensity to force dissolution, the solution of conflicts is an essential mechanism of integration. It is the cumulative experience of solving conflicts that sharpens the capacity to discover areas of mutual compatibility on subsequent occasions of tension. Another factor which makes conflict solution possible is the awareness of reciprocal dependence especially in the field of economic development. A shared ideology may also encourage conflict resolution in a certain society; the most basic ideology for national integration is the ideology of nationalism and national consciousness.[6]

Weiner defines 'national integration' as 'the process of bringing together culturally and socially discrete groups into a single territorial unit and the establishment of a national identity in the context of a plural society'.[7] Coleman and Resberg view national integration as comprising political integration, i.e. 'the progressive bridging of the elite-mass gap on the vertical plane in the course of developing an integrated political process and participant community, and territorial integration or the progressive reduction of cultural and regional tensions and discontinuities on the horisontal plane in the process of creating

---

6. Ibid., pp 335-336.

7. M. Weiner, "Political Integration and Political Development" in The Annuals of American Academy of Politics and Social Sciences, (Philadelphia: No. 358, March, 1965), p. 53.

a homogeneous territorial community'.[8]

Loiria observes that these developmental lines
are only analytically distinct because the means of
achievement overlap in practice; the achievement of
territorial integration requires a continuous process
of creating an ordered society and pursuing a general
but uniform pattern of political education, and the
various modes of socialization which would bridge the
elite-mass gap. Territorial and political integration
require an effective territorial control by the central,
political, administrative and military authorities and
a uniform and constant process of cultural and political education.[9]

Geertz defines the concept within the context of
new nations by stating that it is the aggregation of
independently defined, specifically outlined traditional groups into larger, more diffuse units whose implicit
frame of reference is not the local sense but the
'nation' in the sense of the whole society encompassed
by the new civil state.[10] A recent critical appraisal

---

8.   J.S. Coleman and C.G. Resberg, "Introduction" in
     J.S. Coleman and C.G. Resberg (eds.), Political
     Parties and National Integration in Tropical Africa.
     (Berkeley and Los Angeles: University of California
     Press, 1964), pp. 8-9.

9.   A.L. Loiria, 'Political Awakening in Southern Sudan
     1946-1955: Decolonization and the Problem of Nation-
     al Integration', Unpublished Ph.D. thesis, (Los Angeles,
     University of California 1969) p. 5.

10. C. Geertz, "The Integrative Revolution: Primordial
     Sentiments and Civil Policies in New States" In
     Geertz (ed.) Old Societies and New States: The
     Quest for Modernity in Asia and Africa, (London:
     The Press of Clencee) pp. 105-7.

of the theoretical implication of the concept has been
made by Sklar who tried to show the relevance of class
conflict in solving the problems of the integrative
process in Africa. He believes in a radical analysis
which emphasises the revolutionary possibilities of
change.[11] All these definitions of the concept "national integration" characterise it as a process leading
to the building of new national allegiances and attitudes among diverse groups of people who have been
grouped together by the same political boundaries.

Has the integrative process, in the sense which
has been described, been working in the newly developing countries? No doubt the progressive development of
the national integration process has been hindered by
many problems, the major of which is the intranational
regional movement. One of the manifestations of this
situation is the continuity of the identities of the
plural groups as pointed out above. As a result of
the dominance of these diverse groups a lack of
national consciousness and progressive political and
territorial integrative process arises and regional
loyalties develop as counter demands to national loyalties. The two loyalties conflict because the first is
limited to regional issues while the second helps to
establish a state-national allegiance. The difficulty
of creating this national allegiance is the unwilling-
ness or inability of an individual or a group to feel
part of the nation-state.

---

11. R.L. Sklar, "Political Science and National In-
     tegration a Radical Approach", in The Journal of
     Modern African Studies, Volume, 5 No. 1, 1967
     (London: Cambridge University Press), pp. 1-11.

Connected with regional loyalties are regional and sometimes tribal parties which have been created by intranational regionalism. Political parties are important in creating national unity because national parties are usually formed to solve parochial problems by cutting across different groups, reflecting national goals and common participation and aspiring to bring about national consciousness, which would lead to national integration and national unity. But intranational regionalism hinders these national parties from holding regional particularities in check by allowing regional and tribal parties to spring up. Many examples of such parties are found in African states. In Uganda there was the Kabbaka Yekka in Buganda region; in Nigeria there were the N.P.C., N.C.N.C., and A.G.P. in the northern, eastern and western regions respectively; in the Congo the Konakat party dominated the Katanga region. All these regional parties were dominated by certain tribal groups. In Ethiopia the E.L.P., most of whose members are Muslim, dominates Eritrea. Because of these regional and tribal parties, national consciousness has been weak and progress towards national integration has been very slow. Secessionist movements, which are politically and sometimes militarily organised, are the most serious problem in intranational regionalism.

Colonial policy in some instances led to situations which encouraged later secessionist movements. The colonial practice of having special arrangements for dissident groups in colonized countries resulted in serious limitations which ultimately came to slow down the process of national integration. Buganda was indirectly and separately ruled by the British. The Belgians encouraged the separation of the Katangese

from the Congo. Biafra was directly ruled by the
British while the largest part of Nigeria was ruled
indirectly. Eritrea had first been ruled separately
by the Italians before its annexation to the Ethiopian
Empire. The Kurds and the Armenians in the Middle East
were also treated separately for centuries.

Following Shepherd's opinion that national unity
and internal stability are, in a large measure, determined by the presence of national consensus and public
order, one realizes that secessionist movements can
hardly allow such goals to be achieved. National consensus is used here to refer to the process of developing a sense of common loyalty to national values,
institutions and policies. Public order, on the other
hand, comprises the processes of law-making and its
enforcement. [12] In this respect intranational regional
movements not only hinder the achievement of national
consensus but also seriously undermine public order.
The military activities of the Biafra secessionist
movement, the killing and disturbances that took place
during the Katanga movement in Congo, and the destruction and killings done by Eritrean guerrillas are all
such examples. These incidents created havoc with
internal peace and socio-economic development. They
led to serious political instability which adversely
affected national integration. Still more seriously,
secessionist movements tended to create situations
that endangered the sovereignty of the state itself.
They frequently induced other foreign states, and in

12.   G.W. Shepherd, "National Integration and the
      Southern Sudan" in The Journal of Modern African
      Studies, Volume 4, 1966, No. 2. (London: Cambridge
      University Press), pp. 193-4.

some instances regional or international organizations,
to intervene either to put down the secession or to
help it. In fact nowadays no political struggle which
leads to armed conflict can be considered merely domestic.

The national era, in which the internal affairs
of a nation would on no account be considered the
business of any person or group outside the nation, is,
if not quite dead, shrinking considerably. The international community has seen too much of the havoc which
the internal politics of a state can inflict on the
world beyond its borders. and too much of the inhuman-
ity which may be perpetrated within its borders under
the notion of national sovereignty, to regard all
situations of internal conflict as domestic affairs.
International and regional organizations such as the
United Nations and the Organization of African Unity
can intervene with the intention of putting an end to
secessionist movements due to that world concept of
peace and by that providing humanitarian relief through
reducing the magnitude of killing. Sometimes their
intervention gives the conflicting parties an opportunity to make rational inquiry into the cause of secession.

On the other hand, there is what we call 'other
states' intervention. In all cases the intervening
states are either friends of, previous colonizers of,
or hostile to the concerned states. In the former
case they aim at promoting internal unity while in the
latter they seek to hamper this unity through helping
secessionist movements. Examples of the latter include
the turmoil of Katanga in which the Belgians had an
upper hand, Israeli and French intervention in Biafra,
British support of the Nagas movement in India and

Dutch support for the Ambonese revolt in Indonesia.
Such support, in whatever form it may be, is secretly
given and the accused states in most cases deny comp-
licity.

Foreign intrigues led to considerable political
and socio-economic instability in the concerned states,
hindered the process of national integration, and
fostered intranational regionalism in them. In turn,
strong secessionist movements have encouraged and
induced other ethnic and regional minority groups in
the same state or states to follow the same line. This
is particularly true in Africa where in most countries
circumstances exist which can easily develop into intranational regionalism. The best examples are the movements of Bunyoro, Ankolo, Toro and Busoga which followed
the Buganda intranational regional movement, the eastern rebellions of 1963 and 1964 which followed in the
steps of the 1960 Katanga movement in Congo, and the
development of the Somali group in Ethiopia, influenced
by the Eritrean movement, into a regional political
movement.

Because of the adverse consequences which intranational political regional movements and secessionist
tendencies inflict upon national unity, various political methods have been applied in search of a solution
including decentralization, federation, home-rule or
self-rule (regional autonomy). Although all these
devices have some common characteristics and implications, we are mainly concerned here with regional
government or regional autonomy.

Regional government is used by unitary states to
solve the problems of their minority groups. It means
the devolution of certain governmental powers from the
centre to the region, this devolution of powers can be

in the field of legislation, execution or administration, i.e. political devolution or administrative
devolution. The scope of these powers is determined
by agreement between the region and the centre, but in
all cases central government has the say whether in
the devolution of powers or in changing these powers.
Autonomy implies a group relationship not with a coordinate social body but rather with a more inclusive
power to which it is subordinate or which demands its
subordination. In fact it is an agent of the central
government. There is no rigidity of division of power
i.e. the powers of the region and those of the centre
cannot be written into a constitution and may be
revised from time to time. Sometimes the initiative
for regional government emerges from the central
government itself, this is particularly true of the
imperial states of large territorial compass, or of
multi-national communities. It is also applied by
states which have failed to induce interest in the
continued maintenance of state union on some parts of
their frontiers, especially outlying or ethnically
alien regions. Such regional autonomy arrangements
may be incorporated organically in the prevailing
structure of the state, or may be exceptional arrangements. The latter takes place because of the unique
or special position of the region given regional autonomy.

The case of the Sudan

Sudan is geographically the largest independent
state in Africa, with an area of approximately one
million square miles. Because of its mid-way position
between the Arab World and Africa, Islamic religion
and Arabic culture exist besides African culture.

During Anglo-Egyption rule Christianity began to spread
in the south, especially among educated southerners.
Ethnic, tribal, religious and socio-cultural pluralism
dominate Sudanese society. The five hundred and seventy-
two tribes are strongly based on major ethnic units in
different regions and provinces. In each region there
is one major ethnic group dominating the others, i.e.
the Arabs in Blue Nile, Khartoum, Kordofan, Northern
and Kassala Provinces, the Fur in Darfur Province, the
Nilotics in Bahr el Ghazal and Upper Nile Provinces
and the Nilo-Hamites in Equatoria Province.

Furthermore, the Sudan is bedeviled by a very
serious "north-south" conflict of intranational regionalism between the predominantly Islamic and Arabic-
speaking northern Sudanese majority and the medley of
ethnolinguistic groups of the southern Sudanese minority, led by a western-educated Christian elite. This
problem of regionalism between the north and the south
involves, among other things, differences in socio-
cultural institutions, different historical experience,
numerical imbalance and educational, technical, economic and political inequalities.[13] It is a by-product
of many factors, geographical, social and cultural,
colonial administrative policies and the attitudes of
national politicians and parties, including the role
of the southerners themselves, especially their educated elite. The role of the British administration in
exacerbating the problem was remarkable. However, during
the armed conflict between the two parts of the country
other foreign states, such as Israel and West Germany,
intervened to help the southern political movement. At
first the conflict started as a political intranational

---

13. Loiria, op. cit., p. 5.

regional movement but the failure of post-independence
governments to find a solution pushed the movement
into a new phase, the climax of which occurred during
the first military regime which used force as a solution to conflict. The approaches of all Sudanese
political circles to the problem failed because of
lack of unity and consensus among them. Important
among these were southern intellectuals and southern
politicians, who in most cases had no clarity of vision,
directive, purpose or specific programmes for economic,
social and cultural development in the south and,
above all, the ability to suggest effective devices
for the solution of the problem. Consequently, since
independence the intranational regional problem of
southern Sudan has seriously hampered national integration and created many subsequent problems.

Afro Arab multiplicity in the Sudan

The Republic of the Sudan, like most African territories, is a political but not an ethnological unit.
Although it resembles most African states, particularly those in the Sudanic belt, in its environment,
achievements, problems and potentialities, it is still
unique among them. It differs from them in being a
bridge between Arab Africa and Negro Africa. This
relatively unique meeting point of Arabism and Africanism, which is a result of the geography and history
of the area, is especially conspicuous in the northern region of the country. Initially there was the
phenomenon of racial mixing and intermarriage between
the indigenous negroid groups who used to inhabit the
Sudan and the Arabs or the so-called brown race who
originated in the Arabian Peninsula and migrated to
the Sudan at different times and for different reasons

and motives; so the Arab Sudanese are in fact Arabised
negroes rather than ethnically semitic. The term "Arab"
in reference to racial character cannot be used in the
case of the Sudan; it can be used by anthropologists
in a historical sense referring to those people who
emigrated from Arabia to the Sudan and their descen-
dents and to the indigenous folk who were absorbed
into Arab tribes and adopted their culture. So Arabism
in the Sudan is an acquisition of culture rather than
racial heredity. Mohammed Omer Beshir says in this
respect:

> The true Arabs have always been numerically insig-
> nificant and whenever they settled they intermar-
> ried with the local people whether Nubians, Beja
> or Negroids. The result of all this is the exist-
> ence in the Sudan of today of every conceivable
> degree of admixture between the Brown and the
> Negro and the absence of a culture which can be
> described as purely Arabic and Muslim.[14]

The combination of Arabism and Africanism in the
northern provinces of the Sudan is to a degree and in
a manner unparalleled in any other country. Although
Somalia, Chad, Niger, Mali, Nigeria and Senegal are
all to a greater or lesser degree Islamic and therefore closely connected with the Arab World, none of
them are either wholly or partly Arabic speaking, as
is the case with northern Sudan whose culture is very
much influenced by Islam and Arab culture. Mauretania's
southern regions, in contrast to the southern provinces
of the Sudan, are almost completely Islamized and
Arabized, while its northern region is inseparable

---

14. Mohamed Omer Beshir, The Southern Sudan-Back-
     ground to Conflict (London: C. Hurst and Co.,
     1968), p.5.

from the main body of Maghribi culture and society,
thus it is more of an Arab or North African country
than the Sudan as a whole, or even the northern Islamized and Arabized part of it.[15] According to Mazrui:

> It is therefore the Sudanese more than any other
> group of Arabs that have given the Arabs a deci-
> sive Negro dimension in this racial sense. The
> distinction between Arabs and Negro Africa is not
> dichotomous, but has the complexity of a continu-
> um ... The Sudan has made the biggest single con-
> tribution to the fact that Arabism includes
> a Negro dimension.[16]

By this Mazrui adds a comprehensive and logical continuity to what Abd al-Rahim says. Islam developed an
underlying unity among the northern Sudanese people
and tenuously linked then to the wider community of
the Arab world. Racially they are mainly assimilated
to the indegenous people, but their language, religion
and, to a large extent, their tribal structure, are
superimposed, distinguishing them from the Ethiopians
in the east and their pagan neighbours of western and
southern countries. Despite this degree of cultural
homogenity, ecological diversity, poverty and the
vastness of the country delayed the development of
a closely-woven social unity. From the sixteenth to
the nineteenth centuries a semblance of political

---

15. Muddathir Abd al-Rahim "Arabism, Africanism and
Self-identification in the Sudan" in Yusuf Fadl
Hassan (ed.), <u>Sudan in Africa</u> (Khartoum: University
Press, 1971), p.228.

16. A.A. Mazrui, "The Multiple Marginality of the Sudan"
in Yusuf Fadl Hassan (ed.), op. cit., pp. 242-3.

unity was given to this northern region by the Funj
Kingdom. However, in 1821 the broken kingdom of Sennar
and the whole of northern Sudan was easily captured by
the invading armies of Mohamed Ali.

As for southern Sudan, it witnessed the arrival of
foreign missions and the introduction of non-tribal
administration from Turce-Egyptian rule onwards; but
still it has not been affected by Islamic religion or
Arabic culture. It continues to be an African region
both ethnically and culturally. This is due to many
factors, mainly geographical. The Arabs were unable to
penetrate south because being nomads, they were
accustomed to vast, open areas and not the thick
forests and jungles which constitute the physical
environment of the south. Southern penetration was also
hampered by the Arabs inability to use the river-routes
of the south and to cross the barrier of the sudd.
A further factor is that the inland geographical
position of the south rendered it out of reach of the
type of cultural movement which usually take place
along coasts and near navigable inlets. What is more the
ecological situation of the south is such that it has
retained ethnic southern societies, till recently
there was little intermixing and intermarriage among
them.

So it is not only the racial mixture in the northern region which makes the Sudan an important point of
contact between Arabism and Negroism but also the
division of the country into two segments, a northern
Arabized one and a southern non-Arabized one. This
confirms that the whole Sudan is not quite as Arabized as some people think. On the basis of the 1955-
56 census it was estimated that of the 10.3 million

population of the Sudan about 39% were Arabs, 30% southerners, 13% westerners, 12% Beja and Nuba, 3% Nubians and the rest foreigners and miscellaneous. Using language criteria, 52% are Arabic-speaking and 48% speak other languages.

The Sudan like many emerging states, contains both cultural and social pluralism as a result of the variety of ethnic societies, tribal groups, ecological conditions and historical factors. These different ethnic units[17] and tribes are more or less aware of their origin, ethnicity, history, language, ideological and institutional patterns, ecology and cult,

Some ethnic collectivities in the Sudan are recognized as "tribes" having the characteristics of distinct ethnic units. Thus in northern Sudan, although all Arabs claim Arab descent still there are systems of endogamous connubium which segregate families of clans into closed communities. In southern Sudan also the Dinka, Bari, Nuer, Latuka and Toposa stand as separate communities or tribes which are socially, connubially and territorially closed despite their common language, historical origin and culture.[18] Wider ethnic units which embrace different numbers of tribes also exist. For this reason the population is divided into about 572 tribes whose origin can be classified into 56 ethnic groups. Besides these ethnic and tribal collectivities there are religious sects which almost dominate the northern Sudan.

---

17. Ethnic units refer to those who identify themselves as exclusive ethnic entities having common race (descent) or ethnicity, language, connubium, cult and ethnological conditions.

18. Loiria op.cit., p. 25

Northern Sudan ethnic and socio-cultural pluralism

There are many ethnic and tribal groups in the
northern Sudan. They can generally be classified into
Arabs and non-Arabs on the basis of ethnicity, language,
religion and social modes of attachment. The marginality between the two categories is difficult to draw
because Islamic religion and Arabic culture have affected both of them, however superficial their effect on
the non-Arab category. Moreover, these two categories
geographically overlap and this makes their distinction
less marked. Yet the claim of the first category to
Arab descent and their strong identification with the
Arab World and Islamic religion make possible such
a distinction.

What we call the 'Arabs category' is mainly divided
into two major ethnic groups; the Ja'aliyin and
Juhayna. Besides, there are such groups as the Ashraf,
Rashida and Umayad or Bani Umaya. These groups are not
confined in any geographical or ecological sense. They
are distributed mainly along the Nile as sedentary
cultivators, in the desert and semi-desert areas as
pastoral nomads, and in central Sudan, especially the
Gezira area, as tenants.

They have different social, political and economic
organisations, different patterns of values and orientation all derived from their different ecological conditions which make for heterogenity among the Arabs
of northern Sudan. But superimposed over these local
differences is the ethnic claim among all of them to
have an Arab origin or connection, speak a common
language, Arabic, which is an important cultural
factor of identification and profess Islam as their
religion, with common Islamic institutions, e.g. in
law, connubium and education.

Conventionally the non-Arab category includes the Nubians, the Beja, the Fur, the Nuba and other tribes in southern Funj and Darfur Province. It is difficult to identify most of these as non-Arabs because they have been Arabized and Islamized. Some claim Arab descent and their physiological features are not much different from those of the Arabs. However, the physiological and cultural distinction between the Arabs and the non-Arabs of northern Sudan is not marked. The Nubians have long intermarried with the Arabs and have given birth to such groups as the Kunuz, the Mahas and Jawabira. The Kunuz claim descent from Rabi'a Arab tribe; the Mahas, some of whom have migrated and settled in Khartoum vicinity, claim descent from Juhayna through a certain eponym called Abd al-Aziz Mahasi; the Jawabira claim descent from Jabir Ibn Abd Allah al-Ansari. The Nubians speak a language which is spoken also by the Hill Nuba of Kordofan. The dialects branched from this language include Kunuz, Danagla and Mahas along the Nile, Dair in Kordofan and Midob in Darfur.[19] However, all Nubians are Muslims who use the Arabic language for trade, commerce and education.[20]

The Beja, on the other hand, are pastoralists inhabiting eastern Sudan. The main tribes of the Beja group are Amarar, Busharin, Hadandawa, Bani Amir, Arteiga and Halenga; there are many other tribes, subtribes and families. They have preserved their language which is locally known as Tu-Bidawiya. However, Arabic is increasingly used for religious rituals, external

---

19. G.W. Murray, "The Nilotic Language" in The Journal of the Royal Anthropological Institute. Vol.1, July-Dec.,1920. p.328.

20. Yusuf Fadl Hassan, The Arabs and the Sudan (Edinburgh: University Press, 1967) pp. 142-5; Loiria, op.cit.,

communications, trade and currently in administration and education.[21]

A third group, who have not been completely Arabized and Islamized, are the people of Dar Funj in southern Blue Nile Province. They can be divided into those occupying the plains and those living on the hills. The former have been in close contact with the Arabs and most of them have been converted to Islam and some have been Arabized. But those on the hills are the least affected by Muslim-Arab culture, they live in closed upland communities surrounded by the Arabized Islamized people of the plains. Linguistically and perhaps culturally the peoples of Dar Funj consist of the Gule-speaking groups in Tabi Hills, the Berta and the linguistically related Shilluk, Yakan and Ternasi, the Uduk and Burnu. Generally the degree of Arabization and Islamization decreases from north to south and from plain uphill. However, Arabic is used in administration, education, trade and Islamic rituals, and it is bound to increase in time.[22]

The people of the Nuba Hills are sedentary cultivators, rearing few cattle. Although they live in a common environment they differ ethnically and in local culture and language. They are linguistically grouped into Koalib, Tagali, Talodi, Tumtum and Katla. The tribes of the northern area such as Tagali, some of the Koalib, Dilling, Tira, Moro and Nymmang have been Islamized but their languages, customs and general social

21. A. Paul, A History of the Beja Tribes of the Sudan (London: Cambridge University Press, 1954), p.137.

22. P.M. Holt, A Modern History of the Sudan (London: Weidenfeld and Nicolson, 1961), p.22; Loiria op.cit., pp.50-51.

structures have not been transformed. In fact the
Muslim-Arab influence is still partial, incomplete and
unequally distributed in the Nuba Hills.[23]

Southern Sudan ethnic and socio-cultural pluralism

In the southern Sudan differences of ethnicity,
language and other socio-cultural institutions correspond with the various collectivities known as "tribes".
The term "tribe" here refers to an ethnic category of
people, e.g. Azande, Shilluk, Nuba, who are aware,
often vaguely, of a common historical origin and that
they are culturally different from all other groups
around them. They have a common language, marriage
system, cults and other institutions. Although it is
difficult to classify and survey the ethnic categories
of southern Sudan because of their plurality and diversity, it is possible to use linguistic classification
to analyse the various ethnic categories.[24] Linguistic
classification does not necessarily indicate that an
ethnic group is also culturally and institutionally
homogeneous. This is particularly true in the case of

---

23. Barbour op. cit. pp.172-4; Loiria, op. cit.,

24. There are other classifications such as that used
    by Seligman and Morrison but they are out-dated
    and rather confusing because they combine racial
    and geographical criteria; See C. Morrison, The
    Southern Sudan and Eritrea: Aspects of Wider African
    Problems (London: Report No. 5, M.R.G. 36, Gravan Street,
    1971), pp.6-7, B.S. Seligman, Pagan Tribes of the
    Nilotic Sudan, (London; George Routledge and Sons
    Ltd., 1932). A more recent and neutral linguistic
    classification is used by Greenberg, Stevenson and
    Loiria. See Stevenson, op. cit., p.54.

the wide categories. The tribes of southern Sudan fall
into two broad linguistic categories: the eastern Sudanic comprises, as sub-families, the eastern Nilotic, the
Murle-Didinga (including the Didinga, Longarim and Murle)
and the western Nilotic. The central Sudanic family includes the sub-categories of the Bongo-speakers, the
Kreish, Moru Madi, the Azande and related tribes and the
Ndogo-speaking tribes.

The eastern Nilotic tribes claim to have come from
the south-east. A claim supported by generic linguistic
affinities which suggest either a common ethnic origin
or a prior geographical contiguity. Members of this sub-
category, who are all acephalous in socio-political organization, consist of such representative groups as the
Toposa, Lotuho, Bari and other related tribes. The unity
of these tribes is based on tribal allegiance, identity
and internal peace. Tribal conflicts are dealt with according to recognized patterns of political, judicial and
ritual purification. There are few contacts beyond the
tribe or tribal land; they are hostile people who live
further afield, including those culturally related to
them but vaguely recognized.[25]

The Lotuho-speaking groups are culturally, linguistically, institutionally and organizationally related. The
major groups comprise Latuho, Heriek, Lopit, Lekeya,
Lange, Dengetene and Logir. These groups have developed
individuality and independence as a result of the in-
adequacy of communication and lack of abundant cultiva-
ble and pastoral land. Though not politically united,
the whole of the Lotuho tribe is divided into six major
clans each of which has descended from a common epony-
mous ancestor. The Lotuho claim to have come from the

---

25. Loiria, op. cit., p.55

east while the Toposa are from north-eastern Uganda.[26]

The Bari is an influential tribe in the southern region and dominates the minor tribes speaking the same language. The Bari-speaking tribes of Pojulu, Kakwa, Nyepu, Nyangwara and Kuku mostly live on the western bank of the river and the Mandari around Mangala and Tali. The Bari tribe and Bari-speaking groups seem to have one ethnic origin through common name, language, customs, culture, religious beliefs and institutional practices. Despite this cultural and linguistic unity each of these tribes has its exclusive identity as a distinct tribe, and this is due to the ecological conditions of spatial separation and contact with other culturally different tribes like the Madi, Meru and Dinka. Each tribe consists of component units that are socially and politically independent; there is no centralized political and administrative control.

The Murle-Didinga-speaking tribes (Murle, Didinga and Lengarim) constitute the second category of the eastern Sudanic linguistic family. The Didinga are divided into two main groups; the eastern consisting of Bekora, Leudo and Morukeiyan, and western including Betalade, Thugure, Kadumakuch, Nakeri-Chake and Lomongole. Minor raids over a petty quarrel between the two groups are not uncommon.[27] Although culturally and linguistically related, the Murle and the related Kachipo and Peta are separated by a considerable distance from the Didinga and Lengarim. Each tribe of this category maintains internal cultural entity and

---

26. Ibid., p.56.

27. J.H. Driberg, "A Preliminary Account of the Didinga" in Sudan Notes and Records, Vol.No.1. 1962, pp.208-22.

external exclusiveness. They combine cultivation and lifestock rearing.[28]

The western Nilotic tribes, the third category of the eastern Sudanic family, comprise the Dinka, Nuer, Shilluk, Anywak, Bari, Acholi, Bor-Belanda and Je-Luo. There is no data on their original home but oral traditions indicate that their last habitat was in the vicinity of Rumbek and a slow process of migration resulted in their present distribution. Except perhaps for the Anywak and Acholi, most western Nilotics are pastoralists with an absorbing interest in cattle which possess social and religious values. The western Nilotics are divided into two major groups; the Dinka-Nuer group and the Shilluk-speaking group which comprises the Shilluk, Je-Luo, Anywak, Bari and Acholi. The two groups are linguistically and culturally related and show many similarities. The Shilluk, one of the largest tribes in southern Sudan, occupies the western part of the upper reaches of the White Nile, while the Anywak are distributed along the Akebe Oboth, Agwei and Biber streams. The Bari, who are a branch of the Anywak, occupy the Lepul Hills, east of Bahr al-Jabal whereas the Acholi live in Torit District. The Bor-Belanda and the Le-Luo, who live in Bahr al-Ghazal Province, seem to have been sections of the Shilluk-speakers who remained behind after the migrations.[29]

The Dinka and Nuer may be described as the closest representatives of the western Nilotics culturally and institutionally. The Dinka, who constitute the largest tribe in southern Sudan, dominate Bahr al-Ghazal Province while the Nuer dominate Upper Nile Province.

---

28. Ibid., pp.213-220, Loiria, op.cit., p.59.
29. Loiria, op., cit., pp.61-62.

Despite regional variations in their extensive habitat,
each of these tribes possesses a degree of identity
which distinguishes it as one tribe or a single people.
The two tribes are physiologically alike, and their
languages and customs are too similar for any doubt to
arise about their common origin, though the history of
their divergence is unknown. They are so similar that
the Atwot appears to be a Nuer tribe which has adopted
many Dinka habits while the Jikeny tribes of Nuerland
are said to be of Dinka origin. Moreover, there have
been continuous contacts between the two peoples which
have resulted in much miscegenation and culture borrow-
ing. Both tribes combine cattle rearing, cultivation,
fishing and hunting; cattle play a significant role in
their economic, social, religious and political life.[30]
The Dinka and the Nuer show similarity in system of
social organization, structure of territorial internal
units, seasonal cycles of transhumance and cultivation,
modes of settlement, systems of marriage, inheritance
and succession and the various economic, social religious and political institutions, so the Dinka and Nuer
can be regarded as complementary groups or as one
totality though there is little consciousness of this
totality among the various units of the society.[31] Their
common culture and language may draw them together,
simply as Dinka, in opposition to foreigners whom they
understand less than each other.[32] Evans-Pritchard makes

---

30. E.E. Evans-Pritchard, The Nuer (London: Oxford
    University Press 1940), pp.3-4.

31. Loiria, op. cit., pp. 65-66

32. G. Lienhardt, Divinity and Experience-The Religion
    of the Dinka (London: Ixford University Press, 1961)
    pp. 8-10.

a similar observation about the Nuer.[33] Incidently both
the Dinka and Nuer are among the tribes of Sudan which
have been intensively studied by anthropologists. If
such studies are extended to other tribes, especially
those of southern Sudan, similar identity and exclusiveness may emerge among other tribes.

The central Sudanic family comprises what have
generally been known as the "Sudanic-speaking" tribes.
It is a sub-division of the Chari-Nile group of the
Nilo-Sahara inclusive family of languages. It includes
the Bongo-speaking tribes of the Bongo, Banka, Moro,
Kodo, Beli and Gberi; it also includes the Kreish-speak-
ing and Moro-speaking tribes. These linguistic categories
do not show a continuous territorial pattern of distribution as do eastern and western Nilotic categories. Their traditions of migration are rather vague
and complicated. It seems that most of them came from
the west and south-west in successive waves which are
gradually compressed between the eastern and western
Nilotics.

The Bongo are linguistically related tribes and are
more scattered and diverse than all other linguistic
groups. They stretch in a broken belt from Amadi District in Equatoria Province to Lake Chad. The Ndego
linguistic group of tribes, whom Greenberg groups
together with the Zande-speakers under the "Adanawa
eastern group", at present occupies the central parts
of Bahr al-Ghazal Province from Wau to Daym Zubayr, the
Moro Madi tribes extend from Amadi in a horseshoe bend
through Maridi and Yei, through the north-eastern corner
of the Congo and north-west of Uganda into the Oparilea

---

33. Evans-Pritchard, op. cit., pp. 113-138.

area east of Bahr al-Jabal in Torit District of Equatoria Province.[34]

The components of the central Sudanic family occupy
the Ironstone Plateau which lies almost entirely on the
west bank of Bahr al-Jabal, and which shows diversity
of population and tribes. Here the tribes are agricul-
turalist and, except the Azande, have acephalous patterns of social organization. Intermarriage and close
contact failed to mediate their tribal, cultural and
linguistic identities, especially in the north-west.
The Zande, the only tribe of this group to receive
thorough study,[35] occupies Bahr al-Ghazal Province and
shares with the Bari tribe and Bari-speaking group in
settlement of parts of Equatoria Province. The Azande
who incorporate a number of non-Azande tribes which
have been under a process of "Zandeisation" during the
past century, have been remarkable for their militancy
and ability to resist outside pressures. They were the
culturally dominant group in the province till the
arrival of European and subsequently Arab administration.

To sum up, the Sudan is a socio-culturally diverse
country with many ethnic and linguistic groupings. Many
different large and small tribes have significant socio-
cultural and economic distinct identities which have
evolved from these groupings. These socio-cultural
diversities are the outcome of different conditions of
natural habitat, ethnology and history. Northern Sudan
can be considered as a distinct cultural region because
it is dominated by Muslim-Arab culture. Although there

---

34. Loiria, op. cit., pp. 67-69.
35. Ibid., p.70

are local variations among tribes as a result of different environments, still the criteria of identifying
the aspects of cultural pluralism-ethnicity, language,
religion and connubium show that common cultural patterns predominate over local variations. The relative
economic and political development in this region has
also helped to incorporate these plural groups. Government authorities, especially local government institutions, could be a suitable means to bridge these cleavages.

On the other hand prior to the introduction of
Christianity and the use of the English language in
schools, there has been in the southern region no single
traditional cultural element which might be designated
as a common denominator in characterising the component
groups. What was common among them was the territorial
area which had arbitrarily been delimited by Britain
and incorporated into the Anglo-Egyptian Sudan. Nevertheless the southern Sudan today can also be considered
as a distinct region in the country. Ethnically it has
many groupings of tribes which claim different origin
and identity and different social, economic and religious institutions related to their different environments.
Still similarities can be traced among the linguistically related peoples. All southern culture is African and
negroid in origin and has not been affected by Muslim-
Arab traits except in a very limited and superficial
sense. The condominium regime territorially welded the
three southern provinces into one region, and administratively and politically separated it from the northern
part which has greatly contributed to the exclusiveness
and alienated development of the region. This, no doubt,
has its impact on national integration.

Ethnic and socio-cultural pluralism and integration

National integration is always the main political problem facing new nations, especially African ones because of their ethnic and socio-cultural pluralism. The Sudan's problem of national integration has been more acute because of a multiplicity of Arabic-African culture in the north and the medley African culture in the south.

The main prerequisites of national integration are national consciousness, consensus and public order. nationalist movements, as a vehicle of national consciousness and consensus, began to develop in the Sudan as late as the 1920s, though weak national consciousness started as early as the Mahdist movement (1884-1898) but it was given a religious flavour. The Mahdi inspired Sudanese national feelings against the Turco-Egyptian regime and his aim was to awaken Islamic religious feelings all over the Muslim world and establish a Mahdist religious state, centred at Omdurman. But the idea of Sudanese nationalism as such (i.e. as a patriotic sentiment that would unite all the inhabitants of the Sudan irrespective of tribal, religious or regional differences, did not appear until after the First World War. The primary objective of the Sudanese nationalist movement was to attain independence. The significant landmarks in this nationalist movement were the White Flag League in 1924, the formation of the Graduates General Congress in 1938 and the Sudanisation of administration during 1947 - 1955. The contribution of northern Sudanese to this movement was so great that national consensus emerged among its educated elite, as a sense of loyalty to new national values, institutions and practices. This does not necessarily m e a n that the northern elite had c o m p l e t e l y shed its tribal, ethnic or sectariam attachments but that a minimal consensus of loyalty and pride in the new emerging Sudanese political nation-state existed. The new northern elite, to some extent, spread these national perspectives among different tribal groups and religious sects, creating a limited national consciousness among the traditional illiterate masses. National consensus and consciousness had been so limited that the greatest achievement of Sudan's national movement, which is largely a movement of the educated class, was the formation of an independent state for the Sudan. The Sudanese national movement had been short in duration and dependent on peaceful negotiations which left an adverse effect on the process of national integration and nation formation. Ga'afar Mohammed Ali Bakheit elaborates on this point by saying:

> Paradoxically enough it was independence that
> hindered the process of nation-formation, which
> tended to derive its impetus from the struggle
> against the common foe. Elements of diverse ethnic
> and cultural groups would gradually develop a common
> outlook as a result of joint sacrifices and comrade-
> ship in arms. By the time the national movement had
> been transferred from the protest stage to the war
> of liberation stage, nationhood would have matured
> and the incongruity of state and nation would dis-
> appear.[36]

So the circumstances in which the Sudan attained independence, before even a full scale protest movement had developed created unstable conditions and rendered national integration still a goal to be looked for.

---

36. Ga'afar Mohamed Ali Bakheit, "Native Administration in the Sudan and its Significance to Africa" in Yusuf Fadl Hassan (ed.), op. cit. p.262.

Independence was won before national ideals could be
communicated to the masses, especially in the rural
areas, to direct energies towards the service of national aspirations. This resulted in the isolation of the
politically aware from those whose consciousness developed in the independence era. This led the latter group
to launch an attack on the central government, and
hence the call for federation or regional government
irrespective of whether these were administratively and
financially feasible or not.[37] This applied to the different peoples of the Sudan and particularly to the
southerners whose participation in the national movement,
even their educated elite, was limited and minimal.

Tribalism and socio-cultural pluralism continued to
survive during the national movement era and after independence. British administrators, especially after the
revolt of the White Flag League and the expulsion of the
Egyptians, encouraged tribalism and sectarianism (taifia).
They went to such an extent as to insist that a person's
tribe be put on official documents and certificates. in
schools tribal allegiances were taught and the Sudan was
studied as a political state containing various tribes
and ethnic groups and not as a developing nation.

The system of indirect administration was institu-
tionalized in the early thirties (the Chiefs Courts
Ordinance of 1932); this indirect administration is also
known as native administration. In Africa indirect administration means that Africans, as far as possible
through the instruments of their own indigenous institutions, administered themselves. In the Sudan native
administration was created by the colonial power to
strike at and weaken the national movement. It evolved

---

37. Ibid., p.263.

from a tradition of indirect influence of wide political
connotations in which the revival of tribalism figured
prominently, and so native institutions were built. The
aim being to create certain influences rather than make
use of the most influencial elements available. It was
used to suppress the rural masses, not to promote their
interests. The powers of native agencies at that time
were restricted to judicial fields and collection of
taxes. In 1934 this system of native administration was
confined to areas which were predominantly tribal and
where socio-economic development was not possible in the
foreseeable future; instead there would be a local
government system geared to keep public security and
order, provide social services, train Sudanese in the
art of government, absorb nationalist sentiment and
divert enthusiastic patriotism into the service of concrete constructive ends. The Local Government Ordiance
of 1937 for Rural Areas, Townships and Municipalities
and their 1938 Regulations indicate the role which the
Sudan Government had envisaged for native administration
which was to be absorbed in local government. Thus the
balance of power among the indigenous competing forces
had been tilted in favour of the educated urban class
and the tribal chiefs who were to be united against
ultra-nationalism represented by the traditional sector
of the Mahdists and the modern pro-Egyptian elemantsand
forces dominated by Egyptian culture.[38] So the change to
local government was a change in name because native
authorities had then acquired relatively substantial
powers. In fact local councils had been established on
tribal bases except for those of Khartoum, Khartoum
North, Omdurman and Port Sudan and the other six established at El Obeid, Wad Medani, Kosti, Kassala, Berber

38. Ibid., pp. 260-261.

and Shendi. Others might be established in certain
areas to administer tribal affairs, sometimes such
a rural council would be named after the tribe it was
administering.

The latest opposition to native administration made
itself visible during the October Revolution demonstrations, in 1964; but these slogans failed to gain inclu-
sion in the National Charter. Two months later, al-
Shafi Ahmed al-Sheikh, the representative of the labour ·
movement in the Revolutionary Front of 21st October and
the Secretary of the Sudan Federation of Trade Unions
and the Minister for Cabinet Affairs, submitted a note
to the Council of Ministers in which he urged the
council that the laws governing the functions and conduct of local government councils should be amended in
such a way that the councils would be responsible for
native administration functions. The tribal chiefs and
"nazirs", who would be the most affected by such an
amendment, moved quickly to show that they were perform-
ing important duties i.e. preserving stability, collecting taxes and looking after peace and order; they pointed out that they could discharge their duties properly
only when they were secure in office. They tried to
mobilize their people in support of native administration and against the new attitude of liquidizing it.
Later on the administrative officers showed their fear
that such a liquidization would istrative influence the
fields of security and taxation in a country with a 90%
rural population. In fact they feared that the government authority emanating from them would not be communicated to the sedentary and nomadic rural people.
Consequently the government modified its policy of
liquidization to mean, instead of direct suppression,
introduction of such amendments as to render the former

native administration in line with development. This
meant that the policy of liquidising native administration turned out to be a mere slogan; the continued
survival of the influence of tribal chiefs and "nazirs"
and tribal allegiances, which resulted in tribal collectivities and cleavages, seriously hindered the
process of national integration in the country.

The development of national consciousness and
national consensus among the southerners had generally
been very limited. Their contribution to the national
movement was insignificant, although Ali Abd al-Latif,
the leader of the White Flag League movement was a
Muslim Dinka. This was due to the fact that the modern-
ized and educated elite among the southerners were few.
Even that small group appeared to lack interest or
strong national consensus concerning the emerging
Sudanese nation. Gray described that situation by saying:

> Completely isolated from the north until little
> more than a century ago, embittered by decades of
> subsequent hostility, and administered separately
> until the threshold of independence, the southerner
> feels himself to be an African, while the ruling
> northerner is proud of his Arab consciousness.[39]

This feeling of being an African and therefore
alienated from the new Arab-dominated Sudanese nation
had been expressed by many southern intellectuals until
the time of the Round Table Conference on the South in
1965. The limited number of southern intellectuals and
their limited contribution to the national movement

---

39. R. Gray, "Introduction" in J. Oduho and W. Deng,
    The Problem of the Southern Sudan (London: Oxford
    University Press, 1963), p.2.

paved the way for the northern elite to take over most
of the Sudanized administrative posts. The number of
southern administrators, even in the southern provinces,
was surprisingly small. This was followed by limited
representation of southerners in the first and subsequent national constituent assemblies.

According to Shepherd the establishment of public
order is a necessity in the process of national integration and nation-building. It is the authoritative organization of society around the instruments of government which is represented in law-making and law-enforcement agencies. The strength of public order can be
asserted in terms of the extent of participation of
ethnic and interest groups in the process of law-making
and their co-operation with law-enforcement.[40]

Political parties have always been the instruments
through which integrated plural groups are linked to
the elite. Through practising their rights of discussing and voting in different fields, the masses participate in law-making in the liberal parliamentary system.
Political parties, which are usually organized on national, non-ethnic, non-tribal and non-religious bases, can
play a paramount role in breaking through local loyalties and can thus push forward the process of national
integration. During the two phases of parliamentary
experience in the Sudan, political parties were super-
ficially organized to guide the people along the line
of participation in law-making, but both tribalism and
sectarianism had hindered the role of those parties.
Prior to 1950 the contribution of southerners in national political parties had been minimal at best and it
was always followed with withdrawal. During the 1950s

---

40. Shepherd, op. cit., p.200.

southerners began to organize their own parties but as
was the case with northern parties, tribalism infiltra-
ted into the political parties. So although Sudanese
political parties, northern and southern alike, were
theoretically organised on national bases in reality
they strongly depended on tribalism for membership
recruitment and electoral support, except for the Sudanese Communist Party and the Islamic Charter Front. The
heavy dependence of political parties on tribalism can
be exemplified by the fact that the National Unionist
Party derived its membership and support from the tribes
of Kordufan Province and the Shukriya tribe, the Umma
Party from tribes occupying the central reach of the
White Nile and Darfur Province, the People's Democratic
Party from the tribes of the Northern Province, Kassala
area and the Beja tribes, and the Sudanese African
National Union from the Dinka tribe. Furthermore, northern parties depended almost entirely on northerners for
their membership and support while southern parties
relied on southerners. This reliance of political
parties on tribalism helped to consolidate the tribal
structure of the Sudan and to regionalize the country
into north and south.

The two ideological parties, the Sudanese Communist
Party and the Islamic Charter Front, were dominantly
materialist and metaphysical respectively, and those
were the lines along which they rallied membership and
support from different parts of the country. These two
parties could have immensely helped in the elimination
of tribalism. The Sudanese Communist Party was the only
party which recruited its real membership from the two
regions of the country and whose higher committees were
run by northerners and southerners jointly. Had it not
been for the moral, religious, legal and physical

hindrances put in its path by tribal, religious and
traditional leaders, the Sudanese Communist Party could
have greatly aided the process of national integration.
But apart from these two parties, the interests of
tribal and party leaders often coincided, and the part-
became tribal instruments.

Religious sectarianism: an aspect of pluralism in Northern Sudan

In the Sudan Islam has developed many religious
sects or "turug" which themselves carry divisive part-
icularism. Islamization of the Sudan was largely the
product of the missionary activities of a wide spectrum
of popular religious fraternities or "turug sufia" each
of which centred around the personality and teachings
of a particular saint, "sheikh" or master. These religious "turug" are not like Christian religious divisions
such as Catholicism or Protestantism, nor did they
present such serious cleavage within Sudanese Islam as
existed between Sunni and Shi'a Muslims eleswhere in
the Muslim world. A "tariqa" is a corporate religious
group with an exclusive identity, membership, often
endogamous standardized modes of action among its
members. They operate within the borders of Islam as it
is generally understood and practised throughout the
world of Sunni Islam: but with varying degrees of
emphasis on communal worship on "sufi" or mystical
lines as may be recommended by the founding "sheikh"
and his more important disciples. The main "turuq-
sufiya" in the Sudan have been the Qadiriyya, Shadhal-
iyya, Sammaniyya and Khatmiyya with numerous sub-turuq.[41]
The close link between religion and politics in former

---

41. Yusuf Fadl Hassan (ed.), Kitab al-Tabaqat Ly Ibin
    Dief Alla Khartoum; University Press, 1971) pp.8-9

Muslim societies resulted in the growth of important,
sometimes even bitter, rivalries between some of these
"turuq". Because of this and because he was inspired to
reform Islam by leading Muslims back to the original
sources (i.e. Quran and Sunna), Mohammed Ahmed Al-Mahdi
tried, among other things, to abolish all "turug-sufiya"
including those in which he received his first teachings
as a religious novice. As expected, Mahdi puritanism
was met by stiff resistance and hostility on the part
of the different "turuq", and was particularly disliked
by the Khatmiyya whose principal leader was Sayed Ali
al-Mirghani.

After the overthrow of the Mahdist state, "sufism"
with its different "turuq" revived, gaining more support.
During the condominium Wingate Pasha established an
official "Council of Ulama" through which he tried to
control the "turuq-sufiya", counteracting Mahdism which
stood apart from all religious orders. Ironically enough
after the First World War, Mahdism which rejected
"sufism" and wished to abolish the different "turuq"
itself became a "tariqa". The paradox of these "turug-
sufiya" lies in the fact that they are divisive as well
as unifying factors at the same time. Their unifying
aspect emerges from the fact they were popular, open
and prosyletising associations and cut across tribal
boundaries, and by emphasizing and encouraging mutual
sympathy and co-operation among their followers achieved a remarkable degree of unity of purpose and outlook
among their adherents. On the other hand, they divided
society into various religious orders, hostile to each
other and thus created collectivities bigger than the
tribal ones. The unifying element is weak in the case
of the Sudan where sectarianism encouraged tribalism
instead of cutting through it. The politically involved

religious sects, particularly al-Ansar and al-Khatmiyya, controlled most of the rural population through their control of tribal leaders.

In fact the role played by al-Khatmiyya and al-Ansar in Sudanese politics was so great that they controlled political parties, constituent assemblies and consequently executive and judicial bodies. Thus they controlled the mechanism for bridging the elite-mass gap and creating an integrated political society, i.e. the political parties and the bodies of law-making and law-enforcement. This was done smoothly by the domination of the Umma Party by al-Ansar and the People's Democratic Party, which was later united with the National Unionist Party, by al-Khatmiyya. The leaders of these religious sects, who were also the real leaders of the parties, used to nominate of candidates in general elections and they would usually succeed. The "Taifya" leaders could also nominate supporters into cabinets and thus control administration and economic planning in the country. This resulted not only in the failure of the parliamentary experience but also in segmentation of people into different collectivities controlled by religious sectarianism and tribalism supporting each other. However, public order had been broken several times by repressive actions by the sects or their militant political stand, e.g. in 1954 when the Umma Party, mainly al-Ansar, who were famous for their firm stand against unity with Egypt or even close links with it, demonstrated against the visit paid by Mohammed Nagib, the leader of 1952 Egyptian Revolution. Some demonstrators got out of hand and many people were killed. Another incident took place in August 1961 when Ibrahim Abboud's military regime banned

al-Ansar's celebrations of the Prophet's birthday. Al-
Ansar youth marched in uniform to al-Mahdi tower
through Omdurman; the military junta considered the
march a demonstration and a violation of the law since
demonstrations were banned. The police opened fire and
twelve Ansar youth were killed and three policemen. In
December 1965, due to religious sectarianism, political pressure and the Islamic Charter Front's political
strategy, twelve members of the Constituent Assembly,
all of whom were either members of the Sudanese Communist Party or pro-Communists, were driven out of the constituent Assembly. The consequent public demonstrations
and insurrections affected public order but the government used coercion to put them down. The 1970 incidents
at Wad Nobawi and Gezira Aba show to what extent religious sectarianism in the Sudan could react as a militant
group in the field of politics; this was the case of
al-Ansar and their sympathizers in the Umma Party.
Religious sectarianism continued after the October Revolution of 1964 and the military takeover in 1969 to
adversely affect the process of national integration.

No doubt the six years of Abboud's regime was the
hardest time for both northerners and southerners. It
was the time when the slow process of national integration reverted back to a process of disintegration. The
failure to restore peace in the south led to suppression
and injustice. Tens of thousands of southerners fled to
the forests and to neighbouring African countries and
the Anyanya political and military movement began. The
climax of disintegration was reached when the Anyanya
group raised the issue of separation as a solution to
the southern question. Thus the weak bridge of national
consensus between the northern and southern elite, together with the breakdown of public order in the south,

produced a strong intranational regional movement with
both political and military dimensions. The problem
of southern Sudan has left a deep adverse impact on
the socio-economic development of the whole country.

Manifestation of regionalism in different areas in the Sudan

Ethnic, tribal, religious and socio-cultural
pluralism dominated almost all Sudanese society till
very recently. The condominium rulers exploited a diver-
sive society to strengthen their grip on the country
and to delay as long as possible their evacuation from
it. The easy way to do this was by placing hindrances
on the developing national movement and by creating
and widening cleavages and divisions in Sudanese
society. "In the era 1920-1930 discussions concerning
the development of the various regions of the Sudan on
ethnic and cultural lines of their own were held by
the British rulers. That has resulted in the policies
of regionalism, most prominent among them was the southern policy, which placed influence in the hands of the
British rulers and not the native chiefs".[42]

However, the northern, eastern, western and central
parts of the country can be regarded as different
regions, each having general or sometimes vague characteristics which make it different from the others, e.g.
common ethnicity of tribes, similar or slightly different geographical conditions, similar livelihood or
related historical and socio-economic development.
Still, the south stands apart, it is more African in
ethnicity and culture, and most of its educated people
are Christians while all the other regions are, to a
greater or lesser extent, dominated by Islamic religion

---

42. Bakheit, op. cit., p.260

or Arab culture. British policy and the indifferent, or even irrational, attitudes of the national government towards the socio-economic development of the south helped to crystallize the southern question as the most serious national problem, the solution of which became a burning issue, especially after the October Revolution of 1964. To attain such a goal the Round Table Conference on the South was held on sixteenth March, 1965 at Khartoum. Unfortunately the conference could not reach a unanimous resolution on the pattern of government to be adopted. On the 29th of the same month the conference resolved to set up a 12-man committee to deal with the issue of a constitutional and administrative set-up which could protect the "special interest of the south" as well as the 'general interest of the Sudan'. Besides it had to watch the implementation of the policies agreed upon, to plan for normalization of conditions in the south, and consider means for lifting the state of emergency and the establishment of law and order.

Parties' representatives at the Round Table Conerence were asked to submit proposals on the required constitutional and administrative set-up. The northern parties' members, except those of the Islamic Charter Front, suggested the adoption of the present provincial boundaries to create nine regions out of the nine provinces. Their argument was that the main advantages of regional government lie in the smallness of the administrative units. They opposed the idea of amalgamating the three southern provinces into one region because it would then be too large a region to be administered from one regional capital. The demand of the southern parties for a constitutional set-up which would embue local initiatives for the advancement of the region would be satisfied whether the three southern provinces were incorporated into one region or kept separate. They also argued that if the south was demarcated as one region, this would perpetuate the sense of confrontation between north and south.

On the other hand, southern parties' representatives suggested either the division of the country into four regions, north, south, east and west, or the adoption of the present division in the northern provinces, making six regions out of them and incorporating the three southern provinces into one region. The southern representatives argued that the regional government should be based on division between the north and the south as two distinct units because of their difference in culture, language, religion and race. The duty of the committee was to solve the southern problem and this necessitated the treatment of the south as a 'special' part of the country with an acute problem different from those which other regions faced. Contrary to what the northern parties' representatives suggested, large regional units facilitate aggregation of the citizens' interest. The present provincial administrative boundaries, which were inherited from the colonial administration, were based on tribal considerations and it became the duty of the national administration to adopt a system which would weaken tribalism and so help in the building of a modern nation.

The constitutional and administrative formula was concentrated on the distribution of powers between the two. Therefore, a list containing the powers proposed to remain in the centre and those proposed to be transferred to the region besides those suggested to be concurrent were worked out. These were drawn mainly from the schemes of the National Unionist Party and the

Sudanese African National Union. The distribution of
powers gave the region legislative and executive
bodies while the centre would keep the national legislative and executive machineries; the relationship
between the centre and the region was determined.

The different schemes presented to the 12-man committee by the northern and southern parties and the
general proposals made by the committee, all hinged on
the idea that regional government should not be confined
to southern Sudan only, but extended to different parts
of the country. The northern elite could visualize that
a lack of socio-economic development in some parts of
the country might create problems in those areas similar
to the southern problem.

Regional movements in northern Sudan began about
a decade ago, and their parties or groupings worked
side by side with national political parties. Significant among them was the Beja congress which derived
its membership and electoral support from the Beja
tribes of eastern Sudan; it had ten representatives in
the Constituent Assembly of 1965 and three in 1968,
besides the southern parties, old and new, which had
been working on a regional basis during the second
parliamentary experience, 1964-1969. It is no coincide-
nce that these northern regional parties and groupings
emerged in economically and socially depressedparts of
the country. The real motive behind them was not a call
for separation or regional autonomy, contrary to the
southern regional movement, but was a strongly justified
demand for better distribution of economic activities
and services.

Thus southern parties and northern regional groupings had all been working on a regional basis when all
parties were disolved by the military take-over of 25th

May, 1969. No doubt, particularly during the era 1964-
1969, the acute regional cleavage placed the Sudan in
crisis in the process of national integration, which
expressed itself in territorial disintegration and
lack of reduction of cultural and regional tension and
discontinuities on the horizontal plane in the process
of creating a homogeneous territorial community.

CONFLICT RESOLUTION:
THE CASE OF NIGERIA AND SUDAN
Kamal El Din Osman Salih

The purpose of this essay is to examine the way in which
the conflicts of Nigeria and the Sudan (namely Biafra
and the southern Sudan) were resolved. We will also
discuss the obstacles which stood in the way of conclud-
ing a negotiated agreement and we will see how in the
case of Sudan a peaceful settlement was worked out and
what factors facilitated that.

Nigeria-Biafra: Conflict Resolution by Force

A peaceful settlement was obstructed in the case of
Nigeria because great difficulty was faced with respect
to the reconciliation of the main issues of the civil
war: stopping bloodshed, preserving Nigerian territorial
integrity and guaranteeing the safety of the Ibo people.
Soon after peace talks started, the main issue was not
whether the Biafran state could continue to exist
(federal recapture of much Biafran territory made it
quite clear that it would not survive, but on what basis
would the Ibo people coexist with other ethnic groups
in the future.

Immediately after Ojukwu was granted a mandate by the
Eastern Regional Assembly to declare the Republic of
Biafra on 26 May, 1967, the Federal Government declared
a state of emergency throughout Nigeria. Gowon announced
a decree that would give Nigeria a new constitution and
divide the federation into 12 new states. Northern
Nigeria was to be divided into six states: North-West-
ern, North-Central, Kano, North-Eastern, Benue plateau
and West-Central (Kwara State); Eastern Nigeria was to

be divided into three states: East-Central, South-Eastern and Rivers; Western Nigeria was to continue as one state with the exclusion of the Colony Province, which was to be incorporated in Lagos, from now on a separate state, and the Mid-Western region was to continue as the Mid-Western State. The Eastern Government rejected the planned regrouping of Nigeria, stating that it would not be implemented in Eastern Nigeria.

The Federal Government held the view that a permanent settlement could only be guaranteed if Biafra agreed to withdraw its declaration of independence, recognize the authority of the Federal Nigerian Government and agree to the new 12 states.

From their side the Biafrans were ready to accept a peaceful settlement if it endorsed the following demands:

(i)   That the responsibility for keeping law and order within Biafran territory should be held by the Biafran Government and not the Federal Government.

(ii)   To protect the country against any invasion, the Biafran army must take an oath of allegiance to the Biafran Government.

(iii)   Economically, Biafra must be independent, in the sense of having full control of the economy and natural resources and also in the sense of planning its own economic development.

A compromise was not reached because the Federal Government insisted that Biafra had to denounce secession before a cease-fire, while the Biafrans wanted a cease-fire with no such condition attached. The Biafrans in particular were not ready to move an inch from this entrenched position and continued thus until the end of the war. This was in spite of the fact that they were the weaker party in terms of military strength, clearly shown by the shrinking of their territory in the face of swift federal advances. They were under the illusion that their state would be able to survive, and so they rejected any proposal for renouncing secession. It was this stubborn and uncompromising attitude which defeated all attempts to find a peaceful settlement to the dispute. Below we will illustrate this more clearly by reviewing the Biafran stand in the various negotiations held either under the auspices of the OAU or other international organizations.

First, during the discussion of the Nigerian crisis at Kinshasa OAU summit conference (held in September 1967), it was agreed that a consultative mission, comprising the heads of state of the Cameroons, Congo Kinshasa (Zaire), Ethiopia, Chad, Liberia and Niger, was to be sent to Nigeria in order to review the situation there. After its visit to Lagos on 22 and 23 November 1967, the mission issued a communique saying that:

> Any solution of the Nigerian crisis should be in the context of preserving the Federation's unity and territorial integrity and that, as a basis for the return to peace and normal conditions, the Biafrans should accept the political and administrative structure of the Federation in the form of the 12 states.[1]

The immediate Biafran reaction was that they were not ready to abandon their sovereignty and insisted that in any peace talks Biafra had to be treated as a sovereign state and not as part of Nigeria. They

---

1. S. Cronje, The World and Nigeria: the Diplomatic History of the Biafran war 1967-70 (Sedgwick and Jackson, 1972).

therefore rejected the mission's communique, making it
clear that their stand in this regard was not negotiable.

Secondly, in the Kampala peace talks - arranged by
the commonwealth Secretariat on 23 May 1968 we find the
Biafrans adopting the same inflexible attitude. The
meeting seemed to be about to reach an agreement on
a cease-fire, when suddenly the Biafran delegation withdrew from the talks and left Kampala for Enugu. The
Biafrans justified their withdrawal on the grounds first,
that the federal delegation was exploiting the superior
military standing of their forces and trying to impose
their own conditions rather than negotiate terms and
secondly, the federal delegation was using dirty tactics,
not wanting to negotiate peace and submitting totally
unacceptable proposals.[2] However these accusations were
not true - especially the second one, for the Biafrans
were the ones who submitted totally unacceptable proposals. They (the Biafrans) demanded first an uncon-
ditional cease-fire, and secondly insisted on the withdrawal of federal troops to the position they held
before the beginning of the war. To the Federal Government the latter was a completely unacceptable and unrealistic demand, for by that time the Federal army was
in control of three-quarters of the Biafran territories.
That was the reason why the conferences failed to achieve
results. In his book, The Struggle for Secession 1966-70.
Etieyong U. Akpan makes the following comment regarding
the Biafran demand that Federal troops withdraw to pre-
war lines:...

> But any person with an informed and objective
> appraisal of the situation ought to have realized
> that Biafra ceased to exist the moment practically
> all the non-Ibo areas - namely, Calabar, virtually

---

2. Africa Confidential 14 June 1968, p.3.

the whole of the Ibibio/Annang area, Port Harcourt
and the other Rivers areas, following so they did
the whole of Ogoja were retaken by Federal troops.
It was therefore unrealistic and fatuous of Governor
Ojukwu to talk of Federal troops withdrawing to the
pre-war boundaries... Biafra had no moral or legal
right to expect the Federal Government to withdraw
from areas which are not foreign but its own territory de jure and de facto; areas they regarded as
liberated from the rebels. Even in the absolutely
unlikely situation of the Federal Government's being
willing to consider such a preposterous demand,
these areas were not in the newly created states,
prowd and determined to keep their identities, and
Federal troops could not withdraw except with their
consent. (p.138).

Thirdly, in the Monrovia meeting of 17 April 1969
which was held under the auspices of the OAU Consultative Committee on Nigeria, the Biafrans too rejected
a proposal made to end the war. The proposal submitted
by the Committee was that:

the two parties of the civil war accept in the supreme interest of Africa, a united Nigeria, which
ensures all forms of security to all citizens.....
within the content of this agreement, the two parties accept an immediate cessation of fighting and
the opening without delay of peace negotiation.[3]

The Biafrans rejected the proposal because it
included the words "United Nigeria"; it was reported
that they might have accepted the declaration in principle if these words were replaced by the word "solution".

---

3. Africa Confidential 25 April 1969, pp. 2-3.

To the Biafrans, the acceptance of a "united Nigeria", meant the defeat of their seccession and sovereignty and this was something which they were not ready to give up even though they knew that their fate was about to sealed. The Committee in its communique noted that the Federal Government of Nigeria accepted the proposal but regretted that the Biafran delegation did not.

Finally, when the Emperor of Ethiopia invited both the Nigerians and the Biafrans to Addis Ababa (in December 1969) to resume talks under his chairmanship, it was the Biafrans who obstructed this peaceful initiative. Just before the departure of the Biafran delegation, Governor Ojukwu issued a statement that the meeting was being held, not under the auspices of the OAU, but under those of the Emperor, acting independently,[4] although the Biafrans knew that the Emperor was sending this invitation in respect of his position as Chairman of the OAU Consultative Committee on Nigeria. The leader of the delegation was also instructed to make a similar statement on arrival at Addis Ababa. These statements had the effect of stopping the federal delegation from even leaving for the meeting, and made the embarrassed Emperor issue his own statement affirming that he was acting under the auspices of the OAU. As a result of this impasse the talks never took place and the Biafran delegation returned home by order of their government on 18 December, 1969.

Thus from the review of these peace negotiations we emerge with the following picture: the Biafrans retained a consistently rigid attitude to all attempts at negotiation and mediation, which never changed. When any talks started, the Biafran delegation was always

---

4. S. Cronje, op cit, pp. 317-18.

under strict instructions (from Governor Ojukwu) "to be
rigid, not to allow the talks to last too long, but to
break up the discussions at the earliest opportunity"[5].
Thus the line of rigidity was followed mainly in order
to obstruct any peaceful settlement from being carried
out. For the Biafrans knew that if a flexible line was
adopted this would mean paving the way for the kind of
settlement where the Federal Government would benefit
more than the Biafrans, and would bring to an end their
sovereignty and independence. They were unwilling to
give up their sovereignty so easily; for thousands and
thousands of lives had been sacrificed for the sake of
achieving the goal of independence. In fact by that time
the Biafrans were working hard to obtain additional
diplomatic recognition from various countries. For the
more diplomatic recognition their country had, the
stronger was the likelihood of the world accepting the
fact of Biafra's international existence.

When the Nigerians realized that the Biafrans were
no longer ready to negotiate peace and that their main
concern was to obstruct any peaceful settlement, they
returned to force, the only means left to them. They
launched their last offensive in the battlefield, thus
ensuring a military victory over the Biafrans. This
occurred at the end of 1969 when Federal Government
forces had accumulated sufficient firepower and brought
some co-ordination into their command, as described by
Sols Odunfa in his article "How Ojukwu's dream of empire
became a nightmare", in the Nigerian Daily Times of
2 February 1970.

---

5. N.U. Akpen, The Struggle for Secession 1966-70:
   account of the Nigerian Civil war (Frank Cass,
   London 1972).

On Monday, 12 January 1970, Major General P. Effiong –
to whom Ojukwu had handed over power before he fled to
the Ivory Coast where he was given political asylum,
called upon the Biafran army to lay down its arms:

> I am convinced that a stop must be put to the blood-
> shed... that the suffering of our people must be
> brought to an immediate end. Our people are now
> disillusioned and those elements of the old regime
> who had made negotiation and reconciliation impossi-
> ble have voluntarily removed themselves from our
> midst...[6]

Three days later in Lagos in a formal ceremony
Effiong surrendered to General Gowon making the end of
a conflict which had lasted for two and half years. The
conflict might has been resolved differently if the
Biafrans had adopted a more cooperative and flexible
attitude, but that never happened since the main
strategy of the Biafran leadership was to follow a rigid
line in any peace talks. This strategy cost the Biafran
population a great deal and resulted in a prolongation
of the war and the deaths of more people.

The Southern Sudan: Conflict Resolution by Negotiation

The first attempt to find a peaceful settlement to the
southern problem was after 21 October 1964, when
a civilian government took over power from the military.
The civilian government was convinced that the southern question was not one of security (as it had been
regarded by the military regime of General Abboud) but
"a political problem originating in the social and

---

6. J. de St. Jorre, The Nigerian Civil War, (Hodder
   and Stoughton, London, 1972), p. 401.

cultural differences between the two parts of the
country"[7] Therefore the best possible solution was
a political settlement arrived at by negotiation. Accordingly a round-table conference was convened in Khartoum
(March 16-29 1965) attended by forty-five members from
both the north and south (18 northerners and 27 southerners), plus observers from Uganda, Kenya, Tanzania,
Ghana, Nigeria, Algeria and Egypt. A deadlook was
reached when the two parties (northerners and southerners submitted proposals which were mutually unacceptable[8] The northerners called for a regional government
in the south, composed of a cabinet and parliament
whose major responsibility would be "a Southern Council
for economic development, a Southern public service
commission and a university in the South"[9] The southerners (mainly their two parties SANU and the Southern
Front) submitted two schemes. The first one called for
a plebiscite in the southern Sudan to enable the people
to choose one of three possibilities: federation, unity
with the north or separation[10] The second scheme proposed the creation of two regions in the country, where
each region would be dominant with respect to finance,
economic development, external affairs and defence.
According to this proposal " the two regions would establish an o r g a n i s a t i o n of c o m m o n s e r v i c e s

---

7. Ministry of Foreign Affairs, Peace and Unity in the
   Sudan (Khartoum University Press, 1973).

8. From an interview with Andrew Wiou, Deputy Minister
   of Co-ordination, March 15, 1975.

9. M.O. Beshir The Southern Sudan: From Conflict to
   Peace (Hurst and Company London 1975), p.52.

10. O. Albino, The Sudan: A Southern Viewpoint (Oxford
    University Press, London 1963), p.54.

responsible for the regulation and administration of
external tarriffs, currency and banking, higher education and health, transport and communication, and medical
services", in addition, "a Council of Ministers from
both regions and a Secretariat would be set up to administer the common services".[11]

The northerners rejected the two schemes on the
grounds that both of them would lead to separation. In
their view the first scheme meant the granting of self-
determination (and automatically independence) to the
southerners. The second would ultimately lead to the
creation of two separate entities in the country linked
together by common services. On the other hand the
southerners were not ready to suggest schemes which
would omit separation or independence and thus meet the
demands of the northerners. So when it was felt that an
aggreement was unattainable a decision was made to form
a twelve-man committee (six from the north and six from
the south) to carry on the debate on the future constitutional relationship. The conference thus failed to
bridge the gap which separated the two viewpoints.

Between 1965 and 1969 no peaceful initiative was
undertaken. The different national governments during
this period were too busy quarrelling over power. No
time was devoted to tackling the issue seriously, and
it was only highlighted during elections when northern
politicians felt that they were in need of southern
support to enter parliament. For the sake of winning
that support they made false promises and used corrupt
methods of appeasement, which in turn undermined north-
south relations and reinforced southern mistrust of
the north.

---

11. M.O. Beshir, op. cit., p.94.

It was only with the advent of President Nimeri to
power in May 1969 that prospects for peaceful settlement increased. His regime realized that a military
solution would not be possible. For in spite of army
superiority in terms of equipment and training, it failed
to crush the Anya-Nya. Force would simply complicate
what was essentially a political problem stemming from
the social and cultural differences between the two
regions. Because of these differences the regime made
what was later known as the June Declaration (of 1969)
in which the South was offered regional autonomy within
a united Sudan. According to Andrew Wiou, the idea of
regional autonomy originated mainly from Abel Alier (at
that time Minister of Supply & Industry) who presented
it for discussion to both the Revolutionary Command
Council and the Council of Ministers. The idea was then
endorsed by the two councils, and announced as a policy
on 9 June, 1969.

In order to train southerners for autonomy, new
policies were introduced. Principal among these was
a special administrative training programme and the
creation of a Ministry for Southern Affairs. Some significant economic measures were taken, such as the
initiation of economic, social and cultural development plans and the formation of a special economic
planning board for the region.[12]

But there were many delays in the implementation
of the policy. Those who were charged with its implementation (mainly the Marxist element like Joseph
Garang who was appointed Minister of Southern Affairs)
thought that the best way to solve political problems

---

12. Peace and Unity, p.42.

was by accelerating economic development in the region. The line of reasoning followed was that the solution of the political issue required more than any thing else, economic development which would offer work to the majority of southerners.[13] If the people of the region flourished economically, then their political grievances could diminish considerably. The deficiency in this reasoning was that before funds could be put into the region a high degree of political stability was required, which, in turn was lacking as long as armed conflict continued.

It was only after the removal of the communists from office and from positions of influences, following the abortive coup of July 1971, that the chance for a breakthrough came.

Joseph Garang, who was executed after the coup had failed, was replaced by Abel Alier as Minister of Southern Affairs. According to Andrew Wieu, Joseph Garang constantly blocked any idea of talking with the rebels. Garang was always against the southern view represented by Abel Alier in the Council of Ministers, that there was nothing wrong in negotiating with the rebels. Optimism prevailed that the Government's southern policy would be seriously implemented. According to Alier, the best way to bring about a lasting peace was through a negotiated settlement in which the rebels must participate. His view was shared by other ministers who had also become convinced that a possible solution should not be obstructed by the former refusal to negotiate peace with the Anya-Nya. The rebels had played a great role in the problem's creation and for that reason they had to participate in its resolution.

---

13. Ibid. p.43.

This intention to open talks with the rebels in order to reach a solution was further consolidated by the fact that the war was causing much damage to the economy of the country. Funds which might have been alloted to developmental projects were used to finance military operations in the south. So the country's economic situation could only be improved by finding a peaceful solution.

Due to these factors, permission was given to the Ministry of Southern Affairs to start a dialogue with the Anya-Nya and southern leaders who were living abroad. Accordingly Abel Alier prepared a draft outlining the government approach to regional autonomy. According to Andrew Wieu, Abel Alier set up an advisory committee to draw up proposals on the framework of the expected regional institutions. The committee was divided into three; one dealing with political aspects; the second with socio-cultural aspects; and the last with economic aspects. This document was later (February 1971) sent to different southern organizations outside the country and to those who were in the bush.

Southern leaders in exile were approached mainly by the World Council of Churches.[14] After their tour of the Sudan in May 1971, the World Council of Churches and the All Africa Conference of Churches mission became convinced that the Sudanese authorities were serious about their peace talks. In a meeting which took place in Addis Ababa (January, 1971) between Rev. Burgess Carr (of the All Africa Conference of Churches) and the Sudanese Ambassador in Addis Ababa, the latter

14. From an interview with Samuel Athi Bwogom Director of Sudan Council of Churches (May 27th. 1973).

expressed the desire of his Government to start negotiations on substantive issues. So the moment the mission returned to its headquarters in Geneva, it started making contacts with southern groups in Europe, conveying and communicating to them the desire of the Sudanese Government to enter into negotiations. A positive response came from the southern leadership; as reported by the two representatives of the Southern Sudan Liberation Movement in Europe (Mading de Garang and Dr. Lawrence Wol).

The southern leadership took the decision to enter into negotiations for a number of reasons: first, it was convinced that a military solution was completely impossible and non-attainable. Especially at this time the movement was complaining of shortage of arms, neighbouring African countries previously used as a transit for arms delivery were reluctant at this time to give help because of the new policy adopted by Nimeri's Government to win the support of his neighbours. Secondly, the movement began to realize that the great bulk of southern public opinion was in favour of the new government policy of regional autonomy. Southerners were convinced that the language of force would not solve the problem and that it was better to search for peaceful means for ending the dispute.

The general framework for peace negotiations was agreed upon during President Nimeri's state visit to Ethiopia at the beginning of November 1971.[15] The Emperor of Ethiopia had expressed the desire to end the Sudanese conflict. On this tour President Nimeri was

15. C. Eprile, War and Peace in the Sudan 1955-72. (David and Charles, London. 1974).

accompanied by Abel Alier, who was to play a great role
during peace talks. When Nimeri left the Ethiopian
capital, secret negotiations continued between the
Sudanese Government's delegation led by Alier and Major-
General Mohammed Al Bagheir (Minister of Interior at
that time) and the delegation of the Anya-Nya led by
distinguished southern politicians, like Dr Laurence
Wol and Mading de Garang. In these preliminary talks the
two delegations laid down their general principles
regarding negotiations. The Anya-Nya representatives put
the following conditions as a pre-requisite; first, the
cessation of hostilities, with the Sudanese army confined
to barracks; secondly, the acceptance of the SSLM to
represent the southern people in the negotiations; and
thirdly discussion of the southern problem at a summit
conference held in a neutral African country, under the
auspices of a neutral African chairman.

The conflicting parties adopted flexible attitudes
in these preliminary negotiations, was reflected in the
concessions made by each. For example the Anya-Nya did
not stick to their condition of cease-fire before talks.
Nor did they insist on a neutral chairman. On the other
hand, the Government dropped its earlier condition that
negotiations should take place inside the Sudan. Both
sides realized that an unyielding attitude could prec-
lude cooperation with possibly disastrous results. Only
one issue remained unresolved and that was the question
of the host country. The issue was not settled until
Emperor Haila Selaisse conveyed to President Nimeri
(during a state visit to the Sudan in January, 1972)
his acceptance that Addis Ababa be

the place for negotiation and also his agreement to
play the role of mediator and an agreement was reached
to start negotiations in February 1972.

In an interview conducted with Rev. Carr (Secretary
of all Africa Conference of Churches) in Khartoun in
Februray 23 1975, he revealed that contrary to what
people generally believed, the Emperor never played any
role as a mediator between the two conflicting parties
during the process of negotiation. According to Carr
the Emperor refused to play that role before the start
of the negotiations (in spite of his promise to the
Sudan Government) Rev. Carr gave a detailed account of
what passed between him and the Emperor in a heated
discussion in which each reminded the latter of his
promiss to the Sudan Government in this matter. These
are Carr's words:

I arrived in Addis on Saturday , 12 February 1972,
and was informed that the Emperor never agreed to
be the mediator (as was told by the Sudanese Government) and only that he offered his good offices
for negotiation but not to play the role of mediator. I didn't believe this because it was contrary
to what I have been told by the Sudan Government.
This was the first difficulty which faced us in the
... negotiations. I made consultation with the
Southern Sudan Liberation movement and decided to
open negotiation on Wednesday, 16th February. On
Tuesday evening I decided to give a cocktail party
so that the two groups meet each other in an in-
formal atmosphere. Secondly, that evening I had
audience with the Emperor to clarify his role in
the negotiation. During the conversation the Emperor
confirmed that he would not be the mediator.

A heated discussion followed. I told him that if he
insisted in this attitude, this will ruin the process of negotiation and therefore the responsibility
will be his. Even I threatened him that I would
explode the whole matter to the international press
explaining his reluctance to function as mediator
(as he promised President Nimeri) and that he will
be in a very embarassed position. The Emperor understood this and said that he would decide after speaking with Abel Alier, the Vice-President and Dr.
Mansour Khalid, the Minister of Foreign Affairs,
who arrived in Addis that afternoon. I went back to
the hotel and reported back to the representatives
of the Sudan Government and the Anya-Nya leaders
what occurred between me and the Emperor. Here the
southerners lost their tempers and started shouting
that the Arabs (northerners) had deceived them by
saying the Emperor will be the mediator. The Ethiopian Foreign Minister came to the reception and
joined our talks. The following morning the Emperor
received both Abel Alier and Dr. Mansour Khalid.
As a result of those discussions the Emperor allowed
his foreign Minister to open the meeting and nomi-
nated one of his officials to sit in as observer
at the negotiation table. This observer remained
silent during the whole time of negotiation.

When the conference opened on 16th February 1972,
the first thing discussed was the papers submitted by
the two delegations. In the early deliberations each
side took an extreme position, to the extent that
a feeling prevailed that there was no room for compromise. For example on the issue of the political arrangement, the southerners fiercely opposed the idea of

grouping their region alone against the rest of the country. They asked why there should be a southern region alone, and not a western or northern region. They felt that they would be in the position of a small region against the remainder of the country. There was also deadlock on the military issue; for here the question arose whether all the Anya-Nya troops would be absorbed into the proposed southern army or not. The same applied to the "economic" and "security" issues. When negotiators reached deadlock, a proposal was put forward that a committee be formed (later broken into different sub-committees) to study the two documents submitted. The committee's task was to concentrate its discussion on certain points on which agreement could be reached, while leaving the rest for later.

After deliberation the committee was able to provide the two parties with a "basic law" while isolating the most sensitive issues (economic, military and security matters) to be tackled by three separate sub-committees. The two sides went on discussing the political settlement, incorporating it in the basic law and amending some parts. They did the same for the other three matters after they were reviewed by their three sub-committees. The military and security matters – concerning first the size and composition of the proposed southern army and secondly security arrangements for people coming from the bush – were ones on which the conference spent much time without reaching a compromise at this stage.

During discussions the Government delegation proposed that of the 12,000 troops (the total number of the proposed southern army), the northern share would be 9,000. 3,000 southerners were to be recruited from the Anya-Nya, whose total force was about 10,000. According to the proposal of the Sudan Government, the remainder of the Anya-Nya (About 7,000) would be retained as frontier guards, police and prison forces. This was rejected completely by the southerners, for they could not accept only 3,000 of their troops being absorbed in the regular forces. Their soldiers would have been outnumbered by northerners. When the meeting reached deadlock, the southerners suggested that the conference be adjourned regarding the military issue. Here Rev. Carr (who was selected by the two parties to be the moderator) suggested that the Emperor be invited to use his good offices (for the first time) for mediation between the two conflicting parties. The Emperor responded by calling the negotiators to his palace and suggesting that the total force of 12,000 be divided between them evenly, meaning each side would have 6,000 troops. The Emperor also guaranteed the southerners security against reprisals.[16] This was accepted by both sides. With the removal of this deadlock and with the substantial progress already made in relation to political and economic issues, the two delegations were able to sign at last what came to be known as the Addis-Ababa Agreement, on 27 February 1972. A month later in Addis the ratification agreement was signed by General Lagu on behalf of the SSLM and Dr. Mansour Khalid on behalf of the Sudanese Government.

In an interview Dr. Lawrence Wol talked about the difficulties which faced the ratification process. As was scheduled, the southern delegation left Addis Ababa for Uganda and from there proceeded to meet General

---

16. Eprile, op. cit., p.149.

Lagu in his headquarters in the southern region to
brief him about the agreement. There a general discussion in which senior members of the Anya-Nya armed forces
participated. General Lagu raised a number of issues
particularly in the field of security, in which he
thought the agreement had been rather inadequate. Some
politicians, who felt left out of the agreement had
believed that they could get better terms if they went
to Addis, complained that the agreement had been inadequate. They suggested to Lagu that instead of going
to ratify the agreement, he should inform the Sudan
Government that he wanted further negotiations about
the points he and the others had raised. It was in the
light of this situation that General Lagu felt he should
go to Addis Ababa with a new team bearing in mind the
terms of the agreement on security. He decided to take
eight military advisers and one civilian, Mr. Joseph
Oduho, who acted as his political advisor. He thus left
behind all the members of the former negotiating team.

When the team arrived in Addis they conveyed to the
delegation of the Sudan Government their desire for
further negotiations but this was completely rejected
by the latter on the grounds that they came to Addis
to ratify the agreement and not to enter into any new
negotiations. When General Lagu realized that the Government was firm in its stand, he decided to go ahead
with the ratification process and called back all
members of the first delegation which had negotiated
the agreement to join him in Addis. At that time only
two members of the former delegation Dr. Lawrence himself and Mading de Garang were present in Addis and
they therefore became part of the new delegation. On
27 March the agreement was ratified.

The agreement was embodied in a law called "The
Southern Provinces Regional Self-Government Act, 1972",
and signed by President Nimeri on 3 March 1972. Under
the law the provinces of Bahr El Ghazal Equatoria and
Upper Nile were to constitute a self-governing region
to be known as the Southern Region. It established
a people's Regional Assembly as the legislative body
for the Southern Region and a High Executive Council.
It defined the following as national matters not subject
to the legislative and executive jurisdiction of the
Southern Region's Executive Council or Regional Assembly:
national defence, external affairs, currency and coinage, air and interregional river transport, communications and tele-communications, customs and foreign
trade (except for border trade and certain commodities
which the regional government might specify with the
approval of the central government), nationality and
immigration, planning and public audit (appendix III
to the Act).

The People's Regional Assembly was given power to
legislate for the preservation of public order, for
internal security, and for administration and the
development of the Southern Region in cultural, economic and social fields. The latter related to regional
financial resources, the machinery for regional and
local administration, traditional law and custom,
prisons, state schools, local languages and cultures,
town and village planning and construction of roads,
trade, local industries and markets and traders'
licences, public hospitals, health services, animal
health, tourism, zoological gardens, museums and ex-
hibitions, mining and quarrying, police and prison recruitment, land use, pest control, forest products and

pastures and self-help schemes.

The law guaranteed freedom of movement, citizenship rights, personal liberty, equal opportunities for educa- tion, employment, commerce and profession, freedom of religion and conscience, protection of labour and free- dom for the minority to use their language and develop their culture. The basic agreement provided that Arabic would be used as a working language in the Southern Region, as well as any other local language that might prove useful for efficient administration or under certain practical circumstances. Juba was selected as the capital of the region and the seat of the regional executive and legislative body.

Thus a peaceful settlement was worked out in the case of the southern Sudan. The uniqueness of the settlement resides in its being the result of negotia- tion (this in comparison to Biafra). The conflict was not resolved on the battlefield: but at the negotiating table, and neither of the two conflicting parties could be designated winner or loser, since both emerged with equal powers after the negotiations.

Conclusion

Thus from the review of the method of resolution in each case, we can conclude the following:

That an agreement was reached in the case of the southern Sudan because the two conflicting parties realized that their goals could not be achieved through prolonging armed conflict. They recognised that it was better to lay down their arms and enter into negotia- tions. In actual fact the readiness of the Sudan Gov- ernment and representatives of the Southern Sudan Liberation Movement to enter into negotiations reflected

a reassessment by both sides of what they stood to gain
or lose by the prolongation of the war or by an agreement on the most generous terms which the other side,
in the light of its own interests, would be ready to
concede. The Sudan Government had come to believe that
a possible solution should not be obstructed by the
previous attitude that the Government should not negotiate
with outlaws. In connection with this, it should be
mentioned that the conflict in the southern Sudan was
prolonged for 17 years because during the period 1955-
1970 the southern leadership was in a state of disarray
and fragmentation and this in a way made it difficult fo
the Sudan Government to identify which of these organizations truly represented the southern Sudan (whether
the Anya-Nya in the bush or one of the southern organizations formed by leaders in exile e.g. the Nile Provisional Government) so that it could enter into negotiations. It was only after the emergence of a united
leadership in 1970 under Joseph Lagu (with the Anya-Nya
as the sole authority in the southern Sudan) that the
way was paved for a negotiated settlement.

In the Nigerian situation the possibility of a
peaceful settlement was ruled out completely because of
the existence of an arrogant leadership in Biafra,
whose main concern was to obstruct any peace plan put
forward. The main strategy of this leadership in peace
talks was to follow a rigid, inflexible line. Until
its collapse, the leadership remained convinced that
the Biafran soldiers could stop the federal advance
and save the territory of their fatherland. "Never in
history have a people lost a war of independence" -
this was Governor Ojukwu's repeated assertion which he
intended the people of Biafra to accept as an article

of faith. Because of this firm belief in the existence
of Biafra, the leadership rejected any peaceful initiative to end the war and preferred to continue the
struggle. In this situation, the Federal Government had
no alternative but to resolve the conflict on the battlefield.

With the termination of the war in both the Sudan and
Nigeria, we can now ask whether the real problem has
been solved or whether there is any possibility of the
conflict breaking out again. To answer such a question
we have to look at the way in which the major causes
of each conflict have been dealt with. If they have
been properly handled there can be no danger of the
country falling once again into chaos and disorder.

The main reason for the Ibo secession from the Nigerian federation, was their exclusion from central political office. The Ibo were of the opinion that they
were the group qualified to govern because of their
higher education and economic advancement. They were
resentful at seeing what they considered an ignorant
and less developed people (the northerners) dominating
central power. The Yoruba also shared this grievance
with the Ibo, since they too were excluded from central
power. In order to solve that problem a system of Government had to be developed in which there would be no
chance for one major group to dominate the centre.

A twelve state decree issued by General Gowon on 27 May
1967, introduced a government system which was supposed
to embody this principle. For instead of three or four
large regions the system involved a number of states -
a minimum of twelve, with the possibly of larger number
at some time in the future when conditions permitted an
examination of popular attitudes and an exploration of

the political and economic problems posed by alternative
patterns of division. In the centre there would be a
stronger government than formerly, the states being
smaller would have less effective power and fewer economic resources than the regions had under the older
system, when they were autonomous.[17]

The creation of the twelve states in place of the
four regions has removed the most obvious imbalance
which was not directly ethnic but had ethnic overtones
as the north, east and west were each dominated by
a single ethnic majority. Some states are still in the
position of being either homogeneous or having a single
ethnic majority, East Central is Ibo, Western State is
Yoruba, Kano is Hausa and North West and North Central
are dominated by Hausa. But the overall position is
now such that the ethnic balance within each state or
between states should not be an issue which in itself
could topple the federation, whereas previously the
dominant position of the north and the Hausa within the
north was in itself the major political issue.

In that way the system would reduce the possibility
that any one region could dominate either the centre
or any other regions, because the north, which previously had half of the seats in the Federal Assembly,
would now be divided into at least six states. Thus
the Ibo would no longer fear northern domination, for
according to the principles of the system this could
never happen again. The reaction of the north to its
division into six parts was positive. Opinion generally viewed the new state system as a spur to development.

17. C.R. Nixon, "Self-determination: The Nigeria/
    Biafra Case", World Politics. Vol.XXIV, No.4, July,
    1972, (Princeton University Press), p.483-4.

So after the correction of this main deficiency of the older system - which was fundamentally responsible for its collapse and for the series of crisis into which Nigeria had fallen - we can say without any reservation that the possibility of future conflict is remote.

Now what about the southern Sudan conflict, is it finally resolved? Does the agreement satisfy the interests of southerners and solve their problems or does it fall short of achieving the objectives? To answer such questions we have to recall the major reasons behind the uprising. As we noted earlier, southerners revolted mainly because they felt that they were the most neglected group in terms of political, social and economical development. After independence all the key posts in their region (army, police and administration) were under the direct control of the northerners. Economically their region was the most backward and the least developed in the country. Socially, the inhabitants of the region felt that they were degraded and humiliated by the ruling northerners.

So the question to ask here is whether the Addis Ababa Agreement failed or succeeded in healing these wounds and in redressing these grievances? If we study the agreement closely, we find that it does provide southerners with what they aspired to: self-governing status for their region where they would have full control of their own affairs. According to the second provision of the agreement the southern provinces of the Sudan "shall constitute a self-governing region within the country and shall be known as the Southern region". The region has its own legislative and executive organs. The legislative body (called the People's Regional Assembly) is empowered to legislate

for the preservation of public and or, internal security
efficient administration and the development of the South
ern Region's cultural, economic and social affairs.[18] Whil
the regional executive authority (vested in a High Executive Council) which sits on behalf of the national
President and is responsible to the President and the
Regional Assembly for the efficient administration of
the region, is empowered to specify the duties of the
various departments in the Southern Region provided that
on matters relating to ministers and departments of the
Central Government it shall act with the approval of the
President (of the Republic). Those who are selected to
exercise these legislative and executive powers will be
mainly citizens resident in the Southern Region.

By granting self-government, the agreement was able
to redress the major grievance of the southerners, which
was centred around their region being controlled by
northerners. From now onwards the southerners are direct
ing and controlling their own affairs. The days of
northern control are over, for all key posts are now in
the hands of southerners.

In addition, the agreement spelt out measures to be
taken in order to stimulate economic development in the
region, (in an attempt to remove the economic inequalities which existed between the north and south. For it

18. Among the matters excluded from the jurisdiction
of the Regional Assembly and the High Executive
Council are national defence, external affairs,
currency and coinage, air and inter-regional river
transport, communications and telecommunications,
customs and foreign trade, except for border and
certain commodities which the Regional Government
may specify with the approval of the central Government, nationality and immigration (emigration),
planning for economic and social development, educational planning and public audit.

vested the regional government with the right to levy
duties and taxes (i.e. direct and indirect regional
taxes; revenue from commercial, industrial and agricultural projects in the region in accordance with the
national plan) and to receive contributions from the
Central Government (i.e. funds from the national treasury
for established services, and funds voted by the National Assembly in accordance with requirements of the
region.)   In addition the regional government is empowered to engage in border trade if it sees that certain
essential commodities have to be provided for the region
(those commodities which the regional government may
specify with the approval of the Central Government).
Finally, the agreement stipulates that the region has
to have its own special economic planning board and its
own development budget. All these measures are aimed at
generating economic growth in the region and removing
inequalities.

Generally speaking, we can say that the agreement
has worked well in meeting the demands of southerners,
in satisfying their interests and in correcting the
mistakes of the past. So to some extent, it can be seen
as a victory for the southern cause.

Thus in conclusion we can say that as long as the
past causes of each conflict have been properly handled,
then there is no danger of either country falling once
again into chaos and disorder.

RESISTANCE AND COOPERATION IN BAHR EL–GHAZAL 1920–1922

By Damazo Dutt Majok

The first two years (1900-1901) of the Anglo-Egyptian occupation of Bahr al-Ghazal did not witness any hostile relations between the indigenous people and the alien forces, however, the reluctance of the British forces to give presents to the local people on route from Mushra' al-Raq to Wau resulted in local refusals to provide them with carriers.

Agar Resistance

Resistance to British rule started in 1902 among the Agar in the east and ended in 1922 among the Malual people in the north of Bahr al-Ghazal.

The Dinka Agar have traditionally opposed encroach-ment whether local or external. From the 19th century onwards, the Agar resisted the Nuer for several reasons: firstly, to defend their cattle, women and children; secondly, to check Nuer attempts to occupy their land and make them landless as Nuer invaders from Bahr al-Ghazal did to the Anyuak and Dinka whose country is presently occupied by them. As for external intruders, the Agar have resisted slave traders, Turco-Egyptians, Mahdists and the French.

With such a long traditional hatred of alien intru-sion, they similarly resisted the new invaders in 1902. This antagonism was so inbred that one of the members of the inquiry committee remarked that: "From all our inquiries there was no personal animosity in the attack, simply Agar rooted objection to any form of government which I believe is well known to all travellers in these

parts"[1]. The second cause of resistance was the desire
of the British Government to arrest Manyang Mathiang,
the Agar leader who organized the foray against the Agar
Ban clan and the attempt to recover confiscated cattle.
Thirdly, the instigation by Nuer and a certain northern
Sudanese adventurer, Mohammed Ahmed, of hostility to
the British. Fourthly, acquisition by troops of supplies
from the Agar who were already suffering from famine.

In 1902 a camel convoy commanded by Captain Scott-
Barbour left Shambe for Rumbek. As it forded the river
Naam, it stopped so as to enable the troops to cook
their breakfast and Scott Barbour after photographing
some hippo and shooting an antelope for his men went to
rest in a rakuba (grass shelter) built by Shaykh Manyang.
While he was in the rakuba, many Agars came from the
cattle camp and some of them entered the shelter to
present a gourd of milk and eggs to him. The gift was to
divert attention and he was brutally murdered. The other
Agar outside the shelter who had been watching the
soldiers, killed them all except four who escaped, one
to Shambe and three to Rumbek. Animals and provisions
were all looted.

When news of the murder reached Khartoum and Wau,
British officials reacted promptly and violently. "The
Government determined not to be delayed in its scramble
for the frontier and fearing a general rising, reacted
with extreme violence"[2]. Hence it sent a punitive patrol
against the Agar to revenge the death of Barbour and his
men. Leading 44 soldiers, Major W.H. Hunter Bey, the

---

1. SIR, No. 93 App. B, April 1902, p.6

2. G. Sanderson, Some Problems of Colonial Rule and
   Local Response in the Southern Sudan. C. 1900-1920,
   p.10.

commander of Bahr al-Ghazal bombarded the Agar for one month. "Villages which had any hand in the murder were burnt, the sheikhs shot and their cattle confiscated".[3] The Agar were defeated by modern weapons. After their victory, the British soldiers withdrew to Rumbek leaving behind them burnt villages and forty-two Agar leaders dead, and driving with them tremendous numbers of cattle and sheep.

As Manyang Mathiang was not captured during the first patrol, the British authorities sent a second patrol against the Agar from Khartoum commanded by Stack.[4] This larger force equipped with sophisticated weapons, landing at Shambe, marched against the Agar and for another month systematically devastated their country. Stack burnt huts, confiscated sheep, shields, spears and guns, looted dura and tobacco. He murdered 50-60 men, but Manyang escaped once more to organise further resistance against the British invaders.

In June Manyang attacked Rumbek, but he was driven away by heavy fire. However, again he raided the cattle of chiefs friendly to the Government. This urged the Government to send a force against him. Manyang encountered it but he was seriously wounded. Leaving behind twenty-four dead he retreated to organise further opposition, but died of his wounds. His death demoralised the Agar they stopped being hostile and finally surrendered to the Government. They handed over all their spears to the authorities and as a result the new invaders re-established law and order.

---

3. Report on the Shambe Field Force. SIR No. 94, App. "C", May 1902.

4. The future Governer-General of the Sudan who was assassinated in Cairo on 19, November, 1924.

This bloodshed was in contradiction to the British policy of winning the inhabitants over by friendliness. Moreover, it did not instil permanent fear in the Agar who persisted in their resistance. The Agar were angry about British employment of Atuots in the expeditions. The Atuots paid off old scores helped themselves to Agar women and cattle and enhanced inter-tribal violence. "Besides losing their men in the battle, the Agar had some of their boys carried away by the soldiers to be brought up and recruited in the army".[5] The ex-paramount chiefs of Agar, Bakhit Rehan (Rok Reec) and Khurshid Awedo of the Bongo were among these boys. As they served the Government satisfactorily, they were appointed after the First World War as chiefs to help run local affairs in Rumbek.

Zande Resistance to the British

After the Agar, the Azande of King Gbudwe resisted in 1905. Like the Agar, Gbudwe hated the alien intrusion from the very early days and was hostile to Arab and European interlopers. Consequently he became "the staunchest assertor of Zande independence".[6] In his wars of independence in the 19th century, Gbudwe had fought the combined forces of "Muhammed Abd al-Sammad, Ghatias and Aboo Groon , the ivory and slave traders".[7]

---

5. Interview with elder Muorwal Long Cinkou in Rumbek, November 1976. He worked with condominium forces while he was a small boy and at the age of eighteen was recruited into the army. He participated in several punitive patrols including that sent against Ariathdit in 1922.

6. P.S. Santandrea, A Tribal History of Western Bahr al-Ghazal (Bologna 1964), p.43.

He was victorious and expelled them from his kingdom.
In the same century he resisted the Turco-Egyptian and
Mahdist forces. The former subdued him in 1882 and took
him as prisoner to Deim Zubeir. The latter released him
in April, 1884[7] when they occupied the province. After
his release however he fought his liberators as they
demanded from him slaves and support. He refused to send
these to the Mahdists because he thought himself autonomous and free from Arab interference and decided that he
should fight. Thus he ordered all his sons and Zande
warriors to resist Mahdist encroachment. In the encount-
ter which ensued between Gbudwe and the Mahdists, the
Zande fighters successfully expelled the invaders from
their land. The Mahdists did not reorganise their forces
and renew the battle with him as Karam Allah their commander was ordered by the Khalifa to evacuate the province and suppress the revolt in Dar Fur. The Mahdist
withdrawal had therefore left King Gbudwe as a powerful
and undisturbed leader in Zande country. Thus he remained
for two decades until the occupation of Bahr al-Ghazal
in this century.

Before the Condominium occupation of his country,
Obudwe faced the Belgian forces who coveted his kingdom
to serve their interests in the Congo.

In a battle at a fort on the Mayawa river in 1904,
he lost many of his bravest men. Hence he became dispirited and ordered the withdrawal of his men and abandoned the fight with the Belgians. Although Gbudwe lost
the Mayawa battle, he never forgot the "humiliations
that were heaped on him by his alien captors at Deim

---

7. E.E. Evans-Pritchard, The Azande History and Political Institutions (Oxford 1971), p.340.

Zubair in the north".[8] Thus, "once he was freed, he must have sworn to die rather than to yield again".[9]

After the Condominium forces had occupied Bahr al-Ghazal, Sparkes Bay led a mission to Sultan Tombura's Court in 1901. Having welcomed Belgians and French previously, Tombura thought it wise not to resist the British. Nvuto, the elder son of Ndoruma yielded to British rule as well.

While these Zande Sultans sought friendly co-operation with the Sudan Government, King Gbudwe remained aloof from any foreign contact. Observing his reluctance to accept the new authority, British forces attempted to win "his allegiance by sending him presents, letters of friendships, and even Azande ambassadors who pointed out the benefits of British rule".[10] This, however, did not impress the African King who did not reply to these letters nor send gifts in return. The British sent a mission to win him for the Government, but they failed.

When the French evacuated Mivolo post, the Sudanese authorities tried once more to bring the Zande leader under their control. This last attempt failed too and the officials in Khartoum were now convinced that they should use force against him. In 1904 British forces passed through the teritory of Sultan Tombura who had had strong, cordial ties with the Government since 1901. There were already family rivalries and animosity between Sultans Tombura and Gbudwe attributed to a power struggle over the whole Zande land. These conflicts prevented them from uniting against the external threat.

---

8. op. cit., p.334.

9. Santandrea, op. cit., p.43.

10. Collins, King Leopold. England, and the Upper Nile (Yale University 1968), p.152.

Seizing the opportunity of the British patrol against Gbudwe, Tombura offered the alien invaders his help to effect the liquidation of his rival besides allowing the establishment of a military base in his land, he provided carriers, guides and supplies to facilitate the movement of the invading British forces. British troops marched against Gbudwe with two aims; to annex and administer the Zande land, and to prevent growing Belgian and French political influence in Central Africa from reaching Zande land.

Colonel W.A. "Bully" Boulnois, the Commander and Governer of the province divided the expedition into two columns for strategic reasons. The eastern column of 150 men commanded by Lieutenant Colonel Sutherland marched from Rumbek via M'volo. The western column comprising 600 men and artillery commanded by the Governor himself proceeded via Tombura from the north-west to the territory of Gbudwe.

The British expected strong resistance, but Gbudwe was already exhausted in wars with his nephews Renzi and Bafuko and the Belgians. Hence when the British soldiers reached his territory, they were not resisted. The few who resisted were fired at and escaped into the bush with their leader from the court. During the escape, King Gbudwe was mortally wounded and died shortly afterwards in February 1903. His death resulted in the annexation of Zande land and possibly to the limitation of further Belgian and French encroachments there. The only loser was Sultan Tombura Rewe who having helped the expedition with the hope of territorial gain, received nothing other than tight British control of the whole of Zande land including his own. He was deposed in 1911 by the Condominium Government. The soldiers spread throughout the land forcing remnants of resistance to

submit to the new rule. Being overpowered by alien organisation and technology, the Azande co-operated with
the new rulers because further resistance would have
cost them much loss of life.

Having solved the Zande problem, the British Government negotiated a new treaty with the Belgians in 1906
cancelling the Anglo-Congolese treaty of 1894. The Belgians took the Lado enclave and withdrew from Zande
land in favour of the British Government. This left the
British sole rulers of Bahr al-Ghazal.

Fertit Resistance to the British

The third group of local people to oppose British encroachment were some of the Fertit tribes of western
Bahr al-Ghazal. "At first, generally, most, but not all
welcomed the arrival of the British rule and were prepared to trade their independence for security".[11] This
quick acceptance of the new government was due to past
agonies caused by Mahdist incursions from Dar Fur, Zande
raids and depredations from nearby tribes. Despite the
fact that they hated Turco-Egyptian and Mahdist interference, they were too weak and disunited to oppose
their invasions.

Although at first the Fertit exchanged independence
for British protection, they became disgruntled and
revolted against the new authorities. The leaders of the
uprising were the three powerful sultans Musa Hamid of
Feroga, Murad Ibrahim of Kreish Hufrat al-Nahas and Andel
'Abd Allahi of the Ngulgule tribes. The nature of their
countries helped them to hold out against the Government
for some time. "The great distances beyond the isolated

---

11. R.O. Collins, <u>Land Beyond the Rivers</u>, (Yale Univer-
    sity 1971), p.219.

administrative centres afforded means to escape, while French Equatorial Africa provided a sanctuary from which to plot the overthrow of the British authority".[12]

The motive for resistance was purely religious. The three leaders were fanatic Muslims. One of their grievances was that despite their desire to be annexed and administered from Dar Fur with other Muslims, the British forcibly annexed them to Bahr al-Ghazal. "This was because of their diverse dialects the British officials assumed that they were purely Southern Sudanese and should be adjoined to their kinsmen in western district rather than to Dar Fur".[13] Another grievance was the insistence of inspectors and mamurs on trying local cases which needed Muslim judges following Islamic law. British officials sometimes interfered in their courts to settle marriage, dowry, and adultery cases in ways which were not Islamic. They did not want any longer to serve the 'infidel government. Alien interference also reduced the positions of the sultans or shaykhs as many cases were no longer seen by them because the services and benefits these local leaders used to obtain from their subjects in form of labour in houses or fields, tins of honey and grain as well as meat and tusks were

---

12. Ibid.

13. Interview with elder Murad Angarab in Khartoum, August, 1977. Hajj Murad is a citizen of Kafia Kingi. A Kreish by tribe he lived during his boyhood and manhood at Rodam, Kafia Kingi, Hufrat al-Nahas and Raga. In 1921, he followed his father to Dar Fur when his tribe was annexed to Bahr al-Ghazal. From Dar Fur he came to el Obeid and then Khartoum where he now lives.

interfered with[14].

After the occupation in 1898, some Mahdists who were originally from Kreish, Feroga and Ngulgule tribes returned to their ancestral homes. These brought with them the hope that this Government like the Turkish infidel government would be forced to leave the country when the suitable time to declare the jehad against it had come. Hence when these shaykhs revolted against the Government, it was held by the people that the moment to strike was there. Moreover, the Abbaniya, Risaigat, and Berdi Baggara nomads as well as other Muslim residents in Raga and other stations promised secretly to support them during the uprising. "The Fur tribes even sent their Sultan "Ali Dinar to move at once to deliver them from the infidel and stop paying taxes to the Kufra"[15].

The first to resist the British was Sultan Musa Hamid one of the few local leaders who had originally submitted. In 1907 the Government suspected him of having ordered his followers to murder a black government soldier in Raga. "So he escaped to Central Africa for refuge and to organise his followers against the infidels"[16].

---

14. Interview with Sultan Khoso Muhammed Sughaiar at Khata Paga, January 1977. He comes from Kreish Hufrat al-Nahas that resisted British troops in 1912 under the leadership of Sultan Murad Ibrahim. He claimed to have participated in the resistance and was arrested but released later. He succeeded his father who was appointed by the British in place of Murad Ibrahim after Fertit resistance was repressed.

15. Interview with Shaykh Abd al-Shakur Musa Hamid at Khor al-Saman Raga, January 1977. He is the son of Sultan Musa of Feroge, who together with Sultan Nasr Andel of Ngulgule sent envoys to Khartoum in early 1900 to greet the Governor-General and take flags from him. He was in Qoranic School in 1904 when the British first came to see his father in Raga.

16. Ibid.

But as soon as he reached there, he was arrested by the French and handed over to the British. Subsequently he was exiled by the Government to Sennar and Khartoum where he stayed for six months. By 1908, as his attitude was considered to have improved, he was sent back to Raga. His professed loyalty, however, was only a pretext because when he reached Raga, he immediately escaped again to French territory. Musa's uprising was not bloody. His movement aimed at the expulsion of Christian government and restoration of Islamic rule and previous customs and prerogatives. He was deposed in absentia and his brother Ahmed Fertak was appointed as Sultan in his place.

The next to resist the new Government after Musa were Murad Ibrahim and Shaykh Andel 'Abd Allahi, Initially their revolt, unlike that of Musa, was more violent and bloody threatening British officials in their areas. Murad was deposed in 1908 and subsequently fled to Central Africa where he was later joined by Andel 'Abd Allahi.

When the French came to western district, they made gifts of money, clothes, beads and the like to influential local headmen, women and children to win their cooperation. This induced the indigenous people and Andel 'Abd Allahi to have a high opinion of France and a low opinion of England. Andel believed that France was the greatest of nations, ruled by an emperor who conquered the world. England was a tiny country owing allegiance to a mere woman. England was so poor that she could give nothing, France so rich, as the monthly payments to the Sultan showed, that she did not know what to do with her wealth. "We hear, however", shrewdly remarked the Shaykh, 'that taking, not giving is the rule in French Congo, otherwise it would be a good thing to

follow the givers of presents".[17] By generosity Shaykh
Andel meant besides French gifts also French non-interference in their affairs and their religion. As his intrigues against the Government were discovered, he was
arrested in 1903 and sent to Wau as an outlaw. But on
route, he slipped off to Murad in French territory to
organise resistance to the alien, unislamic rule.

Having organised their men, Murad Ibrahim and Andel
'Abd Allahi marched against government forces at Hufrat
al-Nahas and Kafia Kingi. They attacked and retreated
to Sultan Sanousi of Ndele for safety. But they were
very unfortunate because while they were preparing to
strike once more at the British in the Sudan, the French
marched against Sanusi in 1911 and killed him. Hence the
French occupation of Dar Banda forced them to return to
the Sudan to look for food and guns.

Mustering 300 rifles, Andel searched out and shot
the indigenous people who supported and lived with the
alien forces at the stations. "His depradations, however managed only to alienate the inhabitants, who rejected his exhortations to rise against the government,
and it became increasingly clear that only a dramatic
victory over the troops would persuade the Fertit tribes
to join Andel's uprising".[18] He and Murad invaded Kafia
Kingi in 1912 to crush the few soldiers guarding it,
capture their weapons and possibly occupy it. But they
were defeated. Andel lost his life in the battle and
Murad was wounded too seriously to continue resistance.
Thus the Fertit resistance ended after the loss of many
lives on both sides.

---

17. D.E.E. Service and Sport in the Sudan: A Record of
    Administration in the Anglo-Egyptian Sudan (London,
    1911), pp.222-3.

18. Collins, Land Beyond the Rivers. p.221.

The pattern of resistance showed resemblances to
northern Sudanese resistance movements such as those in
the Blue Nile in 1904 and in the Gezira in 1908. There
as in Fertit people waited without committing themselves
to see if Adam Wad Muhammed and 'Abd al-Qadir Wad Haboba
would have successes over the British forces, just as
the Mahdi had over the Turks. Hence if Andel and Murad
had succeeded in defeating the troops once, resistance
might have spread throughout Fertit land. Fearing to
rush to the resisting leaders, the Kreish remained aloof
while the British crushed the local uprising. Andel's
hand was chopped off and displayed to impress on the
inhabitants the danger of resistance to the Government.
This meant the end of all open resistance among the
Fertit people, because from then on the British kept the
chiefs powerless.

Atuot Resistance to the British

In 1902 the Atuot had offered assistance to the British
forces in suppressing the Agar. But soon they too started to resist the British under their prophet Awo. The
causes of the resistance were increased government pre-
sure to provide labour, taxes and supplies, consequently
under Awo's lead they captured mail carriers, refused
to maintain roads and did not send taxes and supplies
to the administration. Awo did not, however, succeed
because he was killed by the Government while he was
still preparing for full-scale resistance. His death
did not end resistance as the Atuot were determined to
recover cattle confiscated by the soldiers.

When the inspector ordered them to do their duty,
they disobeyed. "A prominent Atuot, Ashwol, refused to
carry out the orders of the inspector, Headlam, and
when troops were sent to arrest him, they were attacked

by Ashwol's followers, the Luac section of the Atuot and Ashwol escaped to lead the resistance".[19] Government attempts to negotiate were in vain for Ashwol, together with his Dar and Dinka "tiit" (diviners) rejected a peaceful settlement and decided to expel the Government from the country. His prediction of destroying alien rule and the prophecies of the diviners incited the Atuot.

British officials called for more troops from Khartoum. "On January 16, 1910 a punitive expedition of 160 officers and men left Khartoum for Wau where they were reinforced by an additional 150 troops already on garrison duty in the province".[20] The troops were rushed from Wau to Atuot in February.

In the encounter with the troops, the Atuot were defeated. They were too weak to resist the well armed British soldiers and surrendered to the Government. Large numbers of cattle were seized and over a hundred Atuot captured. Ashwol gave himself up to the soldiers, having failed to restore traditional authority. Dhieu Alam was appointed in his place to rule the Atuot in co-operation with the Government.

Dhieu's performance was not satisfactory. The Luac Atuot of the former chief disobeyed his orders. Moreover, Dhieu also refused to maintain roods and provide carriers for the Government. Hence he was deposed and Ashwol was reinstated in 1913 as chief as he had professed his loyalty to the British while in prison. This time Dhieu opposed the Government. In ensuing skirmishes with the troops, he was consistently defeated. Many of his supporters were killed without the Government losing a single man. Their losses in April were 300 deaths,

19. SIR No. 174, January 1909.
20. SIR No. 186, January 1910.

thousands of cattle, sheep and goats confiscated and many houses burnt. Dhieu Alam finally surrendered in May 1918 and Atuot resistance ceased.

Although Atuot resistance was suppressed, the Dinka continued their hostile attitude towards the alien rulers. When Manyang Mathiang was killed in the Agar resistance of 1902, he was succeeded by his second brother Dwol as the Agar paramount chief. But in 1911 his younger brother Malual succeeded Dwol and the British faced another administrative problem. In his early days, Malual refused to pay taxes and in 1914 he and his brothers Dwol and Marial drove their cattle in the dry season to the Agar-Nuer border far away from Rumbek to escape government control. He returned in the wet season to his habitual settlement at Luel 33 miles from Rumbek. "Here he set himself up as an independent chief, entered into friendly relations with the Nuer (by paying tribute to them) and withdrew entirely from government control".[21] Moreover, he offered refuge to all people wanted by the British authorities. Hence the Agar considered him an alternative government and it was commonly known among the loyal Agar that when so and so was missing he must have gone to join the 'other government' of Malual Mathiang.

As many deserted to him, his following increased tremendously and threatened the administration. Moreover, his marriage with a Nuer girl in 1916 brought him Nuer moral support. The natural environment was also favourable, long inflammable grass, forests and swamps made his capture almost impossible. Thus due to his petty acts of brigandage and persistant refusal to recognise

---

21. Interview with elder Muorwal Long Cinkou. See foot
    note 5. above.

the new government, he was proclaimed a "rebel" with LE.
10 (increased later to LE.50) on his head. "This had no
effect because of the fact that many of his followers
were individuals related by marriage to the peaceful
Agar Chiefs added to the fear of reprisals on the part
of Mathiang".[22] In addition the provincial police was
too weak to take any measures against him and his band.
In March, 1918, a patrol was sent against him to effect
his capture and destruction of his following and to
confiscate all his cattle, restore stolen cattle to the
loyal Agar and to burn all villages at Luel. Prior to
this in December 1917 Malual had succeeded in winning
over to his side the Agar Shaykh, Wol Attiam with a large
following. He also asked Dhiou Alam for support in
a joint attack on Rumbek, but the soldiers drove him
from the outskirts of the town. This lack of success
foreshadowed his final defeat. As the troops attacked
him at Luel, Malual and his followers took refuge in
Nuer country. The Nuer, however, in spite of previous
good relations, refused to grant him asylum and instead
stole his cattle. Finding himself faced with unexpected
Nuer hostility, Malual returned to Agar land to encounter the alien forces. After having lost over sixty men
and some cattle, Malual was reduced to insignificance,
and the inhabitants became frightened and kept him
in captivity. When Malual found himself powerless, he
surrendered to the British soldiers accompanied by
a large following including his brothers. This was in

---

22. Interview with ex-chief Roc Reec at Pecong, Rumbek,
    November 1976. He was one of the Agar boys captured
    by the British forces in 1902 following the suppres-
    sion of Agar resistance. He was brought up by Rehan
    effendi a Sudanese soldier and later recruited in
    the army. He left the army in 1917 and was appointed
    by the British as Chief over Agar Dinka.

May 1918 two days after Dhiou Alam's surrender. He was
treated kindly and sent to Rumbek where he was kept
under supervision. He was made to attend the hearing
and trial of local cases in the office of the inspector
and he went on treks with him to Agar land. He enjoyed
the same privileges as Dhiou Alam. The Government collected spears and shields from his followers and cooperation thus was effected with the Agar.

Agaakir and Rek Resistance to the British

Having repressed local resistance in eastern, southern
and western Bahr al-Ghazal, the alien forces turned to
suppress those in central district.

In 1903 Areyo (Chak Chak) was established as an
administrative post for the Malual Dinka and Luo. It was
linked to Wau by a route via Kayango. But as a result
of the Risaigat raid on the Malual in 1909, this post
was transferred to Nyamlell in 1911 to cheek Arab raiders.
Nyamlell was still linked with Wau via Areyo and Kayango,
but this route besides passing through thinly populated
areas, was long and affected by tse tse fly. Consequently a new direct route was opened from Nyamlell to Wau
by the British authorities. "Unfortunately, the road
passed through the unadministered Dinka territory west
of the Pongo river which was under the influence of the
old, but powerful Dinka leader Agaakir"[23].

Before the opening of the Nyamlell-Wau road the
Dinka under this local leader were already hostile to
the Government. They refused to clear roads, to carry
and provide the soldiers with grain in the hope of dis-
couraging the Government from establishing itself and

---

23. Collins, Land Beyond the Rivers, p.215.

repeating the same atrocities as the Turks did in their land. Thus when they saw that the road would run through the territory, "they stated that they would not consent to the "Turks" passing through their country".[24]

In spite of local resistance, the Government executed the plan. It recruited local labour to clear the road, built rest houses and dug wells along it. It also made people pay taxes and provide carriers for administrative officials and ordered the inhabitants to maintain the road and keep it open. Resenting this inhabitants, including diviners, rallied to Agaakir to stage a general revolt against British rule. They were joined by the Rek Dinka of central district especially from Mushra' and Tonj who also hated the burden of the alien administration.

Consequently in 1913 the Agaakir people along the Pongo burnt three newly established government rest houses between Wau and Nyamlell. They also invaded the pro government Luo on the road and stole their spears, grain and hoes and escaped into the bush. Moreover, they waylaid government agents who used the road.

Shaykh "Dhal Awat"[25] joined Agaakir in resistance. His people also opposed the building of the road through their land. They removed the marks from places where new rest-houses were to be erected, refused to work, threatened postmen and other travellers who passed through

---

24. Governor, Bahr al-Ghazal Province, Miralai R.L. Feilden's Report on the Agaakir Patrol, 6 April 1913, B.G.P. 1/2/6.

25. The son of Sultan Chak Chak's uncle who remained behind at Awan, Gogrial and was confirmed chief over its people by the Condominium authorities. His son Tong Dhal who succeeded him was deposed in 1926 and Chan Nyal was appointed in his place. Hence chieftaincy was transferred from Dhal's to Nyal's family.

their land. Hence the gallaba who plied between Wau and Nyamlell were alarmed and diverted their cattle over an untrodden road to Wau market. When local uprisings reached crisis point, with inhabitants refused to comply with government orders, the British reacted promptly to punish the delinquents. But before sending a punitive patrol against the Dinka, the authorities first asked Shaykh Agaakir to come to Wau and explain the cause of his resistance and to pay a fine for burning the rest-houses. Being old, blind and infirm, Agaakir was unable to travel the distance from his village to Wau either by foot or donkey. When he informed the Governor of his physical inability to meet him in Wau, the Governer told him that he would come to him and settle the fine.

Therefore, R.M. Feilden, the Governor, took 350 soldiers in March 1913 to the Agaakir territory to check the revolt. As the troops camped at Bol Ashwol 75 miles north of Wau, Shaykh Agaakir sent them two cows, a bull and a bull calf. Moreover, he again instructed his messengers to inform the Governor that he was too infirm to see him personally and to tell him also that the recent troubles were caused by his son Wek and not him-self. "Agaakir's efforts to persuade his men to carry out his orders were greatly hampered by Wek who did his utmost to counteract the influence of his father and was followed by the younger men".[26] Receiving the message, the troops proceeded to the Pongo river, they met Agaakir accompanied by a large following. The old man reaffirmed his loyalty to the Government, but told the troops again that due to infirmity he was unable to control his men and keep order. His excuses for having

---

26. Political Officer's Report on the Agaakir Patrol to O.C. dated 15 March 1913.

no hand in the uprising were not accepted and Channer, the British political officer, held him responsible for local hostility despite his infirmity and lameness. "Channer regarded Agaakir not merely as a leader, but as a chief or ruler who must be held responsible for the actions of his people"[27] Hence he had to pay the fine.

Having been allowed a fourteen day deadline, Agaakir agreed to bring as many cows as he could to avoid bloodshed between his people and government forces in default of payment. "It was pointed out that government had been most patient, but the time had come when the Dinkas must either pay or take the consequences"[28] The imposition of the fine and threats of punishment aroused local resentment to British authorities. Consequently Agaakir was forced to break his promise and condone resistance. As the deadline expired, Fielden ordered the troops to move against Agaakir's villages to confiscate all his cattle. They destroyed houses and captured over 1100 cattle many of which were cows and calves. The inhabitants engaged themselves in skirmishes with troops to recover them, but many of them were killed in the tall grass. Only two government soldiers were slightly wounded.

Having seized a lot of cattle, the soldiers were recalled in April 1913. Agaakir was too weak to continue resistance and surrendered accordingly. The troops returned to Bol Ashwol and drove the cattle to Wau. The object of the patrol, "a fine" sufficient to cover all possible expenditure had been achieved and the country was annexed to the administration. Moreover, the troops efficiency during the patrol astonished the people

27. Collins, op cit.

28. Governor's Report on the Agaakir Patrol, April 1913, B.G.P.,
    1/2/6.

of central district. Their belief that the Government
was afraid of them and that they could disregard its
presence in the country with impunity disappeared.
Agaakir, trying to reconcile himself to the Government,
sent two tusks, five bulls and a cow to the soldiers
saying:

> I am unable to come in person owing to my weak con-
> dition, but I wish to remain a loyal servant of the
> government and regret the action of my followers
> which led to the patrol. I am anxious that all Jurs
> (Luo) who have recently fled from the neighbourhood
> of the new road should return to their home.[29]

The Governor and the Political Officer doubted his
renewed loyalty and insisted that the Dinka leader was
only stalling for time to prepare himself to resist
again, just as he had done before. Agaakir's expression
of loyalty was, however, sincere. If he had wanted to
hold out against the Government, he would have done so.
When he surrendered Dinka of other Ajaak sections,
Buonchuai, Kongder, Shaykhs of the Malual and Abiem
Dinka and those of central district sent reinforcements
and encouraged him to prolong resistance. But he refused
to combine forces with them simply because they had no
concern in the matter between him and the Government to
which he professed his loyalty. Moreover, Agaakir's
insistence that his son should stop being hostile, show
that the old man was not in favour of this from the
beginning. Hence if he had not commanded such great
respect among his subjects, the Government would have
lost more men, more time and more equipment in suppressing them.

The activities of the patrol in burning villages
and capturing cows and calves are to blame for further

29. Ibid.

hostilities in this district in 1922. It was unfair to confiscate 1100 cattle as compensation for grass and mud rest-houses. Considering themselves robbed, the indigenous people nourished deep hatred against the Government and when Ariathdit rose against it, they were the first to support him to revenge their losses, to restore their cattle and lastly to expel the unjust British from the land.

The punitive patrol and surrender of Agaakir did not produce any lasting results among the Dinka. After a very short time they again decided not to serve the Government. They left the roads uncleared once more, attacked travellers and destroyed rest-houses. Seeing these anti-government activities, the British authorities did not, however, hesitate to send another punitive patrol against them despite the withdrawal of Nyamlell troops to the north during the First World War which left Nyamlell and central districts almost unprotected. Thus, "when Chief Mayar Amet obstructed the movements on the Jur river in 1915, few troops were sent against him in the Central District to foil his activities"[30] Nevertheless, he was checked.

In 1917, the resisting Dinkas raided the people of the loyal chief, Chak Chak. Since they had become a real threat to law and order in the area, British troops reoccupied Nyamlell in 1918. The resisters took refuge in the Agaakir area. Their cattle was confiscated and they were forced into submission. In spite of this they

---

30. Interview with ex-chief Monywiir Rehan at Wunrok, Gogrial, December, 1976, who became chief in 1926 as a result of the retirement of his father. He attended many tribal meetings with Baggara, Nuer and other Dinka tribal sections to settle inter-tribal disputes. He retired in late 1940s for reasons of ill-health.

continued to have occassional fights with the British
authorities in an attempt to expel them and return to
their traditional way of living.

The Battle of Nyamlell

Although the Government was sending continual patrols
to punish the resisters, they were determined to violate
the "order" the British wanted to establish. In May
1920, the Malual subjects of chief Anyuon Aturjong killed
four itinerant fellata traders near Khor Malual 12 miles
north-west of Nyamlell. They were murdered partly for
their goods and partly to challenge the mamur of Nyamlell
who was harsh and oppressive to the inhabitants around
the station. The mamur and the police marched from
Nyamlell to arrest the murderers but failed, since they
were hidden from them, but this led the police to open
fire and confiscate the cattle of people who did not
even participate in the murder. Two innocent people
were killed, their cultivation destroyed and their
cattle driven off to Nyamlell. On their way to the
station, the police were intercepted at the river by
a hostile crowd who attempted to recapture the cows.
The insuing battle was very bloody and violent as the
police fought their way back to the station, "the Dinka
followed to attack the Nyamlell Fort, but were dispersed
by machine gun fire; fifty were killed and about one
hundred wounded".[31]

The result of this quick action was beneficial for
the Government and disastrous to local resistance. When
the Dinka realized the power of the Government they co-
operated with the alien authority. Local inhabitants
lost friends, relatives and cattle which were sold by

---

31. SIR No. 310, May 1920, Dar Fur Province 1/15/82.

Public auction and resold in Wau by the traders. This increased their hatred and determination to resist if a new leader arose.

Ariathdit Resistance

Despite the capture of the Nuer prophet Deng Kur and his banishment to Khartoum in 1918 by the British authorities, peace and security were interrupted again when in the central district another prophet arose, a Malual Dinka of the Pariath clan. In 1915 Bol Yell, who later adopted the divine name of Ariathdit, was possessed by the divinity and retreated to far, isolated land where he stayed for two years. "Coming back in 1917 carrying a strange stick, Ariathdit announced to the Dinka that the Divinity had shown him a happy land where there were no governments and he had come to lead the Dinka to that land"[32] Ariathdit demonstrated to the Malual people that he "could raise men from death, he could turn the government's bullets to water and could, as he demonstrated in 1921, deny rain to the Government's Dinka while granting it his own Dinka". In addition to these wonders, Ariathdit had constructed "an audience Chamber (the House of God) capable of holding over 300 men which was far larger than any traditional Dinka structure"[33]

During local attacks on Chak Chak post in 1918 and Nyamlell merkaz in 1920, Ariathdit was suspected and accused by the British authorities of having master-minded opposition and resistance to the Government. There was some truth in this accusation because Ariathdit's hatred of government was deep-rooted. He addressed the people south and north of Nyamlell urging them to fight

32. SIR, No. 332, March 1922.
33. Sanderson, op cit., p.10.

against the British, and visited the unadministered
Dinkas of Abiem to persuade them to overthrow the alien
oppressive Government and substitute it with a Dinka
national government.

His tours took him in 1920 to Kordofan when the Twic
petitioned to him to resolve the cattle dispute between
them and Ngok Dinka of Kordofan using his supernatural
powers to impose the settlement.[34] When he met the Ngok
Chiefs, Kuol Arop and Akonon Alai, he ordered them to
restore the Twic cattle. Chief Akonon refused and
Ariathdit then cursed him. Subsequently believing that
he had been stricken with dysentry by Ariathdit, the
chief surrendered all the stolen cattle to the Twic. As
the cattle went to graze, Ariathdit distinguished the
picketing pegs of the Twic cattle from those of the
Ngok and each Dinka sections was given its own cattle.

Another cattle dispute in which Ariathdit mediated
was between his own section, the Abiem and the Twic. He
ordered the Abiem to return cattle captured from the
Twic, but one of them disobeyed and refused to do so.
Then Ariathdit became angry and told the man: "Go, but
God will see that thing of yours".[35] The man was frightened by his words and accepted Ariathdit's order to divide
the cattle. Ariathdit came to the cattle camp and finding cattle picketed to the pegs commanded the cattle of
the Twic to stand up. Consequently the Twic cattle stood
up and were restored to their owners. Such miracles
bolstered Ariathdit's reputation among the Abiem, Ngok
and Twic Dinkas and they professed loyalty to him as
the sole authority in the land instead of the British.

---

34. SIR, No. 324, July 1921.

35. Interview with Chief Kuac Kuac at Wudhaum, Aweil,
op cit.

As Ariathdit could not visit every area himself, he delegated his agents to preach religion on his behalf in distant places and to mediate in disputes over cattle and murder cases. "He sent emissaries as far as the Agar Dinka and Luo from remoter parts of the country visited him, some settling around his homestead".[36] His ability to stop local fights made him a great contributor to peace among the inhabitants and they flocked around him as a highly respected natural leader. "He told the people that his spirit hated blood and asked them to stay peacefully among themselves".[37] "Even government officials, who had feared that he might become the centre of an insurrection, could not deny him a certain respect"[38] and they admired his achievement of peace which was the main administrative objective in the Bahr al-Ghazal.

But when Ariathdit became a charismatic local leader, government influence over the people was greatly undermined. Considering him an alternative government to the British, people sent him taxes in the form of bulls and refused to make any further payment to the alien government because Ariathdit to them was "a representative of the Divinity and demanded less taxes than the government".[39] Moreover, Ariathdit's popular cry that it was wrong to pay taxes, provide carriers and labour on roads nourished anti-government tendencies among Dinka and Luo in central and eastern districts. His "messengers"[40] and those of his followers who went far and wide to

36. Lienhardt, op cit, p.77
37. Interview with ex-chief Monywiir Rehan at Wunrok, op cit.
38. Lienhardt, op cit,
39. SIR, No. 323, June 1921.
40. Some of these were not appointed by Ariathdit but exploited his hame. See SIR, No. 329, December 1921.

coordinate armed forces and to hear cases, spread
sedition and persuaded chiefs not to pay taxes and to
prepare to fight the intruders. Many were won over to
Ariathdit's side. "Even the Chiefs loyal to the government were compelled to renounce their loyalty to the
government under the threat of destruction of their
crops by blight or drought"[41] Thus when Ariathdit's
tours gained popular support, the authorities felt
threatened and advocated his removal. The Governor noted
that, "If we are to continue to administer the triangle
Nyamlell-Mushra'-Rumbek, Ariathdit must be removed".[42]

Ariathdit proudly went on receiving taxes and fines.
His intelligence network succeeded in deceiving the
Government about his comings and goings. The Wau authorities consulted Khartoum again saying: "Ariendit (sic)
relies on the whole Dinka world to join him".[43] Having
been alerted for the second time, the Intelligence
Department, Khartoum, wired the Governor, Southern
Kordofan describing the situation in Bahr al-Ghazal as
follows:

Ariendeet.... has succeeded to a considerable
extent in undermining Government influence in
Nyamlell and Central District, Bahr al-Ghazal and
has attempted to extend his influence to Gok and
Agar and Rek Dinka of Eastern District as well
as Mareig and Twij and Rueng Dinka on the Bahr al-
Arab in Kordofan. Mesra Merkaz... most police can
do is patrols of roads and telegraph line. Strip

---

41. SIR, No. 328, November 1921.

42. CRO Int 1/20/109 No 2.

43. CRO, Int. 1/20/109, document No. 34A, a letter from
    Governor Bahr al-Ghazal Province, 21st. December,
    1921 to Civil Secretary, Khartoum.

country Nyamlell to Mesra wholly rebellious.[44]

The other outsiders who were also disturbed by
Ariathdit's political and religious propaganda were
the Catholic missionaries. When Ariathdit's agents
travelled from Nyamlell to Wau, Mushra' and eastern district carrying messages to adherents and bringing back
news about the resistance movement, these agents also
went to the Jur (Luo) lands to spread anti-government
propaganda there. Hence being aware that the Jur were
ready to join Ariathdit against the Government and
apostolic work might be interrupted, a priest at Jur
mission wrote to Wau: "We cannot forget that the Jur
peoples are relatives of Dinkas and drink all that is
coming there from".[45]

Chief Lual Dimo near rest-house No. 1 on the Wau-
Mushra' road sent his representative to pay his respects
to Ariathdit in 1921 and to consult him about government
taxes. When this representative returned, he recounted
Ariathdit's miracles which greatly impressed Chief Lual
and his people. He received a spear and was made attorney
general in order to represent Ariathdit in judging cases
and was told to say "I shall soon come to save you".[46]
Besides this representative, many Jur went to Dinks land
to coordinate Dinka anti-government activities with those
of the Jur. They came back and related Dinka readiness
to die for Ariathdit. In all Jur villages on Wau-Mushra'

44. Intelligence 1/20/109, document No. 31B, a telegram
    from the Intelligence Department, Khartoum, 21st.
    January, 1922 to Governor of Talodi.

45. Information on Ariathdit by Hr.X. Magaguoth Catholic
    Mission, Mbili, to Superior Father, Wau Catholic Mis-
    sion dated 19th. November, 1921, B.G.P. 1/1/3.

46. Information on Ariathdit, Ibid.

road Ariathdit's magic influence went on increasing day
after day and was received as a word from heaven. Cere-
monial dances and sacrifices to Ariathdit occurred every-
where in the hope of having good crops. Moreover, people
paid dura tax to Ariathdit before paying it to the
Government.

The gallaba traders in Bahr al-Ghazal had also expressed their readiness to support Ariathdit by all
means. Commenting on the role of these Muslim traders
the missionary wrote:

> I have heard two times that Jellaba (sic. gallaba)
> walking among Jurs for trading purpose said: Aryandid
> (sic Ariathdit) is our black chief: The white chief
> (English people) is (are) powerful but Aryandid is
> more powerful and they are telling fabulous stories
> about him, which introduce and feed subversive
> ideas among these primitive people.[47]

Gallaba support for Ariathdit was not, however,
motivated by sympathy for his political and religious
ideas. Being ardent Muslims, the gallaba had nothing in
common with Ariathdit or the British. They sympathised
with Ariathdit because of their opposition to "southern
policy" which threatened their commercial interests in
the south.

When the British authorities learned of Muslim
support for Ariathdit, the gallaba were confined to
government stations and closely watched. Even those who
went to the Azande and Fertit where Ariathdit was not
supported were seized and forcibly brought to the
stations with threats of confiscating their goods. Thus
the gallaba were discouraged from supporting Ariathdit
further.

---

47. Ibid.

In November 1921, Ariathdit visited areas in the
central district to acquaint himself with the success
of his agents in spreading his movement. He came within
a day's march of Wau and sent a message to the Governor
to come and see him outside the town and discuss provincial affairs with him. Considering Ariathdit his subordinate and his subject, the Governor refused to meet
him outside the station.

While Ariathdit was mobilising his adherents against
the authorities, rumours spread in government circles
that he was planning to start a concerted attack upon
Wau by the whole Dinka population. These rumours were
taken seriously by the British who feared Ariathdit as
a Dinka 'national hero'. R.K. Winter, the Governor,
observed: 'No less disconcerting than Ariathdit's national status - his ability to transcend tribal divisions
and to supersede local "chiefs" and notables was his
skill in political organisation in creating an efficient
network of agents who "worked" the Dinka irrespective
of tribe'.[48]

At first Ariathdit preached against violence between
Dinka sections or between the Dinka and the Government,
either because of his love of peace or because he realised that if he left the Dinka to fight among themselves
or with the Government, he would not attain his aim. He
advised his adherents not to make "hostilities against
the government",[49] and warned the Government not to
attack the loyal Dinka, since any attack on these would
spoil his efforts for peace and security and the Dinka
should be left alone.

---

48. Sanderson, op cit, p.11.
49. SIR No. 325, June 1921.

Ariathdit proved his peaceful attitude to the Government on several occasions. When he saw that his followers had taken five donkeys from Nyamlell, he ordered
them to return them hoping to appease the officials
there. On another occasion his representative was
arrested in Sultan Chak Chak's country for spreading
anti-government propaganda. Ariathdit was asked to secure
his release on payment of ten cows and he accepted the
demand. Moreover, when he heard that some of his adherents had looted a party of the gallaba, he became
annoyed and ordered the return of all the looted property to the gallaba through government officials. Lastly,
as Ariathdit felt that his activities had caused alarm
to the Government, he sent his emissary to Wau for talks
with the Governor. In spite of this British officials
feared that his success as a religious leader would
undermine their authority and the authorities in Bahr
al-Ghazal decided to check Ariathdit's activities before
they resulted into widespread hostilities throughout the
land.

At first they tried to negotiate and in April 1921,
the Governor released Ariathdit's representative from
prison and sent him with a message to Ariathdit to come
to Wau to talk with him promising "a safe conduct back
to his territory whether talks failed or succeeded".[50]
This invitation was, however, rejected by Ariathdit
because according to a government report: "Ariendeet
(sic. Ariathdit) says he will lose his Kujur powers if
a white man sets eye on him".[51] Another reason for refusal was that 'Ariathdit said that his father or mother
never met the white man before and why should he be

---

50. SIR No. 322. May, 1921.
51. SIR. No. 323. op. cit.

asked to do so if the white man did not come to him as
the leader of the land. Moreover, the white man did not
know his language nor did he know his'.[52]

Another diplomatic attempt was made by the Inspector
of central district in May, but this too failed. A third
attempt was made; in September, the Governor sent him
a friendly and influential government chief, Kuol Amet,
from Wau to offer peace if he stopped his activities
and submitted to the Government. Ariathdit expressed his
pleasure and told them that he did not want to have any
hostilities with the British. "He stated that any attacks
on loyal tribes were made against his wishes, and that
all that he desired was to lead a peaceful life, neither
interfering with government of loyal tribes or being
interfered with himself".[53]

Then the Government tried to win back some of his
adherents to British rule through conviction, arrest
and bribery, but this was in vain. Fearing Ariathdit's
influence in southern Kordofan, the Inspector of Kordofan
furthermore "despatched in 1921 an Arab with a gift of
a robe to Ariathdit, however, this was rejected and the
inspector's efforts to win him failed".[54] The Government
was puzzled whether Ariathdit was sincere or simply
waiting for the right moment to attack. It became
seriously alarmed by the actions of certain individuals,
wanting to accumulate wealth claiming to be his agents,
who travelled extensively instigating the Gok and Rek
Dinkas to oppose the Government. Many (e.g. Makuendit,
a Rek Dinka) were arrested by the British authorities
and when questioned admitted to having used Ariathdit's

52. Interview with Chief Kuac Kuac at Wudhum, Aweil,
     op. cit.

53. SIR No. 326, September, 1921.

54. Ibid.

name for their own ends.

Another alarming report was that of a certain northern trader Dirar 'Ali who spoke Dinka dialect fluently.
Dirar told the Governor that Ariathdit had adopted
"a very uncompromising attitude towards the "government".[5]
He added that the person advising Ariathdit not to see
the Governor was an old man "Yor Wal"[56] who was once
imprisoned in Wau by the Turco-Egyptian forces under
General Gordon's administration of the Sudan. Being the
master-mind of Ariathdit's refusal to accept the official call, Dirar claimed that Yor had warned Ariathdit
that if he went to Wau or Merkaz, the British officials
would make him carry stones as Gordon had done during
his imprisonment. Speaking about Ariathdit's military
strength, Dirar Ali noted that in his village (wunding)
alone Ariathdit had a thousand men. Dirar advised the
Governor that: "If soldiers went there, Ariandeet will
I think collect thousands of spear men and fight. The
thing to send is an aeroplane".[57] All this induced British
officials to believe that Ariathdit was a true resister
to the British, that among his adherents were "many
criminals using Ariandeet as a refuge from justice".[58]
Hence, the alien intruders in Bahr al-Ghazal whether
government officials or missionaries unanimously agreed

---

55. CRO. Int. 1/20/109 No. 14A. On a report by Dirar
     Ali to the Governor, Wau. 13 November 1921.

56. Locally nick named 'Yor Amac'. The Malual Dinka
     leader who killed the Mahdist Emir, Abu Mariam in
     1893. See interview with Chief Kuac Kuac.

57. CRO. Int. 1/20/109.

58. Ibid. Document No. 15B.

to denounce Ariathdit as a resister and to crush him accordingly.

The first punitive patrol was sent against a Rek Dinka, Chief Ayok Kerjok near Deim Bashir seventy miles north of Wau. He was an Ariathdit adherent and although he was once a loyal government chief, he became hostile and refused to pay taxes to the British Government. He was supported by his son Kuel Ayok. In 1921, he was summoned by the Government to Wau, but he refused as he professed loyalty to Ariathdit as the sole Government in his land.[59] As Chief Ayok disobeyed the summons, Binbashi Titherington went out to him by steamer on the river Jur to force him and his son into submission. Ajok was arrested and shot on route to Wau. This ruthless and brutal murder precipitated a serious fight in November 1921 between local warriors and troops. "A large number of Dinka obstructed Bimbashi Titherington's force on its return to the river and made prolinged and determined attacks killing one man".[60]

The results of the death of Chief Ayok were twofold: first, the occupation and creation of a government post at Gogrial in 1922 to administer the Rek and Twic Dinka and to facilitate troop movements against Ariathdit in the far north; secondly, many chiefs, even Ariathdit's

---

59. This in the widest sense is not limited only to Dinka if we take into consideration the Dinka calling a Luo of Nuer a Dinka to differentiate him/her from a Northern Sudanese or European. The government meant here is a "Nilotic one" in which the Luo had to fight for side by side with the Dinka as it appears above.

60. A/Governor, Bahr al-Ghazal Province to El Bimbashi V. Ferguson, Nyjong, in a letter No BGP/S.C.R./561, dated 7 November, 1922. BGP/1/2/8.

supporters, were frightened into submission by the
British.

Having silenced the hostile Rek Dinka of Gogrial,
the British authorities started to send patrols against
Ariathdit in 1922. Ariathdit was still mildly disposed
to the British up until Becember 1921, but when his
representative returned from a visit to the Governor in
Wau in 1922, the Dinka became increasingly hostile to
the Government. This might be attributed to the fact
that Ariathdit's agent may have confirmed that troops
were coming against him and Ariathdit was thus unable
to control his adherents.

It was decided that Ariathdit had to be attacked
from three directions, a fact which indicated that he
was to be crushed completely by the intruders. The
Government prepared a large, well equipped patrol in
the belief that "If we are to continue to administer
this triangle, Nyamlell-Rumbek-Mushra', Ariendeet must
be removed at once and all his adherent chiefs punished"[61].
As the troops moved towards Wundiig, Ariathdit's base,
Ariathdit's adherents, consisting of Dinka from Nyamlell,
Kordofan and Mushra' intercepted them at Akuoya on the
Pongo river on 21 February 1922. Deciding to expel
local resisters, Bimbashi Middleton, the commander and
troops first fired into the air, but when none of the
indigenous attackers were hit, they thought that the
bullets had changed into water as Ariathdit had pro-
phesied. Consequently, they charged the troops and
fifty of them were mown down by bullets, a figure con-
tradicted by local sources, according to whom "Ariathdit
alone lost thirty-one of his clan warriors and 150 or

---

61. A letter from Governor, Wau, dated 24th, November,
    1921, to Civil Secretary, Khartoum. B.G.P./1/2/9.
    See also foot note 46 above.

200 men from other Dinka either fell in the field, died
of wounds, perished of thirst in the vast waterless
forests or got lost and died in the jungle"[62].

The Akuoya encounter foreshadowed the future success
of the Government over local resisters. Those who opposed the troops, except Yor Wal's warriors, were the unadministered Dinka. They had mocked chiefs Akot Chak
Chak, Anyuon Aturjong, Awiit Bahr al-Nil, Nyara, Unguec
Ajongo and Dan Marac for cowardice and thought that they
would expel them from the area. This expectation did not
materialise and instead some of them fled with their
cattle and families to loyal chiefs for refuge in the
conviction that the Government was too powerful to
resist. Having forced the local men to retreat, the
troops left Akuoya for Wundiing for further reconnais-
sance and established posts to dump supplies and accom-
modate troops.

When the chief political officer and O.C. patrol
and the last detachment of the "B" column arrived at
Badari on February 25 1922, preliminary operations were
terminated. Then expeditionary forces marched to
Wundiing, the stronghold and headquarters of Ariathdit,
via Ayongdit, Pangab, Kuom and Ariak Riak. No major
clashes occurred en route except at Agaakir. Ariathdit's
houses were locally believed to be impervious to destruction by fire. Hence to destroy that legend the O.C.
B column set fire to them with a Verey light from
a range of 100 yards. "This act had a great effect on
friendlies accompanying the troops who appeared to

---

62. Interview with Chief Kuac Kuac at Wudhum, Awoil,
    op cit. The official report made in BGP/1/2/9 gave
    that 57 local men fell in the field and 13 died of
    wounds later. So the total number killed was 70
    men.

regard the Verey light as a special kind of lightning produced by government at will"[63]

Ariathdit surrendered to O.C. A column at Mareng village on 7 March 1922. Fines were imposed and cattle were collected from all the people involved in resistance to the Government. Besides imposing light fines, the alien forces did not mistreat Ariathdit's adherents as was usually the case after the suppression of local uprisings, such as in the Gezira Aliab and many other areas. The mild treatment of the people was attributed to the fact that they were misled by Ariathdit and by the fact that the Government wanted to co-operate with the indigenous people. They also took precautionary measures in the area to deter them from causing trouble in future. Hence the Dinka and Luo were strongly advised not to call Bol Yel Ariathdit whenever they spoke of him lest they would be inspired to resist the Government again. Consequently, when Ariathdit was caught, he was rushed to Wau for investigation and detention and was not allowed to return to his home where people had faith in his "magical powers which any temporary banishment would affect if he returned"[64] Then the Governor persuaded the Khartoum authorities to transfer him to the north as his presence in the province could undermine security at any time in the future. Therefore, Ariathdit was exiled to Omdurman where he was kindly treated as a political prisoner. However, as he was suspected of trying to escape, he was sent from Omdurman to al-Damer for safety.

After his removal, the Governor and officials visited all the disaffected areas urging the chiefs and

---

63. Report by O.C. 'B' column. B.G.P. 1/2/9.
64. C.R.O. Int. 1/20/109, No. 7.

notables to recognize the Government and to pay arrears
ushur and imposed fines. Having annexed the unadministered areas which had backed Ariathdit against the Government, the British authorities reorganized the administration of the central district in April 1922. Subsequently
northern district was created and Aweil became its new
administrative headquarters and Nyamlell, Wad al-Mek and
Bahr al-Nil military posts were evacuated and troops
families and stores were taken to Aweil. New chiefs in
addition to old ones were appointed to help run local
affairs in the newly annexed areas. A new post was also
established at Gogrial on the Jur river as a winter
residence for an A.D.C. to administer the newly annexed
Twic Dinka. Hence as a result of establishing the two
new posts in the central areas of the Dinka, British
officials were able to control tribal affairs directly.

After these events, the Dinka were peaceful until
the Government allowed Ariathdit to return to Aweil in
1936 and his adherents believing in his magical powers
became hostile again. As Ariathdit "was old and the
government entrenched, however, nothing came of this"[65].
Moreover Ariathdit had to report frequently to the
D.C.'s office at Aweil and the D.C. ordered the arrest
of the Dinka involved and finally instilled feared into
the would-be resisters.

Before the resistance inspectors had stayed at
province headquarters without making regular treks
through their administrative areas. After 1922, the new
administrators - D.Cs. and A.D.Cs. repeatedly trekked
in the rural areas learning the "local languages, customs, problems and respected their feelings which had

___

65. Lienhardt, op cit, p.77.

been neglected by their predecessors".[66] Hence the local people began to understand the new administrators who appealed to them for peace, stability and to increase their efforts to work for themselves and the Government.

The end of Ariathdit's resistance introduced a period of peace in which a beginning was made to effect economic and social changes in the province. It can be seen that resistance was staged by individuals without popular support of other clans or tribes in the province. Since they were isolated the deaths of their leaders and defeat were followed by subjugation and cooperation with the new Government.

---

66. Interview with elder Stanislaus, op cit.

THE ORIGIN AND DEVELOPMENT OF THE ANYA–NYA MOVEMENT 1955–1972

By Elias Nyamlell Wakoson

Introduction

This essay has deliberately avoided the complex socio-economic, cultural and political aspects of the south-north relationship in the Sudan. This has been done successfully elsewhere.

The uneasy relationship between the southern Sudan and the northern Sudan has since independence in 1956 been a thorny issue in the body politic of the Sudan. The worst period of this uneasy relationship was between 1955 and 1972 when civil war raged in the Sudan and, almost tore to pieces the largest and potentially the richest country in Africa. Ironically enough, little academic work has been done by Sudanese scholars on the political and military structures of the movement that led the war on behalf of the southern Sudanese against the northern Sudanese dominated governments at Khartoum. The focus of attention of this essay is, therefore, to examine and explain the origin, development and organization of both the political and military wings of the Southern Sudan Liberation Movement, popularly known as the Anya-Nya movement.

A brief definition of the term 'Anya-Nya' is worth mentioning here. The term 'Anya-Nya' comes from the 'Madi' (an ethnic-linguistic society in eastern Equatoria Province) which means 'snake venom'. The movement adopted this name for reasons which are self-explanatory. The name became universally used for the movement around the middle of 1963. Earlier, guerrilla factions that fought in the southern Sudan were simply referred to as 'freedom fighters' or 'the people of the forest' by the local population. Besides the above references, different localities had different names for the guerrilla factions that operated in their locality. For instance, the Ndogo group of western Bahr El Ghazal referred to as the 'Zua', a folk reference to a tough man.

However, it is important to note that the term 'Anya-Nya was being used loosely to include both the military and political wings of the movement. In its strict sense, it should refer specifically to the fighting forces and not the political factions that operated in exile. Thus it is also important to make a distiction between the political and military wings of the movement. This essay will, therefore, treat the military and political wings of the movement separately (also for easy management), though one should not forget that in the immediate pre-Addis Ababa Agreement period, both worked together under the central command of the Southern Sudan Liberation Movement (SSLM) led by Lt.Gen Joseph Lagu.

One other general fact about the Anya-Nya movement deserves mention here. The movement in many ways was no different from other guerrilla movements which operated in Africa. Basically, their organisational structure, political and military strategies and tactics, and even the type of people (social classes) involved in the guerrilla war (rural illiterate population as fighters led by the urban educated class) form an important denominator to all these movements. Yet there is also an important difference between the Anya-Nya movement and other guerrilla movements that have

operated in Africa since the 1960s. Whereas it has
been fashionable for most guerrilla movements in Africa
to adopt Marxist-Leninist revolutionary principles
(some Maoist) as the ideological motto of their movement, the Anya-Nya movement in many ways had no such
an ideology. In the absence of an 'ideology', the
Anya-Nya movement according to its invariable programmes, was fighting to liberate the southern Sudanese
people from northern-Arabicised-Sudanese domination
with the ultimate aim of establishing a sovereign African
state. Other characteristics the Anya-Nya movement had
in common with similar movements in Africa will unfold
in the course of this essay.

The military wing of the Anya-Nya movement

The establishment of the movement started in 1960
and by 1963 recruitment, training and indoctrination,
organisation of guerrilla bands and civil organisations to help disseminate the aspirations and goals
of the movement to the populace were the major tasks
to be accomplished. No clashes with the national
army occurred before September 1963, though isolated
attacks on soldiers or policemen were common, mainly to obtain arms. Assaults were carried out in
various areas on isolated 'gellaba', village shops,
dispensaries or government stores. However, this
phase was characterised by national army offensives
carried out with all available means - operational
and tactical encirclements, bombardments and ruthless
military offensives against civilians.
The second and last stage of the movement (because
the development of the movement was abruptly stopped
by the signing of the Addis Ababa Agreement in 1972)
was a period of re-organisation and the problem of

establishing a unified military command which the first
phase of the movement failed to achieve. Coupled with
this was the task of establishing close links between
the guerrilla front and the political wing which was to
be seen as the legitimate government in exile. Concurrently the political leadership had internal crises
which paved the way for the military front to interfere
more and more in the political functions of the movement.
This trend of affairs ultimately resulted in a coup de
grace by the military wing and the setting up of military government within the southern Sudan. In retrospect,
the first stage was the hardest, a period of trial and
error. The first groups experienced a period of absolute
nomadism, hardening or seasoning of combatants and administrative organisation.

With regard to initial recruitment, one region,
Equatoria Province had little difficulty in organising
groups. The reason for this was clearly explained in an
interview with Lt.-Gen. Lagu. He stated that:

> The Anya-Nya movement is the continuation of the
> 1955 Torit mutiny. Men like Amadeo Tafeng and Lata'da
> kept the spirit of the movement alive since 1955.
> They grouped themselves in isolated pockets and con-
> sidered themselves as the true Southern Nationalists
> and bitterly resented the presence of the Northern
> army in the South. When Southerners started going to
> the bush to pick-up arms to fight the North, those
> in Equatoria Province simply joined the Tafeng and
> Lata'da groups and continued their struggle.

While in the two other southern provinces of upper Nile
and Bahr el Ghazal it was a difficult task because it
started in a vacum. This is a point of significance

---

1. Interview with Lt.-Gen. Joseph Lagu.

and will be discussed in detail. Once the movement
was started, there was no marked distinction between
the military and political wings of the movement in
the sense that the personnel of the two wings overlap-
ped. Oliver B. Albino (Former secretary for Information of SANU in exile), gave further details.

> We joined the movement at first as fighting forces
> as well as political organisers. It was only
> later when the movement suffered many set-backs
> that a revised policy was established. Due to
> some miscarriages in the early military tactics
> many of the educated and enlightened members of
> the movement were being lost. Then General Lagu
> asked all our educated members to go into exile
> and form a political wing for the movement quite
> distinct from the guerrilla front.[2]

A unique characteristic of southern Sudanese guerrilla forces, unlike most guerrilla fronts in Africa
and the Middle East, is that the fighting forces
remained unified up to the end of the war. This needs
clarification. At the commencement of the movement
each region and locality had its own separate command
with only some formal interactions between these commands. There was no one single high military command
for the whole southern Sudan until Lagu assumed that
post in July 1970. The unity of the military forces
can be viewed in the sense that in most localities and
regions, Generals Tafeng and Lata'da were recognised
as the indisputable leaders and patrons of the different
factions of the movement, especially in Equatoria
Province and western Bahr El Ghazal they were recognised

---

2. Interview with Oliver B. Albino, Juba, 3 September, 1975.

as leaders and commanders-in-chief in principle though
in practice they had little authority in the day to
day activities of the different regional commands.
Albino expressed his viewpoint on this issue as follows:

> The guerrillas were unified by the will to fight
> and eliminate a common enemy, every guerrilla from
> any part of the Southern region was regarded by the
> others as members of their own unit but not belong-
> ing to a different unit.

To proceed to the organisation of the Anya-Nya
movement without examining the propaganda they used to
enlist the support of the masses which strengthened
the movement would be overlooking an important aspect
of the whole guerrilla warfare. Propaganda was of two
main types which complemented each other. There was
propaganda of a national type publicised by politicians
in exile to make known the aims of the war to the
world at large. The other issued from the military
front and was carried out by special personnel known
as political agents (to be discussed later) to educate
the masses on the principles and goals of the movement.
It is the latter that forms the theme of this sub-
section. It should be noted that both propaganda
channels originated simultaneously and worked in re-
ciprocity. Analytically we shall separate the two to
enable us to bring out the essence of each strategy.

From 1960 onwards the processes of propaganda,
recruitment, organisation, collection of arms and
sporadic combat advanced simultaneously.

Propaganda was quite simple, plain and straight
forward. It did not attempt to explain the complex
socio-economic disparity between the south and the
north. Neither did the propagandists attempt to discuss the complicated political issues involved in the

conflict or the cultural clash between Africanism and
Arabism.   These were the concern of the political wing
in exile.   The issues presented to the common man were
obvious events which bore directly on their very existence.   The approach chosen here was most successful in
that the masses were very quick to understand the aims
of the movement.

From the outset, Anya-Nya propagandists were able
to manipulate the political and economic mistakes and
weaknesses of the Sudan Government to the movement's
benefit, since the Government portrayed to the nation
and the world at large a false image of the movement.
It consistently referred to the Anya-Nya as groups of
disorganised poorly armed out-laws, as 'rebels', bandits and/or murderers who had no political goals.   The
ignorant masses in the northern provinces (from whom
the real nature of the Anya-Nya movement was concealed)
took the Government's false propaganda for granted.

On the other hand, the Anya-Nya movement was quick
to expose government fronts and suppressive policies
in the southern Sudan to southerners and the world at
large.   The main target of this Anya-Nya propaganda
was the southerners whom the Anya-Nya wanted to convince
of the just and redeeming nature of the movement. Thus
the guerrilla fighters initially called themselves
simply 'freedom fighters' and were later known as the
'Anya-Nya'.   One of the issues which appealed most to
the people was the re-interpretation of the measures
taken by the Government to kill the movement in its
infancy.   Failing to contain the movement, the undis-
ciplined northern army in the south treated the civilian population very harshly, burning villages, murder-
ing women, children, and the aged.   The Anya-Nya picked
up this point and explained to the people that the

army that went to the south was an army of occupation
and they were at war not only with the Anya-Nya but
with all southerners. It was strongly emphasised that
northerners wanted only the fertile land of the south
but not the people. This reminded the local population
of the slave trade and the Mahdia. Thus reinforcing
the point that the Anya-Nya took up arms to protect
the land and the population from Arab invasion.

The issue of taxation was of great concern to Anya-
Nya propagandists. Taxes paid to rural councils were
condemned by the Anya-Nya as robbery. It was explained
simply to the people that northerners were robbing
southerners of their money which was sent to the north
to build their own section of the country. The most
appealing aspect of this propaganda was the contention
that northerners used the bulk of the money collected
from the south to buy arms for killing southerners.
According to Brigadier Emmanuel Abur, interviewed at
Aweil in June 1975, political agents in meetings with
villagers would often pose the following rhetorical
questions, 'are you ready from henceforth to donate
money to the Arabs to buy arms to come and shoot you
with? To whom do you think you can best give your
money, to us or the Arabs?' One can speculate on the
reaction to such questions. The style of propaganda
made people feel that by paying taxes they were directly collaborating with their own killers in the form of
a donation to facilitate the slaughtering of their
children and raping of their wives and daughters. The
truth of the issue was that the taxation process could
not provide the government services expected by the
people mainly because insecurity at the time prevented
the Government from rendering the required social
services.

Propaganda went hand in hand with other activities,
in particular the formation of a civilian administration in rural areas. Propaganda alone could not have
won the popular support of the populace. Among other
events which gained support from the indigenous populace was the institution of a decentralised system of
civil administration in various localities. An Anya-
Nya administrative officer was stationed in each locality aided in his functions by village notables. The
main objective was to preserve justice, redress individual or group grievances and observe law and order.
This reflected a positive image of the movement to the
masses in that they were not only capable of fighting
but also of running an efficient government, maintaining law, order and justice, in complete contrast to
what the uncontrollable army was doing. Social crimes
were condemned and punishable by the movement. In
short, morality and security were restored in the life
of the people.

Developing mainly out of old socio-agrarian grievances directed against northerners, the secular aspect
of the Anya-Nya movement demanded eradication of inequalities between the south and the north and independence under a southern government. While nationalist aspirations were reflected and symbolized in
a demand to foster southern Sudanese African cultures
together with Arab culture. The clash between Africanism and Arabism is viewed by southerners as involving
the whole continent and not limited to the boundaries
of the Sudan. The moral-religious aspect of the movement has dimensions which contributed to the secular
aims of the revolution. Combined with a reaffirmation
of certain common traditional values and customs, these
precepts provided the movement with a moral force

a conviction that the struggle was just and that right
would prevail over might.

Local customs and traditions which were ignored by
northerners were highly respected and encouraged by
the Anya-Nya. They ruled that any breach of customs
and traditions was a grievous crime punishable by laws
established by the elders of each ethnic group. Jurisdiction over such matters was left to traditional tribal chiefs who commanded great respect among their subjects. The Anya-Nya considered them the cherished
social heritage of the people concerned and any interference would have jeopardized the relation between
the Anya-Nya and the civilians. Rainmakers and sooth-
sayers were respected and were sometimes consulted by
the Anya-Nya on important issues. For the elders, the
freedom for which the Anya-Nya were fighting meant
that there would be a return to the traditional way of
life which the Arabs were on the point of destroying.

At the village level, the Anya-Nya left the administration of villages to the villagers. Those who
came to power did so through village elections. The
whole policy behind this system was to make the villagers conscious of the elementary virtues of democracy
and also made them feel that they were their own rulers.
The imposition of a rigid Anya-Nya authority at the
lowest level would have made civilians feel sceptical
of the 'salvation' spirit of the movement.

In the final analysis, the movement won tremendous
popular support from the masses. The mere sight of the
Anya-Nya in an area reaffirmed the confidence of the
civilians that their own sons were always at hand to
defend them and that there was no chance for northerners to take the south without the support of the people.
The success of the propaganda attracted hundreds of

young men to join the movement.

Except for Equatoria Province, where the bases of the
1955 Torit mutineers were recruiting centres from 1960
onwards. Western Equatoria - the Azande area - Bahr
El Ghazal and Upper Nile Provinces passed through two
phases in the recruitment process. Initially recruitment was disorganised and restricted to each locality.
In the second phase recruitment was organised systematically and universalised in all Anya-Nya occupied
territories. The first phase gives an interesting
picture of how the movement commenced in the three
areas.

In western Equatoria it was less difficult to organise the first guerrilla bands. There were many ex-
service men of the Equatoria Corps who became responsible for the recruitment and military training of the
newcomers. Captain Marko Bangusa was the chief training officer in the region. The system used required
the establishment of recruiting centres for training
new recruits before they were sent to the bigger training centres in Zaire.

It was in late 1965 that the first group of fighters assembled at Nyangera and Bangadi - villages inside
Zaire. The camp started with forty-five men, the
number quickly rose to one hundred. Up to early 1964
the numbers rose daily reaching 1000 men, who received
intensive military training from the ex-servicemen. On
graduation, the recruits took the loyalty oath and were
thus ready for combat.

The camp started with no modern weapons except
bows and arrows, spears, 'pangas' and swords. When an
ex-tax clerk in a chief's court joined the movement,
he offered the sum of Ls.40. The money was used to buy
two second-hand muzzle-loader guns. Immediately after

this, two civilians, one an ex-M.P. the other a trader,
offered two guns to the movement. Thus at that time
the camp was being defended by only four ancient guns.

After the initial three-month training period ended,
a small band of fighters started collecting more guns
from civilians. Receipts were given to donors, those
who were not willing to give their guns were forced to
surrender them. However, the collection consisted
mainly of muzzle-loaders, breech-loaders, magnum rifles
and a few British rifles which had been captured from
the police. Other old types of guns like Remingtons,
Manchesters and shotguns were also collected. It was
not until August 1964 that modern automatic rifles,
grenades and two-inch mortars arrived in the camp. The
main source was the 'Simba' (Congolese insurgents).

The movement in Bahr El Ghazal started in a similar
way. In 1964 a big transit camp was established in
western Bahr El Ghazal at a spot known as 'Ngo Sulugu'.
Here recruits were given military training before being
sent to 'Nyangara' and 'Bagadi' in Zaire. Thus, basic
training in western Equatoria and Bahr El Ghazal was
done in the same places. Those from the further fringes
of Bahr El Ghazal - from Deim Zubeir, Raga and the surrounding areas - had their training in the Central
African Empire near the border town of Mboki. In-
service men were responsible for military training.

With regard to the initial supply of arms, guns of
the types mentioned above were collected from civilians
and receipts given in return. Arms were also taken
from the 'enemy'. In November, 1963, Ferdinand Coi, an
ex-seminarian, who later became a major and commanding
officer of western Bahr El Ghazal central camp captured
two British rifles from the police at Bussere - an educational centre ten miles from Wau town. Coi went to
the police station at Bussere and reported that a fight

had broken out in a village two kilometres from the
station during a drinking party. Two people had been
killed and he needed the immediate help of the police
to stop the fight. Two policement were told to accomp-
any him. On the way he tricked them and killed them
both. He took their uniforms, two British rifles and
one hundred rounds.

In Khor Ghana village 65 miles from Wau on the
road to Raga, a band of guerrilla fighters armed only
with spears, swords and knives attacked the police post
at night. In a night long battle bewildered police
kept firing until by dawn they had run short of ammunition. Then the Anya-Nya launched the final assault
killing most of them and collecting light British rifles.

Individual contributions were also made. George Hilal,
currently a major in the Sudan Armed Forces, deserted
from the police force with one British rifle and 200
rounds.

A unique incident in the history of the Anya-Nya
movement was the case of a Dinka lady, currently
a prison officer in Wau. She had good relations with
the soldiers and in August 1964 invited five soldiers
to supper in her house. She provided drinks and invited
four other ladies to come and dance with the soldiers.
The soldiers enjoyed themselves till about 2.00am when
they all collapsed drunk each with a lady beside him.
The host quietly collected the five automatic rifles
and five hundred rounds, wrapped them in a mattress and
escaped to the forest to join the Anya-Nya force. This
was the biggest contribution by an individual in terms
of arms and ammunition to the movement in Bahr El
Ghazal.

Up to December 1964 no major battle occurred
between the guerrilla fighters and the army in Bahr

El Ghazal except for Bernadino Mau's attempt to capture
Wau. He was injured and captured. After receiving
medical treatment, he was tried publicly and executed
by firing-squad. On 30 December 1964 a major battle
which lasted ten days took place between the Anya-Nya
and the army at Bringi, a village eight miles west of
Wau.[3] In this battle it was estimated that more than
200 soldiers were killed, twelve military trucks destroyed and two tanks burned. Many arms were captured
from the army.

Like the battle at Pachale in Upper Nile discussed
below, the guerrilla band used only ancient guns.
Muzzle-loaders were the commonest weapons with a few
British rifles, shot-guns and breech-loaders and molo-
tov bombs or 'cocktail-bombs' as they are commonly
known. The muzzle-loaders had been modified by the
Anya-Nya, and one gun was loaded with between 60-80
lead balls. One shot of such size fired at a group of
soldiers was likely to injure all and kill many, for
this reason the Anya-Nya used to call it in Arabic
'kulu kum' meaning 'all of you'. The 'cocktail bombs'
were effective in burning cars and tanks and were used
to strike at cars, followed by arms fire. In the confusion, the soldiers were often unable to return fire
until the Anya-Nya had withdrawn to safety.

This particular combat had a tremendous effect on
both the army and the civilians. The army became

---

3. The author on his way from Mboro village to Wau by
   bicycle met the combatants in this particular
   battle who stopped him and told him that if he
   went to Wau he should not return the same way on
   that same day because they had laid an ambush for
   the army. The author followed the development of
   this battle closely and afterwards met the combatants who related the story with minute details.

dispirited and demoralised. The army claimed that the
Anya-Nya were fighting side by side with foreign mercenaries who brought them weapons unknown to the Sudanese army.

The history of the movement in Upper Nile Province
can best be summarised in the words of the military
organiser, Daniel Nyang.[4]

The period before 1960 was characterised by a
general threat to one's life. People were being
arrested and jailed without trial including students.
The policy of the government did very much to encourage the mass exodus of Southerners from the
towns to the bush and hence to the neighbouring
countries. I was among those who took refuge in
Ethiopia and remained there in asylum in a refugee
camp with no idea of organising a fighting force
against the Northerners. It was in 1960 that Philip
Pedak left his studies in Britain, came to Ethiopia
and wrote to me asking me to organise a fighting
force in October 1961. As an ex-policeman with
adequate military knowledge, I accepted the offer
and started my work. My son, I started the movement in Upper Nile, saw its development end in 1972.

Thus in Upper Nile Province, the idea of organising
a fighting force started in 1960, but not until the
second half of 1962 did the real work materialise. This

---

4.   Information on Upper Nile Province is incomplete
     because I conducted field work from May to November
     the rainy season in the south. Motor transport was
     virtually at a standstill and in particular in
     Upper Nile where communication during the rainy
     season is non-existent. For this reason I was not
     able to meet prominent organisers of the movement
     in the province.

period should not be regarded as dormant, it was devoted
to the kind of propaganda which has been discussed
above.

Philip Pedak, the political organiser, called a conference in one of the biggest refugee camps on the
Sudan-Ethiopian border in July 1962 and it was unanimously agreed that Daniel Nyang be vested with sole authority for military organisation and training. Up to
early July 1963 a group of 100 well trained men were
under the command of Nyang. On July 10 this group of
fighters established a base camp on the Sudan-Ethiopian
border a little inside Ethiopia, at a place called
Adeldin.[5] Three years elapsed between the decision to
form the movement and then its tentative beginnings.
Lack of concrete organisation affected development.
But once the movement was started, the speed with which
it consolidated itself and became properly organised
was surprisingly fast.

A significant point about the Upper Nile movement
was that unlike the other southern provinces, the movement was initially dominated by one tribe - the Nuer.
The 100 men who initiated the movement in Upper Nile were
all Nuer. It was only later that 10 Anuak joined the
movement. Not until September 1963 did the other major
tribes of Upper Nile Province join the fighting forces
en masse making the composition of the first fighting
camp a provincial force.

Fighting in Upper Nile started with only three
magnum rifles for the defence of 180 men. In guerrilla
warfare the theory that 'the enemy is the principal
source of their supply' was accurately applied in Upper
Nile. It was on 16 December, 1963 that the first clash

---

5.   Interview: Daniel Nyang.

between the Anya-Nya and the police force at Pachala
police post, manned by twenty-eight policemen, took
place. The operation revealed the bravery and determination of the men involved to begin a war empty-handed
against a force that was well armed with modern automatic weapons.

On the date mentioned above, Daniel Nyang, in command of five unarmed men, advanced from their base and
reached the police post at Pachala at 10.00am. They
hid in the vicinity until 5.00pm, trying to assess the
exact force present. In the evening of the same day,
two policemen were weeding in their garden with their
wives. The policemen placed their guns on a tree
trunk about ten yards from where they were working, the
five men attacked; shouting at the top of their voices.
Panic stricken, the policemen and their wives fled. The
five guerrillas collected the two British rifles with
eighty rounds and retreated. At this point they had
five guns. On the same day the guerrilla band was able
to collect thirty magnum rifles from chief Kourlo
Kusi's village.

The same night the force attacked the police post
at Pachala and in a two hour battle captured the post
killing almost all the policemen. The few that survived
escaped to the bush. The guerrilla force seized a sterl-
ing gun with 150 rounds and a shotgun. They were not
able to collect many guns from this battle because
when the police force realised that they had lost,
they broke all their guns. This was a common army
practice in the south. Breaking into shops and the
police safe the Anya-Nya collected Ls6000, clothes and
food, then retreated to the bush.

On 28 December 1963 the police in Pachala were
replaced by the army equipped with tanks, mortars and

heavy machine and automatic guns. The guerrillas gave
them no time to settle and in an immediate attack,
captured one automatic rifle and 6000 rounds. One of
the guerrillas was killed in the battle which was considered a great loss at a time when they were badly in
need of manpower.

The success of the first two operations at Pachala
raised the morale of the Anya-Nya fighting forces and
above all won tremendous support from civilians. The
effect of the incidents was much greater on civilians,
because although organisational work had started in
1960, no battle had yet ensued and civilians were
becoming sceptical about the ability of the movement
to begin a war. However, the operations convinced them
of the ability of the movement to oppose the army. The
visible effects of this first attack resulted in a rise
in voluntary recruitments. Numbers rose from 180 to
1,000 and more in a short time. Then it was decided to
transfer the base camp from across the Sudan-Ethiopia
border into the Sudan. With this many civilians donated
guns to the movement and in an initial collection 60
magnum guns were obtained. Then the camp was divided
into smaller units with each group operating in a specific area, according to tribal affinities. This action
was based on the principle that a guerrilla fights
best among his own people and in a locality which he
knows.

In the final analysis, the important lessons to
be drawn from the initial activities of the Anya-Nya
can be summed up as follows: first, spontaneous and
voluntary recruitment marked the beginning of the movement; second, no foreign elements participated in
training the fighters, the task was accomplished by
ex-service men; third, the movement started its first

operations with local weapons ranging from 'silent
weapons' - spears, bows and arrows, swords to single
shot rifles, while the army and the police were the
only source of automatic weapons; fourth, the first
operations won popular support from the civilians for
the movement which consolidated it at once; fifth,
neighbouring countries refrained from either opposing
the movement or giving it financial and military support but the moral support which they gave can be seen
from the fact that they allowed preliminary training
centres to operate in their territories.

When military training in neighbouring countries
was completed, the fighting forces moved in and established base camps near the borders while fighting camps
were located near villages and towns. In 1964-65, a well
organised system of recruitment was established along
with a civil administration in rural areas, which fell
under Anya-Nya control. New recruits, after receiving
initial military training at the village level were
sent to the central camp of each region to be register-
ed and a strict oath-taking procedure was administered
before any individual was finally accepted into the
movement.

The oath was usually administered by the regimental
sergeant major of the central camp in front of the com-
mander-inchief of the region and some officers. The
procedure was as follows: the newcomer was asked why he
or she wanted to join the movement; whether he was
ready to suffer without food, clothing, medical care
and undergo all imaginable hardships which might lead
to the loss of his life, to isolate himself completely
from women, whether he could abide by the laws of the
movement. Before taking the oath, the newcomer was told
that the oath he was going to take was based on the

idea that he must be committed and loyal to the movement to the last. He must not betray the movement under any circumstance and must work to liquidate any anti-movement elements even if necessary his own kith and kin.

When it came to taking the oath itself, a Bible (for Christians) a spear, gun and bullets were placed together, then the oath-taker put his right hand on them and repeated the following words after the oath administrator.

I....(name)... promise in the name of Almighty God and those present to work honestly for the defence of my country - the southern Sudan - and that I will execute the orders of my commanders as may be passed onto me and will accept any punishment levied on me should I be found guilty as a result of disobedience.

This procedure of strict recruitment constituted the first efficient Anya-Nya groups. Coupled with efficiency was the fact that the oath seemed to implant courage and obedience in the fighters. Up to 1965, the movement was free from any form of corruption. However, in the second half of 1965 when the strict recruiting procedure was relaxed due to a massive exodus of people to the bush, army 'collaborationists' also found their way into the fighting forces. It was difficult for its ideology and those who joined to act as spies. Generally the groups that joined the movement after 1965 fell into four categories: (1) those who in reality went to work for the Southern Sudan Liberation Movement (SSLM); (2) those who escaped from imminent death; (3) those forced by the conditions of the time, especially after the Juba and Wau massacres of 8 and 11 July 1965; (4) those who were government agents and took the opportunity to infiltrate the movement and report back to the authorities.

Of the four categories of people, groups one and two strengthened the movement while three and four brought confusion to it, which for some time produced adverse effects on military activities. Information leaked before operations were carried out. The location of major camps was known to the army. However, it was not long before the movement discovered those responsible and eliminated them. In the final analysis the strict discipline associated with the movement at the beginning tended to weather later on.

Right from the beginning of the Anya-Nya movement, it relied heavily on village populations for recruitment, supplies, transport, intelligence and some medical facilities. If this support were lacking, not even a single battle could be sustained. Thus, it could not risk separating itself from them.

From early 1965 onwards, the Anya-Nya front organised civil administration of those areas which fell virtually under their control. The structure of this administrative machinery as previously mentioned, was similar all over the southern Sudan except for slight variations in different localities. We shall now examine its structure and organisation is some detail. The chain of command, the hierarchy, can be represented diagramatically in Figure 1. Home guards (village scouts) were highly secret groups drawn entirely from the young people of each village or locality. The home guards were well informed on the whole philosophy of the Anya-Nya regular fighting forces. They were not strictly part of the Anya-Nya movement, thus, they carried no weapons except for the chief scouts who were usually armed with pistols or grenades. In a sense they could be called the militia

Co-ordinating Committee.   Supreme Administration

District Commissioner

Executive   Officer

Political Agents

Village Committees

Recruitment Centres

Home guards (Village scouts

Rural   Population

.........................Channel of authority from top to botton.

The Regional Civil Wing of the Anya-Nya- Administration

Figure 1

of the Anya-Nya movement with only basic military training. Interestingly they were not full time function-
aries. They lived in their own homes and were engaged
in their private occupations but were always ready to
render services for the Anya-Nya and the villagers. For
this reason it was extremely difficult, especially for
a stranger in a locality, to distinguish a village
scout from an ordinary citizen.

The village scouts formed the backbone of security
for the inhabitants in Anya-Nya occupied territories.
Their foremost duty was to warn civilians of an enemy
advance. Though using what one might call "primitive"
traditional methods, they were nonetheless, to all
intents and purposes very efficient. The most commonly
used were horns, woodpipe whistles, drums etc. Each
instrument had a special code to transmit messages of
danger or messages which required the villagers to
assemble for a special purpose.

Working in collaboration with village committees
and political agents, the village scouts collected food
and other necessary provisions for the fighting forces.
They were warned not to use force and any breaches were
severely punished. All donations were accepted, but in
most areas, one tin of durra, groundnuts and dry okra
was set as the standard donation from a household.

At the village level, scouts performed a semi-police
function in maintaining law and order. They transmitted
new policies and programmes formulated by senior administrators to the villagers. As a part of their police
function, village scouts were the most efficient organ
of the movement in spotting and arresting spies who came
from towns to the villages with the pretence of visiting
relatives. They also co-ordinated the activities of their
supporters in the towns with the main Anya-Nya body. For

their paramilitary activities they received orders
from local commanders while for civilian duties they
received instructions from the chairman of each village
committee.

Recruitment centres were manned by an officer sent
from the central regional camp, aided by a local civilian with adequate knowledge of the citizens in the
locality, to guard against enrolling bad elements into
the movement. Recruits were given initial training and
indoctrination by the training officer before they were
sent to the central camp.

In each locality or group of settlements there was
a village committees usually consisting of from five
to ten members depending on the population of the area.
They performnd two important functions under the direct-
ion of political agents. The village committees were
responsible for collecting local rates from the people.
The minimum amount set was 50 piastres and maximum Ls.2
d e p e n d i n g on the economic situation of each region.
Besides this they stored food for the fighting forces.

Within their own regions village committees acted
as administrators with some judicial powers. They sat
as a court to judge civil cases like those of theft,
adultery, rape, feuds, etc. using customary laws. Criminal cases and those connected with anti-Anya-Nya movement activities were sent to the Anya-Nya headquarters
to be tried by a military tribunal.

Political agents were appointed by headquarters
working under a president resident in the military
headquarters. They were engaged in continuous meetings
with village committees to explain the policies and
actions of the movement, and to keep morale high in
times of great hardship. Political agents were all
drawn from students who joined the movement and we can

now see how effectively southern Sudanese students contributed to the success of the movement.

In each locality an executive officer was appointed
by the military command aided by an assistant civil
administrator. Without judicial powers they were responsible for financial and supply matters in cooperation with political agents and village committees. In
official matters they were directly responsible to their
district commissioners.

A district commissioner, aided by three or four
assistants, administered groups of villages covering
a large area. He had judicial, political and administrative power over his district. In each district there
was a senior police officer who helped to investigate
criminal cases, submitting the results to the commissioner for trial. All district commissioners in a geo-
graphic region were responsible to the co-ordinating
committee which was the supreme body of the civil
administration. It comprised members selected from
various districts. In a sense it was like a provincial
board responsible for all administrative and political
affairs in the province. At the head of this committee
was a chairman and a secretary general. The Chairman
was the final authority in both military and civilian
affairs resident in the military headquarters of the
so-called liberated areas.

The coordinating committee included secretaries for
financial affairs, administration, political affairs,
defence, commonly known by the movement as the secretary for special functions who dealt mainly with the
d e f e n c e, weaponry, security etc. The functions of
other departments not mentioned here were vested in the
chairman of the committee.

There was also joint civilian and military board known as the province council whose membership consisted of members of the coordinating committee and area commanders. The council dealt entirely with military issues connected with the theatres of operations and their day-to day activities. Its main functions were allocation of new arms and weaponry to the fighting units, settling disputes among commands , reviewing any tactical situation and final veto over all military issues.

In all these committees any post left vacant due to dismissal or death was filled by election.

Military organization within a region, unlike the civil organization, was less complex in structure, consisting of home guards, territorial forces and mobile forces.

The home guard formed a common base for both civil and military organizations. Besides the functions already discussed under the civil organization, the home guard connected with the fighting forces checked on the passes of guerrillas who came to villages on leave, if they had expired the bearer was arrested and sent back to his unit. Fighters on unofficial visits to villages frequently got involved in corrupt activities and mistreating civilians. It was the duty of the home guards to check these kinds of misconduct.

Territorial forces were assigned special battle areas. They were almost entirely drawn from the people of the locality. The logic of this principle is simply that operating among their brethren they could easily convince them of the national goals of the movement. In times of crises it is a well known fact that strangers cause suspicion. The populace were always ready to protect, feed and help their own. From a purely military

point of view, they made full use of a terrain known to
them since childhood. Ignorance of the environment is
often a serious set-back for guerrilla operations. Any
army defending its own people functions better than
when fighting for strangers or different nationals.

Finally the number of fighters in each territorial
force was determined by the environment and density of
population in the area mainly in order to secure adequate provisions.

The mobile force was drawn from the territorial
forces in different theatres of operations. In some
regions the force was known as the national force.
placed under the command of a senior officer, it had
a variety of weapons ranging from light arms to heavy
armaments such as mortars, bazookas, landmines, anti-
tanks and aircraft, dynamite and T.N.T. explosives.

The mobile force had no specific theatre of operations it operated over very vast regions. Its task was
to be always at alert and to reinforce those forces
who fell under continuous attack from the army. Whereas
territorial forces were tied to a specific theatre of
operations engaged in preventing the army from penetra-
ting their region, breaking bridges and cutting means
of communication, the larger mobile forces attacked
police and army posts, and army garrisons in small
towns.

The army structure came under the final command
of the Chairman of the Co-ordinating Committee. The
link between the civil and military wings can be dia-
grammatically represented in figure 2.

Chairman Co-ordinating Committee

Civil Administration		Military Wings
Home Guards	Or	Village scouts

Figure 2

The logistics and deployment of camps

The initial organisation of camps has already
been discussed. Here we shall deal with factors that
determined the location of camps and the number of
fighters in each. A unique characteristic of the out-
break of Anya-Nya warfare was that from the outset
all camps were situated within the southern Sudan,
a clear contrast with most guerrilla fighting forces
whose camps are usually situated in neighbouring
countries.

There were many factors which determined the location of camps. Major camps were usually situated near
borders with neighbouring countries or deep in the
forests where enemy access was impossible. The tactical
reasons being to secure the rear and thus concentrate
forces on one front, and in case of a major defeat or
setback, a camp could easily be moved to a neighbouring countries. The Iba incident of 1965 was a good
demonstration of this situation. A major camp was situated near Iba in western Equatoria and far from the

ORGANIZATION OF AN INDEPENDENT REGIONAL FORCE

Commander-in-chief: Chairman Co-ordinating committee

CIVIL WING

Commander Mobile Forces

Officer Incharge Ammunition	Off. Inc. First Aid	Off. Inc. Reinforcements	Off. Inc. Intelligence & Operations

Commander Territorial Forces

Commander Theatre of Operations	Commander Theatre of Operations	Commander Theatre of operations

Figure 3

border. The army having located the camp launched
a surprised night attack. In a fierce battle, the army
killed many Anya-Nya and captured weapons and blocked
their retreat.

A similar incident occurred in Raga area in August
1965 where the central camp for the area was located
a few miles from the town. The army launched a midnight
attack and Anya-Nya losses were great. Twenty-two guns
were captured and eight men killed.[6] For a guerrila
movement these losses were too heavy, given the scarcity of weapons in that particular year. Thus, the location of camps and in particular central camps was
dictated by security.

The density of population in each locality could
also determine the location of camps and the number
of fighters. The main reason being to have enough food
and provisions. As a rule, then, the larger the population in a given territory the greater the number of
camps and fighters, while the converse was true for
less populated areas. As the Anya-Nya depended entirely
on civilians for supplies, they were cautious not to
exhaust the resources of an area and leave the people
and themselves in a state of starvation.

As a corollary to the point just mentioned, the
number of weapons also determined the number and location of camps. A well equipped camp had more fighters
than less equipped ones. In areas which were poorly
armed, there were usually base camps from which detachment camps operated over vast areas while the fighting
forces were concentrated in small units. Thus the enemy

---

6. Interview with Kamil Serfadin, Raga 6 July, 1975.
    Kamil formerly a captain in the Anya-Nya movement,
    went to the bush in August 1955. He was a private
    in No 2 Company Equatoria Corps.

were always in danger wherever they went and it gave
them a false impression about the strength of the guerrilla force.

In any given region the headquarters usually keep
the largest number of fighters because the functions
of the headquarters were greater than any of the detachment camps. More men were needed to guard documents,
ammunition and supplies stored at headquarters, and
enough personnel were needed for day-to day activities
and there also had to be reserves for reinforcing
detachment camps. All sorts of communications in the
earlier phase of the movement depended on manpower.
Slight regional variations did occur, but as a general
rule these factors determined the siting of camps and
distribution of fighters.

On the whole the weapons used by the Anya-Nya
ranged from primitive and traditional "silent weapons"
- knives, swords, machetes, bows and arrows, spears -
to automatic rifles, grenades, landmines, T.N.T. explo-
sive, anti-tanks and aircraft.[7] They had a variety of
weapons from different countries, but American, British
Belgian, Chinese and Russian weapons were the most
common. However, none of these countries supplied the
movement with arms. Up to 1964, the Anya-Nya got most
of their arms from within. The turning point came in
1965 when the Khartoum Government made the mistake of
delivering arms given by the Egyptian, Chinese and
Algerian Governments to Simba through the south. The
Anya-Nya intercepted a convoy between Yei and the

---

7.   This author saw in 1966 at the Western Bahr El
     Ghazal central camp a hand bomb which written on
     it in red "poisonous cas" made in West Germany.
     However, the use of this particular bomb was for-
     bidden because nobody knew its effect though it
     was kept in the camp.

Zairean border and captured all the arms and ammunitions. This was the largest arms gain to date.

Following the defeat of the Congolese Simba and
their influx into the Sudan, they exchanged their
weapons for food, clothes, etc. Simba groups who refused
to give up their arms were attached by the Anya-Nya
and their arms taken. The mercenaries brought by the
Tshombe regime to fight the Simba provided the Anya-
Nya with quantities of arms. After crushing the Simbas,
arms captured from them were sold or bartered by the
mercenaries to the Anya-Nya. Trade between the mercenaries and the Anya-Nya was mostly by barter: leopard
skins elephant tusks, rhinocerous tusks, crocodile
skins. There was one Captain Peter (said to be an
American) who was deeply involved in this trade. He
would get money and goods from the Anya-Nya then bring
truck-loads of arms from across the border. There also
existed on a very small scale blackmarketing in arms
and ammunitions from within. It has been confirmed by
many Anya-Nya that some northern army officers sold
guns to the Anya-Nya. This is highly likely because
the army's GIM 3 automatic German-made rifles were the
same calibre as the Belgian made FN. rifles used by
the Anya-Nya. Besides this both guns can use the same
magazines which carry twenty bullets each.

Major arms deliveries to the Anya-Nya started in
1969, from Israel. It was, "strongly believed in
Khartoum... that the Israelis, West Germany and Americans
have stopped up their support for the rebele..."[8] However, these charges were false because the only country

---

8. Colin Legum & John Drysdale, African Contemporary
    Record Annual Survey and Documentations 1969-1970.
    (London & Exeter: William Chudly & Son Ltd, 1969),
    p. 57.

in the world known to have openly given military aid
to the Anya-Nya was Israel. In reality Israel had
every reason to back the Southern Sudan Liberation
Movement. David Martin explained Israeli aid as follows:
Israel aid did not back the southern Sudanese on moral
or ideological grounds. It was simply a means of stab-
bing the Arabs in their backs... By backing the Anya-
Nya (sic) and thereby tying down a large section of
Sudan's army, Israel was able to neutralize effectively the possibility of Sudanese military involvement
in the Middle East Zone. On at least two occasions
Israeli officers were seen inside the Southern Sudan
with Anya-Nya (sic) and air drops of equipment were
made regularly by Israeli planes flying into guerrilla
areas across Ethiopia and Uganda.[9]

A puzzling question for both Sudanese(particularly
southerners) and the outside world, is why the African
countries bordering the southern Sudan did not give
military supplies to the Anya-Nya movement. The situation was pitiful for southerners. In terms of individual countries, Zaire should have had every reason
to supply arms to the Anya-Nya. Before the Simba in-
surgercy collapsed, their principal arms route was
through the Sudan. Besides this, the Sudan Government
allowed Simba to maintain a political office in
Khartoum. In retaliation the Tshombe Government could
have used the Anya-Nya. It did not do this though it
gave moral support to the movement.

Kampala was the seat of the political wing of the
Anya-Nya movement. Having allowed this one finds it

---

9.   David Martin, General Amin, (London: Faber and
     Faber, 1974), p. 158-9.

difficult to understand why the Oboto regime did not offe
military assistance. Ethiopia traditionally had not maintained harmonious diplomatic relations with the Sudan
though a total break did not occur until 1977. Ethiopia
could still have been a source of arms for the movement.

However, considering the general concepts of the
south-north conflict there was justifiable ground for
neighbouring countries to be involved. None the less
there was an important issue which dictated them to
act otherwise. Most of Sudan's neighbours have potentially the same problem of secession as the Sudan-
Zaire, Chad, Ethiopia and Kenya. For this reason they
did not wish to encourage the movement although they
were sympathetic and received refugees. If they had
supported the Southern Sudan Liberation Movement, the
war in all its aspects could have spread over the
borders to neighbouring countries and would have
affected their national unity.

Factors that hindered unification

Many natural factors, practical and technical
difficulties connected with the very nature of the
war hindered the unification of the fighting forces
for a long time. Besides this, rivalry among the
political wings had a negative impact on the movement. There was also the indisputable fact that it
is difficult to bring guerrilla fighting fronts
under a common command, particularly at the beginning
of warfare.

For the nine years of armed struggle, the Anya-
Nya movement fought in isolated pockets. However,
there was nominal unity in western Equatoria and
western Bahr El Ghazal Province. The vast area from

from Maridi through Yambio, Tombura, and up to Raga
area, considered themselves under the command of
General Ali Batala who was recognized in good faith
as the military leader of the whole region. Though
the day-to-day administration and operation of different camps remained under a decentralised system of
administration, important policies and military
arrangements were directed from Ali Batala's camp. He
had the power to transfer commanders of units from
camp to camp and at times did supply the weakest
areas with weapons or in some cases would reinforce
regions that fell under continuous army threat. In
1965 Ali Batala exercised his power by transfering
two Latuka officers from his camp to western Bahr El
Ghazal. One was Captain Lupere and the other Second
Lieutenant Wilson D. Cook. Both were veterans who had
been in the forest since August 1955. He also in June
1966 ordered the deposition of the self-appointed
major and Commander-in-Chief of the whole western
Bahr El Ghazal, ex-school headmaster, Mr Filberto
Ucini Vamvongo and appointed Ferdinand Goi to replace
him.[10]

However, the general factors which hindered unification were as follows: Scarcity of weapons made
guerrillas suspicious of one another in the sense
that weaker units feared domination by stronger units.
Coming under a unified command meant taking orders
from one headquarters. From the security point of view,

---

10. Interview with Habakuk Soro. The author was by
    then in the central camp of Bahr El Ghazal and
    witnessed the coming of Lupere and Cook with the
    official letter of transfer from Ali Batala.
    Batala was a self-promoted general but he deserv-
    ed it because he had been leader in the area since
    the 1955 Torit mutiny.

with very poor means of communication, this was incompatible with day-to day tactical operations. Administration and the rendering of services from a central point was a difficult, if not an impossible task, especially at the beginning when things were not well organized.

There were also differences between political leaders in exile which manifested themselves among the fighting forces and also created difficulties in establishing a unified command. Not until the later phases of the movement was there a single recognized group. Many political factions existed in exile and each claimed legitimacy, which in turn divided the allegience of the fighting forces. In addition, which groups would be ready to surrender their authority to others.

Tribalism also played a great role in inhibiting centralisation of authority. The fear that the centre might appoint foreign tribes to command in different tribal areas was great. It would be the task of headquarters to direct major operations, deploy troops and allocate resources. The fear was that certain areas would be less well equipped, then exposed to continuous army raids. From the military point of view this would give enemy forces the opportunity to use weaker areas as springboards for major operations against other areas. For these reasons units favoured an arrangement in which each tribal group would fight with its own resources and weapons to protect its own homehand and people.

Coupled with the above were two other closely linked factors, security and psychological reasons. Under a unified command, new recruits to the movement would be distributed according to demands for manpower in each region, and were likely to be dispatched to fight in areas where they were not acquainted with the

environment, terrain and life of the people. Psycholo-
gically they would consider themselves mercenaries
fighting in a foreign land. It would take time for
them to get acquainted with the terrain and the people.
To avoid confict between civilians and fighting forces,
it was often though best for each group to fight in
its own locality.

The important principle to be deduced from this
situation is that in guerrilla warfare, centralization and decentralization (in fact localism) are always opposed. If centralism is promoted to its full
sense this is likely to be at the expense of localism.
As a rule, priority would be given to the central
rather than the local authority. In terms of arms,
finance and provisions these might be concentrated in
the centre while on redistribution certain areas are
likely to be over looked. The logical consequence of
such a situation is that charges of corruption and
alliance to one's own locality are made. This is likely
to breed conflict which might lead to armed clashes
between different regions. Favouritism on the part of
the central authority could not be ruled out for this
is a phenomenon inherent in human nature and many
fighters did not want it to develop in the movement.
Proponents of both systems had genuine arguments in
defense of their options. However, difficulty lay in
the fact that a centralized administration, given the
nature of the Anya-Nya struggle, might fail to delegate
reasonable spheres of powers to local regions to ensure
the efficient working of the whole movement.

In the final analysis, since for the first life
span of the movement political leaders failed to organize one unified political leadership for the whole
movement, the fighting forces were not encouraged to

seek ways and means to establish one for themselves.
Besides this, those factors which made it possible for
Lt.-Gen. Lagu eventually to organise an Anya-Nya national command were missing for the great part of the life
span of the movement. However, given the vastness and
difficult terrain in which the war was fought, the
diversity of the population and the spontaneity with
which the movement began it was not possible in a short
period to bring all the fighting forces under one
unified command. Hence, most units fought in isolation.

Feeding, provisions, medical services and education posed difficulties for the movement at the beginning, but they did not affect the armed struggle.
Generally speaking, all these items were obtained
locally by the Anya-Nya. No foreign aid was received
with respect to them. The movement depended entirely
on local subsistence for food. Besides donations from
civilians, the bulk of the food needed for constant
maintenance of the fighting forces was bought by the
movement.. durra, groundnuts, cassava flour, goats,
sheep and cattle. However, starting from 1966-67,
agricultural schemes were established and organized.
In each locality there was an agricultural officer
directly responsible to the Secretary of Agriculture
of the movement. Unengaged Anya-Nya and civilian
volunteers worked on these farms. Two important reasons
dictated the establishment of these farms. There was
a need to secure a constant supply of food for the
camps and it was deemed necessary to make the Anya-Nya
less dependent on civilian resources at a time when
food was scarce. Of course in the heat of the war
civilians were not able to cultivate enough and have
abundant surplus. Besides agricultural products, the
southern jungle provided a luxuriant source of food

in terms of fish, game, fruit and roots. These supple-
mented supplies, especially in years when harvests
were poor. It never occurred in the history of the
movement that food was sought across the borders. Instead the movement traded in meat and dry fish with
Zaire and the Central African Empire.

In each camp there was an organized game department, which dealt in big game and seasoned meat and
skins were bartered for the needed provisions. The
Central African Empire and Zaire were badly in need of
meat and elephant tusks, rhinocerous horns, leopard
skins, crocodile skins, python skins brought high
reyenue and were bartered for clothes, medicines,
bullets, guns etc. Besides the trade with neighbouring
countries there was a constant traffic of black-market-
ing with the towns.

Medicine and clothing were obtained from Anya-Nya
revenue. The medical department was the most important
to the movement. Dispensaries, dressing stations and
hospitals were raided and all drugs taken to the camps.
Native drugs obtained from roots, bark and leaves of
plants provided a substantial supplement to pharmaceu-
tical supplies. Malaria, the commonest disease in south,
could easily be cured with the roots of a small dwarf
shrub known in Ndogo as "Visiri", a sensitive plant
that turns its shoots in response to the position of
the sun. Jaundice which the local people believed to
be incurable by medical science could easily be cured
by native medicines.

Initially, health services were administered mainly by the Anya-Nya both for fighting forces and civilians. Ex-nurses, medical assistants and those who had
some previous experience in the medical field shoulder-
ed the responsibility of running medical services,

except in the case of surgery and complex fractures.

From early 1967 onwards, the movement established
medical schools in the base camps. According to Brigadier Emmanuel Abur there were two types of courses
for nurses, one a 45 day course and the other a course
ranging from three to six months for senior nurses to
man different units. Up to the end of 1967 there was
at least one trained medical officer for each area
and locality. Two persons who rendered invaluable
medical service to the movement both in terms of training and treatment were Dr Clement Khamis and Dr Ajou.
Writing on medical services in the movement, Cecil
Epprile commented:

> In spite of incomparable difficulties, medical
> services were set up by the Liberation Movement
> ... that there was one recognized medical centre
> for the training of medical personnel all over
> the South. Fifteen dispensaries had been set up
> in Eastern Equatoria under the civil administra-
> tion of the liberation Front, and two dispensa-
> ries in the central area of Western Equatoria.
> The other areas of the country were served by
> Anya-Nya military medical centres.[11]

Thus, despite serious shortages of drugs, medical
services were better established in Equatoria Province
than in any other area.

In the so-called liberated areas the movement
undertook the task of organizing people to show that
they were capable of administering their people. In
their efforts to establish services for civilians
they built schools, chapels and dispensaries in each

---

11. Cecil Epprile, War and Peace in the Sudan
    1955-1972. (David Charles, London) p. 101.

locality. The movement began building schools in late
1967, it was not able to build schools earlier because
of the scarcity of weapons to defend them. Like the
medical services system, the educational system was
well established in Equatoria Province. According to
Lt. General Joseph Lagu,

> After establishing some security and administra-
> tive measures in the countryside, the movement
> started to attend to aspects of life in the South
> which up to then had been neglected. It set up...
> schools, so that now there were about 200 elementary
> schools in Juba and Yei districts alone. The move-
> ment had established cotton industries in Zande-
> land and, by early 1971, soap, salt and cooking
> oil were also being manufactured there as well.[12]

There were about 500 elementary schools under Anya-Nya
administration each from 150 to 200 pupils. Teachers
were enrolled from among ex-schoolmasters and students.
Some literate adults were given instruction to pass on
to pupils to supplement the shortage of teachers.
These schools were on British lines Arithmetic, geography, nature study, English, hygiene and vernacular
were taught. Despite acute shortages of books and
educational facilities, coupled with lack of funds,
the movement pushed ahead with its educational programmes supervised closely by commissioners of education
appointed for each region.

It should be explained why schools were not established in All Anya-Nya occupied areas. In some places

---

12.   Grass Curtain, Vol. 1, No. 4 April 1971, Joseph
      Lagu, "The Dynamics of Co-operation between the
      Anya-Nya and the People", p. 6.

there was a lack of security for schools,children and
teachers. In such areas resources could not be used
for both military operations and providing security
for camps and schools settlements. Where there were
also difficulties in getting food, it would not be
advisable to concentrate children in large numbers.
The movement was attempting to overcome these difficulties in the early 1970s up to the signing of the
Addis Ababa Agreement, and Anya-Nya built schools were
incorporated into the educational system under the
Ministry of Education after the Peace Agreement.
Peace and Progress recorded that:

> There are in Equatoria 334 schools which were set
> up by the Anya-Nya and are supported by local com-
> munities. They are mostly sub-Grade Education.
> Some have primary classes. An estimated 65,000
> children are attending these schools. They are
> staffed by 1,100 teachers now paid by the Regional
> Ministry of Education.[13]

The important conclusion to be drawn concerning
the movement is that from late 1964 it was already
necessary for the Anya-Nya to give systematic attention not only to further military action but to the
political, economic and administration organization
of territories which fell virtually under their control.
Schools, medical services, trading posts and a systematic effort to raise production in certain crops were
given priority.

---

13.   Peace and Progress 1973-1974, (Published by the
       Regional Ministry of Information, Culture,Youth
       and Sports, Southern Region, Juba), p. 30.

The military faction

The war started with some disagreement over when operations should start. However, actual fighting started with little agreement between the fighting forces and political leaders, but in the end the opinions of the political leadership prevailed. When Lt.-Gen. Joseph Lagu joined the movement in 1962, he was made the secretary for special functions whose duty was to organize military training for the fighting forces. According to Lagu:

> In my view I wanted first to train the soldiers then equip them. Only after that can we think of beginning our operations. I thought it was premature to strike at the enemy because we had inadequate weapons. However, the political leaders were very impatient and rejected my point of view and decided to carry on the war with whatever little arms we had.[14]

Lt.-Gen. Lagu's concept of the war is an orthodox view usually employed in conventional warfare, where mobilization, general preparations and tactics are planned in advance. Lagu's attitute is understandable given his military background as a captain who served in the Sudan Armed Forces, nonetheless, the beginning of the Anya-Nya operations with scarce weapons had in fact very little effect on the development of guerrilla warfare. The initial tactics of the Anya-Nya were to cut the network of communications and road transport between various towns, villages, army and police posts and the three southern provincial capitals. Telephone lines were the first means of communication that were

---

14.   Interview with author.

disrupted by the Anya-Nya, followed immediately by intensive efforts to cut road communications by destroying all small bridges. Before 1968-69 when the fighting forces had no dynamite or mines to blow up bridges, manpower was used for breaking large bridges. The tactical effectiveness of this measure was that army movements were greatly restricted, enabling the Anya-Nya to have greater control over rural areas.

The exact picture of the situation in the south was that units of the armed forces were completely cut off from their provincial headquarters. A striking example was the case of the garrison at Tombura. From early 1965 up to the middle of 1967 the army there resisted total defeat by the Anya-Nya without any reinforcements provisions or weapons from Wau or Juba. Their uniforms were all torn and they moved about in rags. In that difficult situation the army made an approchement with the civilians in the town and a modus vivendi with Anya-Nya on these terms: That by no means could the army leave their barracks except for marketing and neither would they fire a single bullet at the Anya-Nya. On the other hand the Anya-Nya were allowed to move freely in Tombura with their guns and visit their relatives if they wanted. Though the Anya-Nya could easily have overcome such a weak garrison, one issue deterred them: the army had gathered in their garrison a large number of civilians, mostly women and children. In case of any attack they would have slaughtered all of them and destroyed the town before their final defeat.

In the final analysis, the destruction of the network of communications in the south was the most effective tactic. The Government incurred heavy financial expenditure in an attempt to reconstruct communications

which were continuously being destroyed. This tactic
of systematic destruction of government services was
used as propaganda in 1969-70 by Joseph Garang, Minister
for Southern Affairs, (who was executed in July 1971
after having participated in the abortive communist
coup), to discredit Anya-Nya action in the eyes of
civilians:

> We will construct : you destroy: We will build
> schools; you burn them down: We will build Hospitals
> you destroy them: We will build roads; you burn
> and break bridges. It shall be the people of the
> south to decide for themselves: Who is building
> and who is destroying. In the end, it is they who
> will determine who shall be the political leaders:
> Those who are destroying or those who are building.[15]

Such simple-minded propaganda was not likely to
convince the civilians who had thrown their lot in
with the revolutionary war. Garang's misconception in
his message to the "rebels" and civilians was that he
thought of the Anya-Nya actions as "destruction" for
its own sake without a goal. However, these destructive
measures were only one of the means used by the Anya-
Nya to force the Government at Khartoum to acknowledge
the political goals for which the war was being fought.
In conclusion, a simple-minded answer to Garang's question
can be echoed from his message that "those who were
destroying are now the political leaders of the South".

In terms of military operations the Anya-Nya
employed orthordox guerrilla hit - and-run tactics
throughout the course of the armed struggle, mainly
outside towns and far away from villages. The Anya-Nya
were cautious throughout not to fight battles near

---

15.   A Revolution in Action, op. cit. p.25.

villages because in retaliation the army would turn on
the villagers and massacre them and devastate their
villages. Most effective was the method of felling
huge trees or digging deep trenches across roads. The
army on encountering such obstructions, usually stopped
their convoys to find a way around. In such instances
they came under fire for five to ten minutes then the
guerrillas withdrew before the army got into a position
to return fire. These surprise attacks were very effective and in most cases regular army soldiers fled from
the battle.

The effect of national politics on the movement

In terms of domestic national politics the remarkable effectiveness of Anya-Nya activities had more
influence on the Abboud regime than on successive
Sudanese political regimes. For the first time since
the civil war started, both southerners and northerners questioned the concept of the use of force to
solve the knotty southern problem. What was evident in
the eyes of the population was that the military government had failed by use of force to stop the insurgency.
There was a tremendous increase in army salaries and
a large part of the national budget was spent on
military equipment. The civil service became corrupt
and inefficient, in particular the civil administration in the south lost control over the mounting power
of the army. In the face of this general confusion the
army lost its grip on the country's problems. General
opinion throughout the country was that 'the place for
the military is in the barracks and not politics'.

Abboud's regime realised that force had failed to
solve the southern problem and set up a commission of
inquiry in September 1964 to report on the factors
which hindered harmony between north and the south and

to make recommendations on how best to consolidate
stability in the country without infringing on unity.
This was the first attempt by the military regime to
solve the southern problem. However, debate instead of
being constructive, attacked the regime's southern
policy, and a revolutionary situation spearheaded by
the university students was quickly built up which led
to the downfall of the military government.

A caretaker government known as the United National
Front elected Sir el Khatim el Khalifa, an education-
ist with over ten years experience in the south, as
Prime Minister. Second in command in the cabinet was
Mr Clement Mboro, an experienced southern administrator and politician, who was made Minister of Interior
responsible for security in the whole of the Sudan.
The United National Front recommended liberal reforms
which called for a return to parliamentary democracy,
liquidation of military rule, immediate elections for
a constituent assembly and the revival of free press,
freedom of association, etc., cancellation of all laws
which restricted freedom and the lifting of the state
of emergency except where security might be endangered.
This last item was in fact an allusive reference to the
southern Sudan.

With regard to the south there was a commitment to
seek a peaceful solution while denouncing force. Sir el
Khatim el Khalifa in his first policy statement acknowledged that the southern problem was "the most urgent
national issue of our time and therefore must be tackled
very quickly and energetically", and re-affirmed the
concept that "force is no solution to the vital human
problem which has so many facets, social, economic and

cultural",[16] Thus, for the first time in the history
of the south-north conflict a northern leader acknowledged the dimensions of the conflict. Sir el Khatim
el Khalifa went further and appealed to the nation
saying,"let us establish confidence in the Southerners,
accept Southern intellectuals as leaders of the South".
As an educationalist appealing to educated elements in
and out of the country, he assured southern intellectuals that they were no longer "tools" in northern
politics. At this time the two most popular southern
political parties were the newly created Southern Front
and Sudan African National Union which was most active
in exile. The Sudan African National Union lost no
time in responding, they asked for a general amnesty
for all refugees, the release of all political prisoners and those under detention and recognition of the
Sudan African National Union as a political party as
a condition for its participation in the forthcoming
conference.

At this particular juncture remarkable changes
occurred on the fighting front. The army reduced its
military operations and in response the Anya-Nya also
brought their operations to a standstill. Armed Anya-
Nya soldiers were seen moving freely in towns and
villages. There seemed for some time between October
1964 and June 1965 some signs of the situation in the
south returning to normality. Some schools were re-
opened. Rumbek Secondary School was re-opened in Kasala
in the academic year 1964-65, Juba Commercial Secondary School was re-opened in Khartoum. Southern civil
servants were transfered back to the south. However,

16. Prime Minister's Speech, "Policy of the Caretaker
     Government on the South", (Ministry of Information
     and Labour Printing Press, 1964), pp. 1-3.

the atmosphere of normality was shattered again by the
failure of the Khartoum Round Table Conference to
reach any solution to the southern problem.

It appeared that southern politicians were serious
that the Conference should find a solution. On 20
January, 1965, a three-men committee of S A N U
meeting in Kampala prepared the following conditions
for their negotiations with the northern political
parties:

1. (a) SANU undertakes to appeal to all Southern Sudan-
       ese to call off fighting throughout the South-
       ern Sudan.
   (b) The state of emergency should be lifted through-
       out the Southern Sudan as soon as there is
       positive response to this call.
2. (a) The Governmennt shall undertake to ensure
       personal safety of all negotiating parties and
       all others who may attend.
   (b) The state of emergency in Juba town shall be
       lifted for the purpose of the negotiations.
3.   The conference should find a solution to the
       problem of the Southern Sudan.

The Southern Front being very optimistic of the
outcome of the conference, in a nine-point memorandum
warned SANU factions abroad that the conference was
desirable and should take place anywhere. The Southern Front pointed out that:

The Northerners have admitted that the South has
a case and they have accepted the call of the
Southern Front that the Southern problem has to
be solved by peaceful means. ... should SANU
neither manage to send in a delegation to the
talks nor give the Southern Front mandate to enter
into the talks, the Southern Front will be forced

to enter the talks.

However, the conference took place from 16 - 29 March, 1965. Its terms of reference were to discuss constitutional links between the south and the north and it was attended by seven observers from Algeria, Ghana, Kenya, Nigeria, Tanzania, Uganda and the United Arab Republic. During the conference, northern political parties were united and offered regional self-rule to the south in areas where it could manage its internal affairs. Southern political parties were divided over leadership and other fundamental issues. The Southern Front was willing to accept a solution which would enable the south to manage its own affairs but insisted on the principle of self-determination.

However, with regards to the Sudan African National Union it seems the differences were strategic. The strategy was to start from an extreme bargaining position and then settle for a more moderate one, i.e. to start by demanding full independence for the South but accepting a federal status if negotiations came to a stalemate. The extremists led by Joseph Oduho and Aggrey Jaden stood for separation. The moderates led by William Deng Nhial stood for a federal solution. Another southern party led by Santino Deng and Philimon Majok was unpopular with southerners because it advocated complete unity with the north under a unitary government. Its unpopularity was also due to its close links with the overthrown military junta.

Southerners expressed diverse views which were reflected in four alternatives: unity with the north; federation; seccession through war and independence through constitutional arrangements. These differences were averted when they shifted to a strategy of immediate plebiscite in the south under the Organization of

African Unity's supervision.

In the final analysis, the Round Table Conference
reached no solution and adjourned to reconvene three
months later, which did not take place. It was inevit-
able that the conference would fail, because southerners presented irrational and incompatible goals which
were connected with their suspicion, fear and dislike
of northerners, and once negotiations have begun
incompatible goals cannot be changed or abandoned,
thus the chances of resolving the conflict are slim.
However, the absence of a third party to mediate between
southerners and northerners coupled with a lack of
committed and unified leadership on both sides also
contributed to the failure of the conference.

One fruitful outcome of the conference was the
establishment of a twelve-man committee to seek
a practical political solution acceptable to both the
south and north. it achieved some success in that it
made northerners see the magnitude of the genuine
grievances of the southerners. The committee on 26
June, 1966 recommended regional self-government as the
most appropriate constitutional arrangement for the
country.

The constitutional and administrative arrangements
suggested by the Twelve-Men Committee were the same as
those outlined in the Southern Sudan Regional Self-
Government Act of 1972 which was later incorporated
into the Addis Ababa Agreement for the Southern Region
of 3 March, 1972. There were, however, two points of
contention. One was over the territorial division of
the country and the other over the appointment of
a president for the regional government. Southerners
insisted that the country be divided into four administrative regional governments. The three southern

provinces constituting one region - the southern region;
the eastern region consisting of Blue Nile and Kassala
Provinces; northern region consisting of Khartoum and
Northern Provinces and western region consisting of
Kordofan and Darfur Provinces. The northern political
parties were content with preserving the existing
administration.

However, these two points of differences were
referred to an all Sudanese political parties' conference in October 1966. Northern parties insisted on
maintaining the provinces as they were. With regard to
the appointment of heads of regional governments there
was a suggestion that the President of the Republic
should nominate three persons and the regional assemblies elect one of them as head of government by a simple
majority. However, a further draft proposal suggested
that if the regional assembly rejected the first list,
the President would present another list, and in the
event of the failure of the regional assembly to elect
one person one month from the date of nomination, the
President would appoint one as head of the regional
executive council.

This was the main issue which caused the failure of
constitutional talks. In an interview with Khartoum
News Service in June 1965 Mr Clement Mboro alleged that:

> If the Northern political parties accepted our view
> that the Regional Assembly should elect the Presi-
> dent of the Regional Government, we could have
> solved the Southern Problem a long time ago. The
> mere fact that the North was to elect a leader for
> us was to give the South a government without powers
> and void of the basic principle of democracy which
> advocates that the governed should elect their
> governors. Thus, we were not able to move from

square one.

In further pursuit of a solution, the recommendation of the Twelve-Man Committee which was discussed
by the all Sudanese political parties conference was
referred to a national committee which incorporated
it into the Draft Constitution, which was presented to
the General Assembly in January 1968 but the Government of the day under Mohamed Ahmed Mahgoub failed to
implement any of these resolutions.

It was evident that constitutional talks under the
Mahgoub government were likely to fail because he advocated the use of force against the Anya-Nya. In his
first parliamentary address, Mahgoub declared that his
government "would continue to seek a peaceful and
democratic solution to the Southern Problem and would
end the policy of appeasement and leniency in dealing
with outlaws and those who support them". It would
order "complete disbandment of arms, and end completely
the fanatic bands that play with security", and it
would "order the army to follow the oriminals, return
the state of law and punish the mutineers".[17]

Thus the door for appeasement, reconciliation and
negotiation was closed. The background to the failure
of the Round Table Conference can be seen from the
point when in June 1965 the political parties returned
to power, who were themselves parties in the negotiations. They were naturally prejudiced against their
opponents and biased in their views. The result was
increased pressure from the rightist group who advocated an Islamic constitution, which alienated all
southerners. The Mahgoub government increased military
activities in the south, which resulted in more bloodshed and was the time of the unfortunate Juba and Wau

17.   Khartoum News Service (K.N.S.), 25 June, 1965.

incidents of 8 and 11 July 1965 respectively in which
innocent civilians lost their lives. These two dates
are well remembered all over the south because on the
8th of July 1965 the army carried a general shoot-out
in Juba and burned many houses. In Wau on the night of
the 11th hundreds of southerners were killed by soldiers
at a wedding party.

The Southern Front boycotted the 1968 election on
the basis that the atmosphere was not conducive to
elections. The Umma and National Unionist parties
advocated elections is the north pending those in the
south. This was rejected by the People's Democratic
Party and the Communist Party as fostering separatism.
However, when elections were held, twenty-one "Gella-
bas" were declared unopposed as representatives of the
south. Ten of them thereafter joined northern political parties and this marked the end of the dialogue
between the south and the north. Following these events
the Southern Front withdrew from the cabinet while
William Deng who was willing to play politics with the
north at this juncture lost his life at the hands of
northern soldiers on 5 May 1960 on Tonj-Rumbek road.
His death was a shock to southerners and was followed
by a massive exodus to neighbouring countries and the
bush. The magnitude of the exodus in 1965 can be clearly seen from pupulation records for some towns in the
southern Sudan.

The political parties' regime lasting from June
1965 to May 1969 could be regarded as the worst period
in the civil war in the south. This was also the time
when the outside world took note of the plight of
southerners. In a letter of protest to Mohamed Ahmed
Mahgoub's government in August 1965, the Southern Sudan
Students Union (S.S.S.U.) in Nairobi pointed out that:

Your Excellency, we condemn wholeheartedly and
protest against the non-implementation of the
Round Table Conference on grounds of security. ...
We now understand by "security measures", mass
killings of innocent Southerners is testified by
the recent blood-baths,... of more than 1,400
southerners in Juba and Wau. ...! We wonder whether
the implementation of the resolutions of the Round
Table Conference means first the extermination of
Southern Sudanese, politicians, civil servants,
students, and other innocent Southerners - men,
women and children.

Population records

TOWN	1963	Sept. 1965	December 1969
Juba	18,000	7,000	65,000
Maridi	4,000	29	15,000
Yei	3,000	N I L	8,000
Yambio	2,500	N I L	8,000
Nzara	5,000	200	9,000
Torit	3,000	N I L	11,000
Tombura	2,000	110	15,000

Source: El Buhuth, Periodical Review N.C.R. Vol. 1
(Khartoum University Press, 1974.

In an appeal to the OAU Secretary General in the following month, SALF made clear that:
We hope the urgent need for a peaceful settlement
of the South-North Dispute will outweigh all other
considerations,... As the Honourable Mr Murumbi,
Kenya's Minister of External Affairs had rightly
pointed out..., force will not do in the South -
North conflict. ... It is ... deep conviction that

> this problem be included on the agenda of the OAU
> Summit meeting at Accra in October ... It is only
> too obvious that the OAU will be taking too great
> risks in the heart of the African Continent.

African students had also showed great concern for
a democratic and peaceful settlement to the southern
problem. In an appeal to the Prime Minister of the
Sudan, Kenya United Students' Organization presented
various protests that:

> The entire Kenya Student community do hereby empha-
> tically deplore the inhuman actions of the mass
> massacres that occurred at Juba on 8th and 9th
> July 1965. We deplore in the strongest possible
> terms the total persecution of our African brothers
> in the Southern Sudan and even the Northern portion
> which comes directly under your jurisdiction. ...
> Only a democratic approach to the problem of the
> Southern Sudan will ensure peace and bring a right
> solution to the Southern Sudan crisis.

Finally, a strong condemnation of northern action in
the south came in a joint memorandum from the students
of Ethiopia, Congo (Leopoldville), Malawi, Nigeria,
Kenya and Uganda to the Sudan Government in July 1965
which they concluded with the following five points of
course of action:

1. stage a solemn protest against your government
    which uses Nazi methods of calculated and systema-
    tic genocide.

2. Believe this action is a direct challenge and
    threat to African Unity and as such it must be
    stopped at once.

3. call upon our governments to raise the issue at
    the OAU meeting in September and to defend the
    Human Rights Ordinance of the United Nations

Charter to which they are committed.

4. appeal to peace-loving countries to come out in defence of the human rights of 4 million defence-less African Minorities.

5. call upon UNESCO and the world Students' Organizations to intervene in favour of the Southern Sudan students who are denied education.

In the final analysis, the military and political activities of the Anya-Nya movement were complementary. What is significant is that a change of policy at Khartoum affected the activities of the movement and vice versa. Coupled with this was the fact that the southern political factions were agreed at one time that the south-north conflict could best be solved peacefully. What inhibited an earlier peaceful solution was the attitude of Khartoum regimes towards the problem and a lack of unity among southern political leadership. The world at large also looked for a peaceful and democratic solution.

THE POLITICAL LEADERSHIP OF THE ANYA-NYA

The initial political organisation

A unique characteristic of the southern Sudan liberation movement is that unlike others it started with armed conflict in the absence of a political organization. In this sense, the movement was one of resistance rather than revolution. A resistance movement is initially characterized by the quality of spontaneity and then it is organised. While a revolutionary guerrilla movement is organized and then begins functioning this holds true if one considers the 1955 Torit Mutiny as the beginning of violence in south-north relations. Though many arguments had been put forward for the failure of the 1955 uprising, the most

important reason was that it was ideologicaly vague
and disorganized.

The political wing of the Anya-Nya movement is
said to have started activities in 1962 with the Sudan
African Closed District Union (SACDU). This is not true.
The idea of setting up a political organization for the
southern cause in exile began in December, 1960 and was
spearheaded by Dr Saturnino Lohure, Joseph Oduho,
Aggrey Jaden, Alexi Mbali and Pancrasio.

In Uganda in 1961 this group founded the Sudan
Christian Association (SCA)., this name was adopted
for various diplomatic reasons. First, the organizers
wanted to cover up the political objectives of the organization. Secondly, the Ugandan government would not
have welcomed such a political organization for she
could have been accused by the Sudan government of
harbouring subversive elements. Lastly, there was the
idea of enlisting the support of Christian organisations to give material help to the new movement hence
the name "Christian Association". Coupled with this
was the idea of reflecting the concept of religious
persecution in the southern Sudan under the Abboud
military government. This organization, however, addressed itself mainly to the task of raising funds for
refugees in neighbouring countries and improving their
living conditions.

The first political organization in its strict
sense was set up in 1962 in Leopoldville (Zaire) by the
same group. It was named the Sudan African Closed
District Union (SACDU) This organization with Dr
Saturnino as the acknowledged patron and figurehead,
Joseph Oduho as President, Marko Rume Vice-President,
William Deng Secretary-General and Aggrey Jaden, Deputy
Secretary-General was short-lived. Its name was changed

because it neither reflected much of the southern
Sudan nor was there anything in it that could implicit-
ly reflect the southern Sudanese struggle. In its
functions the movement followed in the steps of the
SCA with the additional task of providing material
help to the fighting men in the southern provinces.

What seemed strange was that, despite its commitment to the cause of the fighting men, the SACDU was
not able to establish close ties with the leaders of
the fighting forces nor was it able to supply any
weapons for the guerrilla forces. In addition, southerners within the country did not have a clear idea
of the existence of the movement in exile. The difficulties at this phase of the movement were clear. No
country showed any sign of interest in the southern
problem, thus the movement was not able to get help.
Besides this, the movement did not start by laying
down a clear ideological commitment which might have
enlisted the support of one of the big powers at a time
when the cold war was at its peak.

After the dissolution of SACDU a new political
organization known as SANU was set up in 1962 in
Kinshasa (Zaire). The same group that organized the
SCA and the SACDU occupied the top offices of this new
organization still maintaining Dr Saturnino as patron.
The activities of SANU at this time were very obscure,
especially to those within the Sudan. None the less
this was the time when harmonious relations between the
political wing and the fighting forces were established.
The most noted activity of SANU was the propaganda published in French with the title "The Southern Sudan
Liberation Movement". In the same year SANU founded
a magazine called the Voice of the Southern Sudan, published in London, publication ceased in mid 1964.

The main tasks which SANU addressed itself to were
political propaganda, raising funds for the movement,
looking after the welfare of southern Sudanese refugees in neighbouring countries and trying to consolidate itself. SANU, however, made great strides in
explaining the aims of movement to the masses in the
southern Sudan and exposing the policies of the Sudan
government towards the south to the world at large.
The ideas of William Deng and Dr Saturnino spread to
all corners of the southern Sudan, but because of the
repressive policies of the Abboud military government
no one from within was able to identify himself with
SANU though many people worked in secret for it. For
security reasons, the three leaders Aggrey, Deng and
Dr Saturnino were referred to as 'the trio'.

In early 1964 SANU transferred its headquarters
from Kinshasa to Kampala (Uganda) where the political
environment was more accommodating. Already at this
time seeds of rivalry were sown in the organization.
The first of these quarrels manifested themselves over
a suitable name for the organization. There were a lot
of suggestions such as - South Sudan Land Freedom army
(SSLFA); Azanian Secret Army (ASA) and Anya-Nya.
William Deng in a letter to Joseph Oduho said the
following on the proposed names:

> If by your contention you mean to say that (Anya-
> Nya) is the official name, then it should have
> been discussed by SANU executive, since it has
> not been discussed, the three names: ASA, SSLFA
> and Anya-Nya REMAIN UNOFFICIAL AND SHOULD BE LEFT
> TO THE ARMED FORCES WHO ARE DIRECTLY CONCERNED...
> if SSLFA is adopted as the official name, I can-
> not see how it can divide the South any more than
> can ASA and Anya-Nya... Names may not divide but

actions such as yours certainly can.[18]

Apart from the above mentioned names, Sudan Pan-African Freedom Fighters (SPAFF) was alleged to have been suggested by Dr Saturnino. His main objective was that with such a name the Pan-Africanists would easily support the movement. This name was rejected on the grounds that it reflected nothing connected with the Southern Sudan cause.

However, the main issue which was beginning to divide SANU leaders was not merely a quarrel over names for the organisation. The core of the contention can easily be grasped from a message from Oliver Batali Albino to William Deng:

> I have lost all hopes in the re-organization of
> SANU itself. Tribalism and regionalism are obvious-
> ly being sustained to enhance individual ambitions.
> Another discouraging attitude to those who would
> work for reorganization is that "this is SANU
> which we formed, if you like it join us, if you
> dont then start your own party and let us see"...
> the present leaders are partly responsible for our
> people's sufferings because disunity among us is
> what the Arabs are working for.[19]

It was evident that the exploitation of tribal and regional affiliations for political and personal ambitions was an important factor in the crises in SANU's

---

18. SANU File of records and correspondences. 25 Feb.,
     1965. As early as August 1963, the name Anya-Nya
     was in existence in some parts of the Southern
     Sudan in particular Eastern Equatoria Province.
     In an interview with General Joseph Lagu, he said
     he had been an influential person in seeing that
     the name Anya-Nya was adopted for the movement.
     This is obvious because 'Anya-Nya' is the 'Madi'
     word for 'Snake poison' and Lagu is a Madi.
19. Ibid.

leadership. None the less SANU was able to hold elections despite all the disputes among the leaders. Joseph
Oduho the out-going President managed to convene for
the first time in the history of the political organization a general national convention in Kampala between
7 and 16 November, 1964. Elections were carried out
with the following results: Dr Saturnino Patron of the
organization, Dominic Murwel-National Chairman, Aggrey
Jaden-President, Philip Pedak Lieth-Vice-President,
Joseph Oduho was given the post of Secretary for Legal
and Constitutional Affairs. At this national convention
William Deng, one of the founding fathers of SANU, was
absent, for this reason he was not elected.

For the first time SANU appointed emissaries to
USA., USSR., Britain, Tanzania, Kenya, Zaire, Ethiopia
and the Central African Republic. At the end of the
convention, the President-elect, Mr Aggrey Jaden, in
his inaugural speech, criticised the conflict in SANU
and for the first time declared the ultimate goal of
the movement. Jaden announced that:

> Countrymen and brothers, at this stage of our move-
> ment it is now absolutely important that more than
> ever we need UNITY OF AIMS. To be united does not
> mean to abolish differences of opinion or points
> of view... but it is very necessary that we must
> be united in our common and final goal which is
> independence from the North.. We must try to bury
> our personal, tribal or sectional interests for
> the sake of our beloved country...only unity will
> be our strength.[20]

The emphasis on unity reveals that SANU was suffering
from internal disintegration. This kind of personal
and sectarian rivalry within political parties is

---

20.   Ibid. November, 1964.

a common feature of the politics of new states. And it is usually the prominent political leaders who cause splits in their party ranks.

SANU up to 1965 remained one political organization for the southern Sudan liberation movement despite obvious internal friction. However, the organization had two important achievements. The official declaration of the final goal of the movement which was total independence from the north. The adoption for the first time in the history of the organization of democratic procedures for electing its leadership. In reality this was only a gesture to enlist the support of the southern masses for the party. In practical terms, the group that started the political movement in exile did not want to part with the leadership and were not even prepared to do so. Looking at the personalities of the movement, it is obvious that no changes occurred til the Addis Ababa Agreement. The same personalities continued to dominate the political leadership in the southern Sudan.

The real crack in SANU came when there was a change of government at Khartoum. The caretaker Government of Sir el Khatim el Khalifa which came to power after the overthrow of Abboud's military regime in October 1964, announced policies which seemed to promise prospects of a negotiated and peaceful solution. This change of government in the Sudan with a new peaceful orientation towards the south had a remarkable effect on SANU. Conflicts over what policies to be pursued to meet the changes in the Sudan divided the leaders in exile. This conflict ended with William Deng's desertion of SANU and he came in and formed a political party with the same name. William Deng was then expelled from SANU-outside because he decided to play politics

with the north with the aim of accepting federation as
a solution. However, through-out 1965 up to early 1966
SANU-outside remained united under the leadership of
Aggrey Jaden.

By early 1966, serious disagreements arose between
Jaden and Oduho, finally Oduho broke off from SANU and
formed the Azania Liberation Front (ALF). Jaden and
his group then changed the name of their party to Sudan
African Liberation Front (SALF).

From January 1966 to August 1967 there was a kind
of anarchy in the political leadership of the movement,
activities almost came to a standstill, while inside
the Sudan Mahgoub's government became extremely barsh
with civilians and the Anya-Nya to the extent of almost
paralysing the activities of the "rebels". At the same
time SANU-within and the Southern Front were in a power
struggle over who should be the legitimate representative of the southern people. Southerners were very
much disillusioned with the divisions and conflicts
among their political leaders. At this time the southern population thought that the south was lost to the
north. Conflicting view were held on the deusion of
William Deng however most southerners saw it as a surrender to the northerners.

Disunity in Anya-Nya political leadership was an
issue of great concern. The Southern Students Union in
exile played an active role in reconciling the different
factions of the political leadership in exile. In July
1965 a commission to compromise SANU and ALF was formed
entirely of the Southern Sudan Students Union (SSSU).
In the early findings of the commission, it came to the
conclusion that there was a need for change of names
for these organisations.

(1) Williams SANU inside the country (Sudan) which aims

at federation is in confusion with the actual
SANU which works to liberate the South. The difference should be made clear by change of name.

(ii) Since SANU is not fighting to liberate the whole
Sudan, there should be a name given to the land
we are fighting to liberate and the name should
be born in the party.[21]

Efforts to reconcile the two political factions succeeded. In August 1965 SANU and ALF issued a joint statement of reconciliation:

1. We members of SANU and ALF have agreed under the
new name of Sudan African Liberation Front (SALF).

2. Under the conclusion of unity the two organizations
have agreed to reliquish their former names, SANU
and ALF.

3. The two organizations have agreed on a common aim
of total independence for the Southern Sudan, and
on the common policy of applying force to achieve
this end.

4. The two organizations to support the Anya-Nya as
an individual body before and after the achievement of independence.

5. The two organizations have agreed to adopt the
leadership of SANU for the new organization. Dominic
Muorwel National Chairman; Aggrey Jaden President
and Philip Pedak Vice-President.[22]

Following the reconciliation agreement, the new organization came out with a new well defined policy. In
a joint statement, the following policy was declared on

21. Ibid.
22. Ibid Agreement on unity reached between SANU and ALF meeting
in Kampala (Uganda), 25 and 26 August, 1965. However, the
conflict in the organization was not resolved finally because
it persisted until J. Lagu took over leadership of the movement in 1970.

28 August, 1965.

1. The SALF is pledged to fight for the final aim of achieving full independence for the South and the establishment of a sovereign state from the Northern Sudan.

2. The SALF strongly condemns the Arab Northern Sudan in their bid to perpetuate Arab domination over the South. We condemn the Arab line-up comprising Algeria, United Arab Republic, Syria and Jordan in supporting the Khartoum Arabs in their atrocities against the South. We also protest strongly against the foreign powers, particularly Russia and China who are supporting the Arabs in exterminating the Black Africans of the Southern Sudan and against the Western countries who are giving military and financial aid to the Arabs of the Northern Sudan.[23]

At this juncture, the exiled leaders realized all the drawbacks in the movement and they undertook a strategy of unity against a common enemy. The important point in SALF's policy was the strategy of achieving the ultimate goal of the movement by force. Force had been emphasized at this time for reasons which were obvious. After the failure of the all Political Parties Round-Table Conference at Khartoum in March 1965 to reach a peaceful settlement of the southern problem, all the old suspicions of northern Sudanese were revived. The mere fact that immediately after the conference civilian massacres were stepped up made southerners conclude that the north was out for a total war of genocide. The exiled leaders then adopted the motto "force confronted by force". The Juba and Wau incidences of 8

---

23.   Ibid.

and 11 July, 1965 respectively left no room for doubt
in the minds of southerners. Similar statements on the
use of force were also issued by the Anya-Nya and
circulated in a pamphlet as follows:

> Our patience has come to an end and we are now con-
> vinced that only the use of force will bring about
> a better decision... from to-day onwards we shall
> take action..for better or worse...we don't want
> mercy and we are not prepared to give it.[24]

From this time the movement realized the need to
make its impact felt on the international arena, hence
the condemnation of both eastern and western powers
together with the Arab countries. The implicit policy
of non-alignment adopted by the movement was in a way
disadvantageous because it would alienate the movement
from potential supporters. The world of the early 1960's
was that of bi-polarization, as such those liberation
movements who did not identify themselves with any one
of the world main ideologies could not expect help
from any of the big powers and their allies.

By 1967 great efforts were being made to remedy the
anarchy in the political leadership of the movement
which was based on tribalism, regionalism and individual rivalries. It goes without saying that the period
prior to 1967 experienced serious weaknesses in the
movement which was kept alive only by the presence of
the enemy and the dedication of every individual to
redress the plight of the southern people. However,
a turning point came in early 1967 when the political
headquarters of the movement were transfered from exile
to Lomiliria in Equatoria Province; later in the same

---

24. Quoted in, Mohamed Omer Beshir, The Sudan: From
     Conflict to Peace, (C. Hurst and Company: London,
     1975), p. 52.

year the headquarters were transferd to Angundri near
the Sudan-Zaire border.

With the rivalry which persisted in the political
leadership, the military men came to the conclusion
that the politicians were of little use to the movement and that it was time for them to intervene to
save the movement from collapse and reorganise it.
This is a common feature manifested at national level
in most African, Asian and Latin American domestic
politics. The army is easily convinced that they have
a role to play in politics on the ground that they
wish to redeem their people from corruption and to
accomplish a task which politicians have failed to do.

The Angundri convention of 15 August, 1967 was
called by political and military leaders. This was the
first time in the history of the southern Sudan liberation movement that they officially sat together to
discuss the common issues which faced the movement.
At the Angundri convention the following resolutions
were agreed upon:

1. The first national government was formed and
   named the Southern Sudan Provisional Government
   (S.S.P.G.).

2. The convention passed a resolution transfering
   the political headquarters of the movement from
   exile to the bush in the southern Sudan.

3. All other political organizations were dissolved
   and both the military and political wings were
   united.

4. The first national flag was created.

5. The convention decreed that there should be
   annual and regular conventions of this kind.

Another success of the Angundri convention was the
formulation of a well defined foreign policy to be

pursued by the movement.

The SSPG envisaged,

1. close cooperation with all liberation movements in Africa for the liberation of southern Sudan from Arab rule;

2. opposition to imperialism, communism and racism;

3. support for all international peace movements;

4. support for a greater East African Common Market;

5. opposition to religious or racial rejudices and discrimination among the members and supporters of the SSPG, and with this understanding the desire to negotiate and cooperate with any Arab Government.

The new policies formulated by the SSPG reveal a drastic change in its politics, at this juncture it was real-ized that rigidity worked against the movement. It could not get substantial material help from anywhere because of its non-aligned policies. Thus, the movement envisaged it necessary to ally with other liberation movements in Africa in the hope of getting military aid from them. Opposition to imperialism, communism and racism are political slogans to which most African states and governments respond. Such slogans were intended to[25] show the outside world the magnitude of the southern problem and to put it on the same footing as other liberation movements like SWAPO of Namibia, FRELIMO of Mozambique, PAIGO of Guinea-Bissau and the liberation movements in racist Rhodesia and South Africa.

The idea to enlist support from international peace movements was motivated mainly by the fact that to achieve total independence from the north by force as the movement had envisaged earlier was not a practical

---

25. Interview with Clement Moses. See also M.O. Beshir The Sudan, op cit. p.61.

proposition. It thus remained for the movement to investigate the possibility of a third party to mediate in order to bring about peaceful negotiated settlement to the southern problem. This became a reality in that the success of the Addis Ababa Agreement was brought about by the mediatory efforts of the World Council of Churches (WCC), the All African Congress of Churches (AACC) and the Sudan Council of Churches (SCC).

Support for a greater East African Common Market was just a political tactic on the side of the movement. The core of the idea was that if the southern Sudan achieved independence from the north through a military victory, it would be on bad terms with the north, at least in the early days, thus it was necessary to secure the good will of East African countries through which the south would have international trade outlets.

The establishment of SSPG reveals a great deal about the political leaders of the movement. It shows that they had reached political maturity and could make comprehensive and tactical political moves rather than being rigid in their policies. Internal rivalry had been recognised as a great divisive element and source of weakness in the movement in the face of a powerful enemy. Total alienation from the military wing created difficulties in formulating a general policy for the overall success of the movement. Military personnel needed to be represented in the top hierarchy of policy and decision making.

Despite the formation of the SSPG as the legitimate administrative system for the southern Sudan, individual rivalry over the leadership of the government never ceased. In late 1968 when these conflicts became apparent and Aggrey Jaden failed to convene a national

convention as decreed by the Angundri Convention he
abdicated as head of government and fled to Nairobi.
The acting President Kamillo Dhol convened a national
convention on 29 March, 1969 at Balgo-Bindi near the
Sudan-Zaire border.

The Palgo-Bindi convention adopted all the resolutions of the Angundri convention with the following
additions:

1. The name of the SSPG was changed and the Nile
   provisional Government was adopted with Gordon M.
   Maysa as the President and a Republic the "Nile
   State" was declared.
2. Separation from the north was the basic policy,
   while federation could be accepted as the least
   compromise.
3. The idea of any autonomous status for the south
   was completely rejected.
4. The idea of a representative government continued.[26]

The name "Nile State" was adopted for the southern
Sudan Republic for the following reasons:

1. The movement at this time had a definite target,
   that is to free the Southern Sudan from Arab domination, hence the need to have a name that should
   have no connection with the word "Sudan".
2. The economic potential of the Southern Sudan is
   believed to be based on the River Nile. Besides
   others the papyrus is considered of great economic
   potential. Other issues like fisheries, hydro-
   electric power, communications were also in mind.
3. From the geographical point of view, all the rivers
   in the Southern Sudan pour into the Nile, and all
   come from all over the Southern Region. For the

---

26. Ibid.

reason just mentioned the Nile is considered as
a symbol of Southern Unity.[27]

Other names were also proposed but they were all rejected. Azania was rejected because it was a small
country on the East African coast and did not reflect
anything connected with the historical background of
the southern Sudan. Fashoda was proposed and rejected
because it was a name given by the British colonizers
and to maintain it would be to keep colonial memories
fresh in the minds of the people. Nilotia which seemed
to be an acceptable name was rejected because it
reflected ethnic tendencies since all southern people
are not Nilotics.

The reason why the Nile provisional government
rejected the idea of autonomous status for the southern Sudan was clearly explained by the NPG's Foreign
Secretary, Mr Arkangelo B. Wengi to Mr Joseph U. Garang,
Minister for Southern Affairs, in Kampala in 1969 when
the latter met the leaders of the NPG After the meeting,
the former stated that:

The NPG felt the North should have regarded autonomy as a proposal rather than a solution to be
imposed on the South. The NPG feared that if they
relinquished the armed struggle and the Revolutionary Government fell from power, the South would
again be unprotected. They looked for a Southern
settlement that would have external guarantees...,
so that whichever party or group ruled in Khartoum,
the South would have some sense of security.[28]

---

27. Ibid.

28. Africa Digest, Vol. XVI, No 5, October 1969, p.91.

It is clear here that suspicion of northern motives
was one of the crucial factors which prevented agreement on any suitable formula for the southern problem.
The harder line, separation from the north, reflected
more or less a retaliatory policy in response to the
worsening situation in the south, since by this time,
heavy tanks, jet fighters and bombers were being
employed by government forces in the war. Southern
politicians were also encouraged by the prospects of
military training and aid from Israel, and the Anya-
Nya Government was keen to manipulate the weaknesses
of the Sudanese army in the south. A large portion of
the Sudanese army was employed on the front line in
the Middle East and there was no great fear of substantial reinforcements if the situation tilted in
favour of the Anya-Nya.

After the formation of the NPG a proper re-organiz-
ation of the whole movement was instituted. Provincial
commissioners were appointed for all southern provinces,
helped by junior administrators. Every region had its
own commanding officer directly responsible to the
commander-in-chief of the region who worked in close
coordination with the Secretary of Defence of the whole
movement. At the regional level there was close coordination of the activities of the fighting forces and
the civil administration. The structure of both the
civil and military administration at this time can
best be represented diagramatically.

The Nile Provisional Government despite being a popularly elected and good organization faced a series
of internal crises. In this particular government
tribalism and regionalism made smooth functioning
very difficult. The reason for the conflict in the
NPG was clearly because the majority of ministers were

from Bahr El Ghazal and Upper Nile provinces.

Minister of Devence: Anya-Nya Government

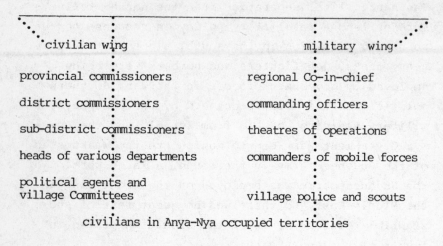

civilian wing   military wing

provincial commissioners   regional Co-in-chief

district commissioners   commanding officers

sub-district commissioners   theatres of operations

heads of various departments   commanders of mobile forces

political agents and
village Committees   village police and scouts

civilians in Anya-Nya occupied territories

Figure 4

The people of Equatoria province being disappointed
with this government formed a number of self-proclaimed
governments. In late 1969, General Amadeo Tafeng who
was the commander in-chief of the armed forces, dis-
agreed with Mayen the President of the NPG and formed
the "Any State". What happened was actually an attempted
coup d'etrat. The Azande tribe, under the leadership
of Michael Tawil, backed by Colonel Samuel Abujohn
refused to acknowledge the NPG. They formed a government known as the "Sue River Revolutionary Government"
and created a state known as the "Sue Republic". These
crises soon paralysed the efficient working of the
NPG and made the atmosphere conducive for an army take-
over by Joseph Lagu.

With the crises in the NPG Joseph Lagu worked hard
to dislodge the politicians. Lagu had been dismissed
from the NPG because he refused to work for the movement, after not being appointed commander-in-chief of

the armed forces. In his own words, Lagu confessed that:
'I was disappointed with the whole movement and kept
out of it. I could not envisage myself working under
illiterate generals. I know Tafeng was appointed Commander-in-Chief because he commanded strong tribal
loyalties in Western Equatoria but I had a strong influence at this time all over the Anya-Nyas.

The people of Eastern Equatoria recognised me as
the only military leader'.

Lagu henceforth busied himself with his military
propaganda that blamed the politicians for the weaknesses of the movement because of their continuous
quarrelling among themselves. He made it clear that he
was the one who supplied arms to the movement and that
the politicians should step down and allow military men
to run the affairs of the movement. Since weapons were
brought in his name (because he was responsible for
arms supplies) he tried to convince the Anya-Nya that
these were his personal achievements. This had a remarkable effect on the fighting forces who were badly in
need of arms. Coupled with this was the fact that Lagu
was a brave soldier and a dynamic and pragmatic personality with military knowledge that none of the other
generals possessed. Besides the factors mentioned above
sporadic armed clashes among the Anya-Nya were a common
feature of this period of crises. It was evident that
Lagu's idea of forming a unified command to stop bloodshed was welcomed by all.

In July 1970, Colonel Lagu announced the formation
of the Southern Sudan Liberation Movement and declared
that the Anya-Nya fighting forces were the sole authority
in the southern Sudan. For the sake of the unity of the
movement and to prevent terrible bloodshed, the leaders
of the NPG stepped down on 3 July, 1970 and accepted

the leadership of Lagu. All other self-proclaimed
governments and political organizations dissolved themselves and declared their support for Lagu's leadership. What occurred after Lagu's take-over was that
those who did not accept his leadership followed the
policy of non-interference and most of them retired
from active political life. Those who showed some signs
of opposition to Lagu's government were dismissed from
active participation in the movement.

In the final analysis, the main cause of the army's
intervention in political activities was unceasing
rivalry among political leaders. There was also the
crucial issue that if the movement was not unified it
would not get much military did from abroad. The other
important advantage of having a unified command was
that any prospective peace negociations would be done
directly with the Anya-Nya and not with opposing factions
of the movement. The Anya-Nya would then become an
equal negotiating parties with the Khartoum Government.
It should be noted that for a long time successive
regimes in Khartoum refused to recognise the Anya-Nya
and negotiate with them. The Anya-Nya were called
'rebels', 'outlaws' 'bandits' etc., and the belief was
that only force should be used against them. The clear
fact is that if the Anya-Nya forces were not unified
under one command the Addis Ababa Agreement would have
not succeeded because certain factions would not have
accepted a peace agreement concluded in favour of one
of them. Thus the unity which Lagu brought to the movement to achieve a peaceful solution to the southern
problem.

Besides the points discussed above which caused
friction in the political leadership of the Anya-Nya
movement, another important factor deserves attention.

Individual ambitions and the struggle for power were
the real core of the issue. The social backgrounds of
political leaders reveal significant facts about their
struggle for power. Almost all exiled leaders were
once people who held important positions in the Sudan
civil service, some were ex-MPs others had once held
ministerial posts. Thus, their standard of living could
be said to have been high by Sudanese standards. In
exile to maintain this same standard, one must be
a member of the executive committee of the political
organization. Being in this position they could avail
themselves of facilities such as residence in first
class hotels, free movement from country to country,
financial help etc. from host countries. It was mainly
for this reason that the military leaders decreed in
the Angundri Convention that "whoever leads the movement must reside with fighting forces in the bush in
the Southern Sudan". This provides a psychological
explanation for the continued individual struggle for
power which resulted in disunity in the Anya-Nya political leadership.

However, in the final analysis, it is undoubtedly
a fact that the political leadership of the movement
rendered inestimable services to the overall success
of the SSLM. Their efforts in petitioning the United
Nations, the OAU African Liberation Committee and OAU
Commission for Refugees, explaining the plight of the
southern masses to the world at large, the supply of
information about the situation in the Sudan to the
world press and their diplomatic activities on behalf
of the movement could not have been tackled efficiently
by the fighting forces. Their contribution to the movement was the actual fire that kept the movement alive
for twelve years. Even under Lagu's military command,

the political leaders were recalled to negotiate the Addis Ababa Agreement. The success of a guerrilla movement lies in the activities of both its military and political wings.

THE CHRISTIAN CHURCH IN THE SOUTHERN SUDAN BEFORE 1900

By Philip Chol Biowel

Formal education in the south hardly existed in any
form before the Angle-Egyptian conquest of the Sudan
in 1898. Soon after it, however, various missionary
societies expressed their desire to send missions to
the country to evangelise. The new administration was
not prepared to allow Christian missions into the
northern Muslim part of the country. Therefore, pro-
selytization was permitted to take place among the
pagan tribes of the southern Sudan only.

That was not, however, the first time for the
Church to come into contact with the inhabitants of
the White Nile. Before 1900, there were unsuccessful
attempts to establish the Christian Church in the
southern Sudan. The attention of the Roman Catholic
Church was drawn to the area as far back as 1844. This
interest was aroused by fears that a Protestant mission
might be sent there. Similarly, the spread of Islam to
this newly-discovered territory was also expected. Consequently, Pope Gregory XVI created the Vicariate
Apostolic of Central Africa in 1846. One of the Roman
Catholic societies, 'Propaganda Fide', was delegated
responsibility to carry the Christian message to the
Sudan. In 1846, a small party of missionaries was formed
to meet this objective. It reached Khartoum in February
1848. Unfortunately, the leader of the group, Ryllo,
died only four months after arrival in Khartoum. He was
succeeded by another member of the group, Don Knoblescher.
The formally approved objectives of the mission were
"To convert the Africans of the Sudan to Christianity;

to assist the Christian merchants in that country, and finally to suppress the slave trade".[1]

Since Khartoum was the seat of administration, the mission made its headquarters there from which future expeditions to the White Nile region were to be launched. From the start life was extremely difficult for the first missionary pioneers. Their health and finances soon seriously deteriorated. 'Our expedition resembles a hospital', wrote Knoblescher in 1850, 'and our means are exhausted'.[2] The revolutions of 1848-49 in central Europe had hampering effects on the mission in the Sudan. The sacred college of Propaganda Fide declared in 1848 that "It was no longer in a position to help the mission and permitted its abandonment.[3] As a result, financial help was not always forthcoming and the condition of the missionaries became grim. Nevertheless, the tiny group in Khartoum decided to hold on. They turned their energies to cultivation to support themselves.

Fortunately, this state of isolation did not last long. In mid 1849, when their position was still extremely difficult, help arrived from Rome. Meanwhile, the Khartoum party had not been idle, in spite of the difficulties. They bought boys of various negro tribes from the slave markets in Khartoum, and with their collection of outcasts the mission established a day and boarding school. While teaching them the rudiments of Christianity and literacy, they were at the same time students of their own pupils, making efforts to learn

---

1. E. Toniole and R. Hill eds The Opening of the Nile Basin 1842-1881 (London 1974), pp. 1-2.

2. Ibid, p.4.

3. Ibid, p.7.

the languages of the different tribes on the White
Nile. They also accumulated information pertaining to
their character, habits and customs.

The perseverance of the mission gave it a measure
of progress in the educational field in Khartoum. The
British trader, John Petherick, mentioned the existence
of the school in 1850, but added that "the school was
for the education of negro children who have been principally supplied from negro families on the White
Nile"[4]. But the mission had not by then any intention
to prosleytise in the northern Sudan. Apparently, no
mention was made of Muslim children attending the mission school at this early date. The object of the mission was the White Nile region in the so-called pagan
south. With such meagre resources, the prospects of
founding a mission station had to be delayed until the
beginning of 1850. This delay was partly due to the
difficulties which faced the mission, but government
policy on monopolizing the ivory trade played a major
role. Due to this policy, traders' freedom of movement
along the White Nile was restricted. They were in most
cases forced to travel with a government escort. Without this, the mission would probably have benefited
from private help. Such assistance was necessary,
because it could not muster an expedition of its own.

On the return of Don Angelo Vinco, one of the missionaries, from Europe with financial aid, the situation began to improve. The Governor-General, Khalid
Pasha Kusru, gave permission to the Pre-Vicar, Knoblesçher,
to travel south. He, with two missionaries, left
Khartoum on 13 November 1849 for Gondokoro. Government

---

4. J. Petherick, Upper Egypt and Central Africa (London
   1861), p.131.

permission, was, however, conditional. The Governor-
General directed that "the Pre-Vicar should refrain
from buying ivory as for several years the monopoly
had been taken over by the governors of the provinces"[5].
This condition was tantamount to calling off the mission to the south since one of its objectives was to
buy ivory in order to pay for transportation. This
restriction was, however, lifted when Knoblescher
produced a letter from the Austrian Consul in Cairo
which made it clear that "government monopoly above
Aswan was abolished as stipulated between the Sublime
Porte and the European Powers"[6].

After this bond between commerce and Christianity,
the missionaries were able to travel south for the
first time. Though their journey was difficult, they
had a friendly reception early in 1850 from the Bari
tribe in Gondokoro. A prominent Bari chief, Nyigilo,
came with a large crowd to meet their boat on 9 January
1850. Two days later, the Bari chief of Bilinyany,
Shubek, paid them a visit. Nyigilo accepted Knoblescher's
request to allow the two missionaries to settle in his
village, but he asked that they should give him firearms to protect his people against the neighbouring
Lotuke tribe. Nyigilo felt that protection for the
Europeans should not be rendered free and realized that
his friendship with the mission was an opportunity to
acquire arms to further his own aims in the field of
trade. This was probably the first African reaction to
European missionaries in the southern Sudan.

Don Knoblescher was not prepared to provide an
African chief with firearms, which could have been used

---

5. Toniole and Hill, op cit, p.56.
6. Ibid, p.54.

for tribal wars. On the other hand Nyigilo saw it
necessary that there should be a token of friendship
on the side of the mission, if his protection was
needed. This misunderstanding created a rift between
the two sides. Lack of knowledge of each other's
customs and traditions was perhaps the reason for this
misunderstanding.

Neither the White Nile traders nor the administration in Khartoum were willing to allow the missionaries
to settle among the Bari at Gondokoro. One of the commanders of the government boats admitted later that
Khalid Pasha, "had secretly ordered that the three
Europeans should be brought back to Khartoum at all
costs".[7] It must be recalled that relations between the
inhabitants of Gondokoro and the traders, though not
completely hostile, were not always cordial. A fear of
strangers had sometimes prevailed among the native
people. This combined with the agitations of the Turks,
made it difficult for the missionary pioneers to find
ready accommodation with the Bari. The Turks might have
been apprehensive about leaving the missionaries behind
for commercial reasons. Knoblescher had gone to the
south for religious purposes, but, at the same time, he
had insisted on buying ivory during his stay there to
cover the expenses of the expedition. Faced with this
difficult situation, the missionaries were reluctantly
forced to return to Khartoum in January 1850.

This first journey to the south convinced Knoblescher
of the absolute necessity of asserting the independence
of the mission. That was possible only if the mission
could manage an expedition free from government supervision. But to do this they needed enough money to buy

7. Ibid, p.73.

their own boats, which was not possible at the time.

Back in Khartoum, Knoblescher decided to travel to Europe to seek financial and diplomatic assistance for the mission in the Sudan. While the Pre-Vicar was still in Europe, the Governor-General of the Sudan, 'Abd al-Latif Pasha, imposed new restrictions on the White Nile traders. One of them stipulated that traders' expeditions to the south should be undertaken with government troops. The Government claimed that this measure was essential to protect traders from the tribes among the White Nile. But one of the traders, Brune Rollet, refused to comply with these restrictions and placed two of his boats at the service of the mission. Angelo Vinco, one of the two European missionaries managed to make an independent trip to Gondokoro in January 1851.

Meanwhile, Knoblescher's mission to Europe was successful. He gained the support and assistance of the Austrian Government. The young Austrian Emperor, Franz Joseph, agreed to be the patron of the mission to Central Africa, which was now stationed at Khartoum. The Emperor used his influence to obtain a firman from the Ottoman Sultan for the mission and in order to protect and strengthen the mission in the Sudan, an Austrian Consulate was opened in Khartoum. This development prompted the Austrian Consul-General in Cairo to write that the Consul in Khartoum, Dr Reitz, "would further the interest of the Mission in all directions under his control and therefore we hope would best promote both the fame of Austria and the spread of Christian civilisation in the Sudan".[8] In fact the Austrian Consul in Khartoum persuaded the Government to

---

8. R. Gray, A History of the Southern Sudan 1839-1889 (Oxford 1961), p.26.

remove the restrictions it had imposed on both European traders and the mission. But shortly afterwards
embarrassed the mission with its traffic in ivory and
perhaps even slaves.

Another development took place which was in the
interest of both the traders and the mission. 'Abd-al-
Latif Pasha was recalled and his restrictions were
abolished. 'Abbas I, the Viceroy of Egypt from 1848-
54 instructed 'Abd-al-Latif's successor, Rustum Pasha
Jarbas, not to obstruct private expeditions to the White
Nile. By this breakthrough, it seemed likely that the
forces of commerce and Christianity would be able to
bring European civilization to the isolated pagan tribes
of the southern Sudan. From that moment the White Nile
region became a focus of attention in Europe, where
influential circles began to follow events closely.

Meanwhile, the new Vicariate to Central Africa was
officially entrusted by Pope Plus XI, to Knoblescher as
Apostolic Vicar. When Mgr Knoblescher arrived in Cairo,
he had an audience with 'Abbas I from whom he "obtained
a firman... to buy a good 'dahabiah' at a cheap price
from the Ministry of Transport".[9] The boat gave the mission a measure of independence from both the traders and
the Government, which it had lacked before. It also
strengthened its hope to establish a station at Gondokoro.

Knoblescher returned to Khartoum towards the end of
1851, with funds and a group of missionaries. In December
1852, he sailed for Gondokoro, with three missionaries.
On arrival there, he bought the mission a piece of land
from one of the Bari chiefs, Lutweri. Most of the chiefs
were now friendly, probably because they had stayed with
the missionary, Angelo Vinco. Perhaps they realised that

9. Ibid. p.27.

despite what the Turks led them to believe during the
first visit, the missionaries were harmless. The occasion of buying the land was marked by a large gather-
ing of the Bari tribe. Many of the chiefs, as reported
by the missionaries said: "The stranger must buy a
field for himself and his friends; he may grow trees
on it and instruct our children, and because the strangers have nothing in common with the robbers and murderers from foreign lands, the chiefs bind themselves to
ensure that no one damages their possessions".[10]

By now the missionaries were assured of Bari support. Knoblescher decided to build a home for the mission which contained a school and a church. He then
returned to Khartoum with a strong feeling that the
Church would survive in the heart of Central Africa.
But this enthusiasm was indeed short lived. When the
Pre-Vicar went back to Gondokoro in April 1854, he
found the mission at its lowest ebb. Two of the three
missionaries who manned the station had died in January
and March respectively. The third had moved north to
open a new station among the Cic Dinka, between Shambe
and Bor, which he named Holy Cross. Therefore the mission station at Gondokoro was virtually deserted.

As mentioned earlier, the missionaries had gone to
the south in the company of ivory traders. Three of the
forty boats that reached Gondokoro in 1854 belonged to
Vaudey, the Sardinian Vice-Consul in Khartoum. In
pursuit of his commercial interests, he planned to
attack the Bari. Knoblescher's attempts to dissuade
him had not only failed but one of Vaudey's boats was
anchored near the mission. Its presence there made the

---

10. Toniole and Hill, op cit, p.7.

Bari 'think that the Mission was a party to the expected attack'.[11] Gunshots were fired at the inhabitants
on the river bank from that boat. But the fighting
that followed led to the death of Vaudey himself. In
this way, the presence of the traders in the area endangered the mission.

Although Knoblescher played the role of a peace-
maker during the fighting, the mission's prestige
among the Bari was seriously impaired. The traders
activities made it extremely difficult for the mission
to maintain peaceful co-existence with the Bari. Moreover, the high death toll among the missionaries dras-
tically reduced their numbers. What is more the southern Sudanese were not yet prepared to allow their
children to attend the mission school or to be converted
to Christianity. Faced with this precarious situation,
the Pre-Vicar was compelled to abandon the mission
station at Gondokoro and returned to Khartoum. Mission
buildings there were entrusted to the chief of the
village, Lutweri.

So far missionary activities were confined to three
stations on the White Nile; Gondokoro, founded in 1850,
Holy Cross established in 1853 and Kaka which was founded later in 1862 among the Shilluk. However, the impact
of these three stations on the surrounding population
was apparently insignificant. There were hardly any
converts and few received missionary education. Indeed
the lack of evidence makes one doubt whether they
existed at all.

Gray sums up the various factors that led to the
failure of the mission to Central Africa by writing;
'The total unpreparedness of the Southern tribes to

---

11. Ibid, p.9.

encounter the impact of the outside world was matched
by a complete ignorance on the part of the missionaries
and traders of the values of tribal society'.[12] The inhabitants of the White Nile could not distinguish the
ivory trader from the missionaries. Both came in the
same company, possessed similar weapons, and were
identical in colour. They both tended to communicate
with the inhabitants in Arabic. The traders' rapacious
demands for ivory and later slaves jeopardized the
evangelists' work. On the other hand, the missionary
was never an effective mediator since the mission had
no administrative power to maintain peace between the
warring parties.

The lack of administrative machinery in the south
at this time made the position of the mission unten-
able. Before 1860, the interests of the Turco-Egyptian
administration in the southern Sudan were purely commercial. It was only after 1860 that Khedive Ismail
decided to establish some form of administration in
the south. The move came as a result of European pressure to bring the White Nile slave traffic to an end.
Before this date stations such as Gondokoro and Fashoda
were government trading outposts occupied seasonally
for commercial dealings with the inhabitants. But they
had no administrative contacts with the surrounding
population. Local officials were unfriendly to the mission in spite of central government's apparently favourable attitude.

All the frustrations that faced the missionaries
during their brief stay in the south and the severe
loss of life among them, discouraged their supporters
in Europe. By 1859 funds and recruits were scarce and

---

12. Gray, op cit, p.32.

in 1860 Gondokoro was finally abandoned. One of the
missionaries, Morlong, continued to pay brief visits
to Gondokoro and Holy Cross between 1861-33, to
witness the spread of violence between the traders
and the inhabitants. In 1861 a large group of
Franciscan fathers arrived at Khartoum from Rome.
They tried to establish a mission station amongst
the Shilluk, but were forced to withdraw due to bad
climatic conditions.

Meanwhile Daniele Comboni, a young priest from
Verona, started to build the fortunes of the mission
in Khartoum. After 1871, he decided to direct its
efforts towards the inhabitants of the Nuba Mountains,
but for the remainder of the 19th century, the mission
ceased to play any direct role in the southern Sudan.

After the final withdrawal from the south in 1860,
the missionaries persuaded the Austrian Agent in the
Sudan to take action with regards to events in that
part of the country. Josef Natterer, then the Consul,
wrote a strong letter to his superior in Cairo condemn-
ing all traders, 'there were no longer merchants but
only robbers and slavers on the White Nile'.[13] At the
same time Knoblescher bitterly protested against the
traders' occupation of the mission station at Gondokoro.
He alleged that Christian children from mission stations
in the south were among slaves sold in Khartoum and
demanded 'direct orders from the highest authority...to
produce an ending impression and redress against this
open evil'.[14]

The reports by Natterer and Knoblescher were for-
warded to the Foreign Office through the British Consulate in Cairo. They also attracted the attention of other

13. Ibid, p.73.
14. Ibid, p.76.

European governments to the southern Sudan. Petherick, the British agent in Khartoum, was instructed by the Foreign Secretary 'to use his utmost influence to stop these Rassias'.[15] Nevertheless, both the British Government and the public continued to regard events on the White Nile as a relatively minor affair.

The triumphant return of the British explorer, Captain Speke, from the lakes region in 1863, had however, helped enormously to emphasize the importance of the White Nile Kingdoms of Buganda, Bunyero and Karagwe. The White Nile was suddenly seen to be the natural and most practicable means of access to this area. The President of the Royal Geographical Society, Murchison, suggested that the British Government encourage Khedive Ismail to extend his powers over the reaches of the Nile. But this suggestion was viewed with distrust by the Foreign Office and other interested bodies. Colquhoun, the British Consul in Cairo, stood firmly against it saying 'supposing the Egyptian Government were allowed to establish its authority at Gondokoro... that frontier then would be closed to territories of the equatorial kingdoms mentioned by Captain Speke'[16] At the same time the importance of the White Nile to missionary work was emphasized in 1860 by a protestant missionary, Robert Arthington. In a report submitted to the Foreign Office, he pointed out the importance of the inland waterway for the rapid evangelisation of Central Africa. Arthington went on to condemn the destructive slave trading activities in the region by saying that 'these wicked cruelties hinder me from planting mission stations promptly along the upper Nile and sweeping with the Gospel around Victoria'.[17]

---

15. Ibid, p.168.
16. Ibid, p.168.
17. Ibid, p.170.

The next important event, which followed these torrents of protests and individual opinions on the situation in the southern Sudan was Baker's expedition to Equatoria in 1869. Although an employee of the Egyptian Government Baker's expedition was viewed in Britain as a symbol of European civilization and commerce. In a leading article, on 15 August 1873, the London _Times_ observed 'The magnificent prospects opened up by Baker's expedition may stir even the sluggish government of Egypt into energy'.[18] Lord Derby wrote to Baker that 'your expedition cannot fail to have extended British influence in Egypt... I know nothing that is going on in the World just now so remarkable as the steady and rapid progress which we are making in opening up Africa, and it is evident that the road must lie mainly through Egyptian territory'.[19]

But the expedition did not attract the admiration of those who were hoping to introduce Christianity and so-called legitimate commerce into Equatorial Africa. In a discussion organised by the Royal Geographical Society in 1873, a certain Dr. G. Campbell expressed clearly the stand of the religious groups in the country. He remarked that the expedition raised the whole enormous question whether Central Africa was to be Christian or Mohammedan and whether it was to be free or a slave-holding country. According to him 'if the expedition was to succeed Mohammedanism would be triumphant and Christianity extinguished'.[20]

Baker's expedition helped to bring together humanitarian forces in Britain to clamour for the defeat of

---

18. Quoted in ibid, p. 172.
19. Ibid, p.174.
20. Ibid, p.175.

slavery in the southern Sudan, namely evangelical
abolitionists, explorers and Christian missionaries.
These three groups insisted on the introduction of
Christianity and legitimate commerce, as remedies to
the then prevalent state of confusion in the southern
Sudan. Baker himself had made an appeal to the Church
of England in his book Albert N'Yanza, published in
1865, to save the pagan tribes of the Nile Valley. He
recognised the difficulties that had faced the first
missionary pioneers in the area, but he wrote in 1876
'a sensible missionary might do good service by living
among the natives and proving to their material minds
that persons do exist whose happiness consists in
doing good to others'.[21] Sir Samuel Baker was known for
his dramatic appeals to the emotions of the British
public. But some of his statements on the southern
Sudan did not represent the real situation in the area.

Such exaggerated statements from respectable personalities like Baker, were reassuring to himanitarians
and missionaries. But the situation in the White Nile
region, as far as missionary activities was concerned,
remained uneventful. Faint voices continued to be
heard demanding the intervention of the Church in the
southern Sudan. Gordon Pasha, the Governor of Equatoria
between 1874-76, advised the Church Missionary Society
to establish a mission station in his province. Gordon
suggested that the CMS could do useful service in
Zandeland in the southern Sudan。

However, Gordon did not minimise the difficulties
which the mission could meet if his advice was adhered
to. In a letter to his sister he wrote: 'The apostle
of Christ who could undertake a mission similar to what

21. S.Baker, Ismail (London 1876), p.115.

he had proposed must be a man who has died entirely to the World'.[22]

Reports by Baker and Gordon with regard to the prospects of mission success in the southern Sudan aroused interest among their countrymen, but no practical steps were taken. The attention of the Church of England was diverted to the East Coast of Africa, while the Roman Catholic Church had been discouraged during the 1850s. The Mahdist revolution of the 1850s, however, put an end to the lingering phantom of the church in the Sudan. The Roman Catholic Fathers who were working at Dilling, in Kordofan, were captured in 1882. By 1885 most of the Christians in the Sudan were either prisoners in El-Obeid and Omdurman or were converted to Islam.

But throughout the Mahdia, the Roman Catholic Church kept a Sudan mission in exile, based in Cairo. Protestant Church interests had been directed to the Sudan by Gordon during his governorship of Equatoria, and particularly in 1875 when he helped a CMS party enroute up the Nile to Uganda. His death at the hands of the Mahdi, on 26 January, 1885, stimulated the CMS to prepare for the time when the Sudan would be open to European civilization.

Just a few weeks after his death, the CMS pledged itself in a meeting held at Exeter Hall to establish a Gordon Memorial Mission for the Sudan. Subsequently a sum of £3,000 was raised to meet that purpose as soon as the Mahdist state would be overthrown. The death of Gordon as well as Christian Zeal to find converts in

---

22. G.B. Hill, Colonel Cordon in Central Africa 1874-1879 (London 1881), p.13.

a country that was considered to be inhabited by
Muslim fanatics and black pagans prompted the CMS to
enter the Sudan soon after the reconquest. In fact
the CMS was more interested in evangelizing during
the first years of the condominium in the northern
Sudan, where Gordon had met his death. Until 1905 it
was reluctant to start work in the south.

Having obtained the necessary funds for work in
the Sudan, the CMS dispatched Major F.T. Haig to Sawakin
between 1890-91. He recommended the immediate establishment of a mission station at Sawakin, which, he felt
'would act as a Vanguard to forward moves into the
interior'.[23] This recommendation, however, did not win
the support of the committee, because it was felt that
such a mission would be ineffective if the Mahdist
state remained in control of the Sudan.

The enthusiasm of the CMS to penetrate the Sudan
was revived in 1898 after Kitchener had stepped up his
offensive against the Mahdist State. In July that year,
Baylis, the CMS secretary, made an announcement that
the committee was willing 'to accept offers of service,
with this field in view; Egypt and the Sudan, and the
committee should consider whether some expedition of
a preliminary character might not be sent from the Mission in Egypt to Khartoum as soon as the way for such
a step was clearly opened'.[24] Just ten days after the
defeat of the Mahdist at Kerari, Dr. F.J. Harper, the
representative of the CMS in Cairo, was instructed to

---

23. R.O. Collins, Land Beyond the Rivers: the southern
    Sudan 1898-1918 (Yale 1971), p.285.

24. R.Hill, 'Government and Christian Missions in the
    Anglo-Egyptian Sudan 1898-1914', Middle Eastern
    Studies Vol.I (1965) No.2.

see Lord Cromer, the British Consul General in Egypt,
on the possibility of sending a mission to the Sudan.
After consultations with Kitchener in Khartoum, Cromer
gave a negative reply. Both Cromer and Kitchener refused
permission for the missionaries to start work in
Khartoum on the grounds that, 'the Sudanese were fanatic-
al Muslims who would strongly object to Christian
efforts to convert them and any such reaction would
endanger both the government and the missionaries'.[25]

The new Government, however, gave the CMS an alternative by urging it to start work in the pagan south.
This proposal was unenthusiastically accepted by the
general committee of the Society. The offer was regarded as a diversion from Khartoum, 'the place where
Gordon had died and where his death could best be com-
memorated'. The CMS persistently continued to press for
permission to proselytise among the Muslim population
of Khartoum. In February, 1899, the House of Laymen for
the Province of Canterbury passed a motion, suggested
by Sir John Kennaway, President of the Society, which
deprecated the prohibition against missionaries travel-
ling to Khartoum. A series of memoranda were subsequently sent to the Foreign Office and the British High Commissioner in Cairo which demanded the removal of all
restrictions imposed on missionary societies in the
northern part of the Sudan.

But Lord Cromer and Kitchener were adamantly opposed
to any missionary work in Khartoum that might threaten
the newly founded administration. Cromer promised the
northern Sudanese that there would be no interference
whatever in their religion. The argument on the part of
those who called for missionary freedom in the northern

---

25. Collins, op cit, p.284.

part of the country was viewed, in the words of Robert
Collins, "in terms of religious liberty, on the mis-
taken assumption that the principles, rights and
liberties of Great Britain had been incorporated into
the Anglo-Egyptian Sudan".[26]

The CMS did not take up the proposed Fashoda
station in the south. Instead the idea of founding
a permanent station there was quietly postponed. A re-
connaissance party was suggested to proceed to the
southern Sudan, but this was a pretext to enable the
missionaries to reach Khartoum. After the death of the
Khalifa in November 1899, Kitchener announced that
foreign traders were free to enter the Sudan. This was
soon followed by a similar permit to the missionary
societies, but on condition that they did not discuss
religion with Muslims. Dr Harper and Bishop Gwynne of
the CMS were the first to visit the Sudan that year.

The Roman Catholic Church felt that the reconquest
of the Sudan would automatically reinstate them. But
Kitchener was not prepared to accept the old order with-
out question. During his first visit to England after
the battle of Kerari, he sought to replace the Austrian
Mission to the Sudan with English Catholic missionaries.
His plan was not accepted as both Bishop Reveggio and
Austrian Emperor, Francis Joseph, strongly opposed it.
When the Austrian missionaries, Ohrwalder and Bishop
Reveggio visited the Sudan in 1899, Kitchener "was
furious and declared cold war against them".[27]

The attitude of the Sudan Government towards the
Roman Catholic Church was extremely cool. Kitchener
rejected their request to occupy the old site and

---

26. Ibid, p.283.
27. Ibid, p.283.

reluctantly allowed them to settle on a new site. such a stand from the Governor-General made it clear to the Roman Catholics that the mission should be prepared for less cooperation and encouragement from the British administrators in the Sudan. But with the death of Reveggio in 1900 and the transfer of leadership to Bishop Franz Geyer, a more flexible cleric, relations began to improve between the two sides. With this newly-founded government confidence, Bishop Geyer managed to open up a new era for the Roman Catholic Church in the southern Sudan.

BRITISH RELIGIOUS AND EDUCATIONAL POLICY:
THE CASE OF BAHR EL—GHAZAL

By Damazo Dutt Majok

In Bahr al-Ghazal Islam and Christianity were the
religions accepted by Condominium rule. "Islam was not
a new religion as Christianity was".[1] Among the non-
Nilotic areas of the province its influence had long
been felt. The agents of Islamization in the nineteenth
century were Muslim ivory and slave traders, Turkiya
officials and the Mahdists who invaded the province for
their own interests. As they mingled with the local
population, some chiefs, notables, commoners and women
(through marriage) became Muslim. Islamic names super-
ceded local names and inhabitants adopted Muslim dress,
customs, beliefs, ways of life and the Arabic language
besides their own tongue. Thus Western District, the
stronghold of the Islamic faith, became completely
islamized and up to this time Islam prevails despite
colonial attempts to restrict it. Islamization also
took place among the Azande and Nilotes neighbouring
Muslim settlements, but not on a large scale in the
central, northern and western parts of the province.

---

1. Interview with elder Stanislaus 'Abd Allah Paysama
   in Wau, December 1976. Elder Paysama was born in
   1905 at Bindisi, Dar Fur and was taken by Catholic
   Missionaries from there to Wau where he grew up.
   He had his elementary and intermediate education
   in Wau and was sent to Khartoum in 1917 to learn
   Arabic. Subsequently, he served as a teacher, clerk
   in the Civil Secretary's Office, translator and
   a sub-mamur before joining politics on the eve of
   independence. After this, he became an M.P.,
   President of the Liberal Party, leader of Opposition in the Senate and a minister several times.
   He retired from politics in 1967 to lead a private
   life in Wau.

Other agents of Islamization were Muslim intruders who reached Bahr al-Ghazal from the west. 'These included the mixed Muslim population of Furanjs, gallabas, Bornouse, Dajo, Nuba, etc.. who came to work at the copper mines of Hufrat al-Nahas in the early 19th century'[2] Pilgrims from West Africa who travelled via these mines to Mecca played an equally big role in introducing Islam into the area. Islamization was peaceful on the basis of marriage, friendship and mutual cooperation. Faqis preached Islam and led prayers and were thus able to win many for the faith. None of the indigenous people opposed these Islamic preachers and teachers, who became very popular.

Other agents of Islamization in the province were the southern Mahdist armies "when these returned to their homes from the north after 1898, they persuaded some of their tribesmen or relatives to become Muslims"[3]. Muslim soldiers who made up the forces which occupied Bahr al-Ghazal played an important role in the spread of both Arabic and Islam among the local population.

---

2. Interview with Shaykh Abd al-Shakur Musa Hamid at Khor al-Samam, Raga, January, 1977. He is the son of Sultan of Feroge Sultan Musa; who together with Sultan Nasr Andel of Ngulgule sent envoys to Khartoum in early 1900 to greet the Governor-General and take flags from him. He was in Qoranic School in 1904 when the British first came to see his father in Raga.

3. Interview with elder stanislaus 'Abd Allah, op cit. Throughout the south these returnees grouped themselves in parts of towns and called themselves and their residential areas malakis meaning private settlements paying no allegiance to any traditional leaders, but subjects of the ruling regime. Some of them were government officials, soldiers and traders and freely mixed with inhabitants.

Most of them "were Southern Sudanese who were taken to
the Northern Sudan during slave trade days, Turkiya
and Mahdiya".[4] As they were manumitted during the early
period of the Condominium, those who wished to return
to Bahr al-Ghazal were allowed to return to their
families. Very few, however, stayed in the countryside
where their relatives still lived a harsh and simple
life, the majority took up residence in towns and
became detribalised.

In the towns they mixed with Muslims - soldiers,
traders, exiled Egyptian and Sudanese officials, started
to build mosques and Qoranic schools. Islamic teachings and practices were widespread in every town or
station in the province as a result of the Muslim
presence.

During the first three years of Condominium rule
in Bahr al-Ghazal, Christians were very few indeed
compared to the tremendous Muslim population. Even
those Christian soldiers and merchants residing in
towns and stations took no interest in or had no time
to preach and convert Africans to Christianity. "The
early years of the Condominium did not witness government's consistent action to check Islam gaining ground,

---

4. Interview with ex. chief Rik Reec at Pacong, Rumbek,
   November 1976. He was one of the Agar boys captured
   by the British forces in 1902 following the suppression of Agar resistance. He was brought up by Rehan
   effendi a Sudanese soldier and later recruited to
   the army. He left the army in 1917 and was appointed
   by the British as Chief over Agar Dinka.

but allowed Muslims to do as they wished"[5]. As the government troops resided at the posts, northern traders came to these centres both to trade and to spread Islam, just as they did during the Turkiya and Mahdiya.

The Governor-General, Wingate, observing that the whole of Bahr al-Ghazal was threatened by Islamic influence, embarked on a preventive policy and in 1910 he wrote:

> It is needless to repeat what you know so well, namely, that for one Christian officer or official who goes into the Southern district there are hundreds of Moslems each of whom by the very nature of his religion appeals to the Blacks very much more than the Christian religion can. If, therefore, we are to succeed in Christianising these Southern tribes, it can only be done by very much greater missionary activity than exists at present and I can perfectly encourage and facilitate such missionary work.[6]

Wingate hoped that a Christian, African population in the south would deter Islam from spreading from Bahr al-Ghazal to other African countries.

---

5. Interview with Sultan Khoso Muhammad Sughaiyar at Khata, Raga, January 1977. He comes from Kreish Hufrat al-Nahas who resisted British troops in 1912 under the leadership of Sultan Murad Ibrahim. He claimed to have participated in the resistance to the British forces and was arrested after the suppression, but released later. He succeeded his father who was appointed by the British in place of Murad Ibrahim after the Fertit resistance was repressed.

6. Quoted by R.O. Collins in Land Beyond the River: The Southern Sudan, 1898-1918 (New Haven 1971) p.306.

In 1904 the Governor of Wau opened the first
school in Wau for teaching the children of colonial
officials and soldiers. Soon the school was dominated
by Muslim children. The Director of Education, Currie,
closed it for the following reasons: firstly, he
thought that lack of funds would not allow the school
to achieve the required results; secondly, the appointment of a Muslim teacher would result in the establishment of Islam which was not the desired goal. Therefore,
he preferred the employment of Lebanese teachers to
check Islam and Arabic. This policy was supported by
Wingate:

> I am not at all keen to propagate Islam in countries
> in which that religion is not the religion of the
> inhabitants. As a Governor, I do not intend
> interfering with religious beliefs and prefer to
> leave all that in the hands of the missionaries.
> Then again the language comes in, the language of
> Bahr al-Ghazal is not really Arabic, and therefore
> if any foreign language is taught, it ought to be
> English.[7]

This policy did not, however, check Islam. At the
end of 1904, the Government fearing the spread of Islam
stopped reading, writing and arithmetic in Arabic in
schools. For the same reason British officials in the
Sudan approved the coming of missionaries to preach
the Christian faith instead of Islam and to make English
the language of communication instead of Arabic. Previously relations between missionaries and British administrators had not been cordial, but in the face of
the threat of Islam the Christian societies were allowed

---

7. Quoted by G. Warburg in The Sudan Under Wingate
   (London 1971) p.116.

to "establish both schools and churches in the South".[8]

Having divided the south into spheres of influence "to avoid a scramble among the missionaries as well as confusion of mind on the part of the local population regarding different Christian teachings";[9] Bahr al-Ghazal was assigned to Catholic missionaries as an operational zone. Being close to the northern Sudan, Bahr al-Ghazal was more Islamized than any other part of the south, a process which continued even during Condominium rule. Hence the British Government considered this a vital area in which Muslim influence had to be checked. Thus, since the Roman Catholics had past experience of this province and were in a better financial position, they were allowed to establish churches and schools there to discourage the further spread of Islam.

In January 1904, Bishop Francis Xavier headed a handful of missionaries, fathers and lay brothers, into as it was said: "If not the unknown, at least the uncertain". They reached Wau in February, "the welcome they had received from the officials, from tribal chiefs and from the population gave rise to great hopes in the hearts of the first bearers of the Gospel, for the future of the church in Bahr al-Ghazal".[10]

---

8. M.O. Beshir The Southern Sudan: Background to Conflict (London 1968) p.30

9. Verona Fathers' Mission The Black Book of the Sudan an Answer (Verona 1964) p.14.

10. Verona Fathers' Mission The Golden Jubiles of the Bahr al-Ghazal Mission (Verona 1956) p.1.

Since Islam was generally practised in Wau with its medley of tribes and ex-soldiers, and Arabic widely spoken, Bishop Geyer established his first missionary station at Kayango north - west of Wau in Golo land in March 1904 amidst a salvo of rifle shots and joyous shouts from the population. Having erected a grass and wooden chapel and some huts, he returned to Wau. In April, he delegated two fathers and a brother from Wau with a message to the Luo chief, Dut Akot, to the east in Mbili village. The indigenous people received them cordially and as a result of local friendliness, the clergy established a second missionary station in the province at Mbili. In 1905, the fathers returned to Wau where they opened a third mission which became the centre of the already established missionary stations in the rural areas, soon (in 1905) schools were opened at Kayango and Wau.

Despite the prompt establishment of these stations, the missionaries encountered much hardship and opposition from the local population, "Indifference, contempt and persecution, hidden and overt",[11] long distances and difficult communications, lack of money, absence of a common language except Arabic in the pidgin form. Unsalubrious climate and widespread diseases and lack of permanent tribal settlements also slowed down their progress. Malaria, dysentry and many other diseases killed half of them and weakened the survivors so that their work almost ceased, yet they carried on. There were however, other factors which inspired them to endure.

---

11. Ibid.

A certain gallaba who had a strange vision at night
came to meet and relate the truth to abuna (father) in
the mission. He told him: "Last night I was without
impurity, and an old man with a white beard drew near
to my bed and commanded me to come here and repeat
three words: ezra (sow), osgi (irrigate), esbur (have
patience)."[12] Having delivered the message to the superior father, the trader left the mission. His message
was considered to have come from God assuring his
Servants of success.

Another source of inspiration and encouragement
for the missionaries were the civil authorities. Wingate
for example wrote:

As Governor of this country and according to the
dictates of human prudence I ought to tell you
retreat.... but as a Christian I tell you hang on
and continue your work despite all the losses or
rather because of them. It is not possible that
the Good God will not take into consideration the
heroic sacrifice of so many young lives and not
blame you and your work in the future.[13]

In 1912 the missionaries reached Zande land and
opened missionary stations there. After having worked
two decades among the Golo, Luo, Belanda and Zande
tribes, they opened Kwajok mission in 1923 for the
Dinka and Luo. Similarly in March 1926, they opened
Deim Zubair mission to serve the Belanda Bviri,
Ndogo and Kreish tribes.

From this network of stations evangelism gradually
increased. The missionaries had two main goals: "Firstly, to evangelise the people and secondly to teach them

---

12. Ibid, pp.5-6.
13. Ibid, p.6.

how to read and write in order to prepare them for
their work".[14] On February 28 1907, Father Paolo
Meroni, Religious Superior of the Mission in the Sudan
baptised the first eight Christians, six boys and two
married men at Kayango. This was the first baptism
ever administered in the whole of Bahr al-Ghazal. It
was the beginning of the campaign to eradicate Islam
and Arabic. Others were baptised in Mbili in December,
1913 and catechumenates were established in all missionary stations for teaching the Gospel and baptising
local men and women.

On 24 May 1919, the Verona sisters reached Wau for
the first time to work among indigenous women and
girls to prepare them for baptism. The arrival of the
sisters added more weight to the evangelisation and
resulted in an increase in converts. The sisters were
sent to work at Kayango and Kwajok in 1923 and 1927
respectively. Christianisation steadily continued in
areas where security and order prevailed, especially
among the non-Nilotes who were docile and loyal government subjects.

---

14. Interview with His Grace Archbishop Ireneo Wien
    Dut Akot in Juba, November 1976. His Grace was born
    in 1912 at Mbili Catholic Mission. His father Dut
    Akot, one of the local chiefs who cooperated with
    missionaries in the early years of the Condominium,
    sent him to the school at Mbili in 1920 where he
    was taught catechism, reading and writing the verna-
    cular. He was baptised in 1923 and in 1925 was sent
    to Wau Primary School to read the Gospel, English,
    Arabic, etc.. He was in Intermediate School (1931-
    1935), had philosophical courses 1936-1944. He was
    ordained in 1944 as the second southern Sudanese
    Catholic Priest, consecrated as the first Sudanese
    Bishop in 1952 and first Archbishop in 1973.

Nilotic areas were left alone until security could be
permanently established.

Missionary educational policy was: "If a native
wishes to read, he must first be baptised".[15] Consequently the first missionary schools were catechist schools,
held in huts, chapels or under shady trees where people
were taught the Gospel to prepare them for baptism.

Prior to missionary control of education, the condominium authorities had opened the first school in Wau
in 1904 to train carpenters, brick-layers and masons,
supposedly recruited from all those who came to the
school. But the Muslim children of northern soldiers in
Wau dominated the school and it was feared that this
would indirectly encourage the spread of Islam. As
a result Wau government school passed to the missionaries in 1904.

Bishop Geyar divided the boys into two schools.
Muslim boys were sent to the regimental school to be
taught in Arabic by Muslim teachers. But this school
did not function at all, hence Muslim parents sent
their sons to the missionary school.

The educational policy of the British Government
was to instruct the inhabitants in their own languages
and English as the lingua france instead of Arabic.
Therefore, in the bush or village schools which relied
on visiting missionaries, boys were instructed to read
and copy the Bible in the vernaculars and received
rudimentary health education. Thus Islam and Arabic
were excluded. Those who passed the examination at the
end of the second year attended third year. In elementary schools boys learned English and received religious
training for four years. In intermediate school (six
years) all subjects were taught in English except

---

15. Quoted by Beshir, p.31.

religion which was taught to them in the vernacular. Again the goal was the eradication of Arabic and Islam, which were considered inseparable by the British authorities.

Despite colonial attempts to eradicate Arabic and supersede it with English, using the missionaries to execute this policy, diverse obstacles retarded progress. There was a shortage of teachers, because of the language policy and limited financial resources. British reluctance to employ northern teachers, European refusals to teach for low salaries in bad climatic conditions also presented difficulties. Moreover, many indigenous chiefs refused to send their children to mission schools and some of them overtly became hostile. For example the students of the Wau school were from Jebelawi,[16] pupils also came from Zande land and from French Equatorial Africa. "With the exception of Azande, however, the students who attended mission schools were invariably the out-casts and misfits of the southern Sudanese societies - orphans, refugees and disowned".[17]

Apart from baptism and western education other weapons were applied to eradicate Islam and Arabic. These included the establishment of local army and police to replace northern Sudanese, the removal of Egyptian mamurs following the assassination of Sir Lee Stack in Cairo and their replacement with A.D.Cs. after the First World War. The activities of British officers who allowed more mosques and other Islamic institutions to be constructed were prohibited. Furthermore, Friday

---

16. A name applied to those refugees who fled from Bahr al-Jebel during the Turkiya and who had settled around Wau.

17. Collins op cit p.319.

was abolished as the traditional day of rest in 1919 and Sunday observed by all people. Finally the southern policy was initiated to check the massive entry of northerners into the southern Sudan.

Considering these measures an antidote to Islamic propaganda, Wingate approved them without consideration for future consequences. Thus the gallaba could only trade in the south with special permits. Local men, under British officers, were recruited to replace the Egyptian army in the south. Consequently the Equatorial Battalion was created in 1917 in Mongalla province and some of its men 'were sent to the Bahr al-Ghazal to replace Egyptian soldiers'.[18] Despite the Governor-General's insistence on the creation of a local army, a lack of British officers and educated southern Sudanese made the realization of his plans very difficult.

Although the gallaba were checked, some of them whose mothers were indigenous women from Bahr al-Ghazal stealthily hid themselves among their maternal relatives and traded without government interruption. Moreover, the policy was not approved of by some inhabitants who passively resisted the British authorities by hiding their gallaba cousins. Thus in the real sense British attempts to get rid of Islam, Arabic and northerners in the province had only temporary success.

"In 1914, 1915 and 1916 missionaries continued to enlist more boys for the schools in Wau, but their attempt was not a success".[19] The Nilotes sent their sons to cattle camps. The few who remained at home participated in cultivation or other manual work. A few

18. Interview with ex.Jehadiya Cigai Wut, op cit.

19. Interview with ex-chief Monywiir Rehen, op cit.

Nilotic and freed slave boys who were sent to school
were taught Christianity and English as well as Arabic.
As they mingled with Muslims in Wau they were exposed
to harsh treatment by local, detribalised people who
professed Islam and spoke Arabic, who did not tolerate
Christians and stoned missionary boys. Moreover, when
the missionaries tried to persuade the chiefs to send
their sons to school, on many occasions they were sent
away or beaten. Subsequently they did not trouble themselves to visit these local leaders. Thus, in areas such as
Aweil in northern Bahr al-Ghazal missionary success
was restricted despite the establishment of British
military posts there. Local hostility being the major
obstacle to conversion.

Since the chiefs considered the sending of boys to
missionary schools a kind of human tax, they only sent
'adopted' sons or slave boys to schools with the belief
that these boys would not return to them and so would
not worry them very much as they were not their legitimate sons! [20] Moreover, besides these boys, they sent
"useless boys of their own who would not do well at
Gospel learning and kept at home the best sons who it
was hoped would spread their fame abroad in other
tribal areas".[21] These also succeeded to chieftaincies.

---

20. Many of my informants, especially the Nilotes,
    expressed this opinion as they suspected the new
    invaders of being no better than their predecessors
    who had enslaved many of their men in the past.
    Therefore, they argued that if they sent many boys
    to school, they would not return to them.

21. Interview with elder Stanislaus 'Abd Allah Paysame',
    op cit. This view and that of other informants is
    a doubtful one, I believe the main reason for not
    sending their boys to schools was that the parents
    employed them in herding and farming.

Thus the number of boys sent to missionary schools was not large and the intake did not increase.

Boys who entered village, elementary and inter-mediate schools were taught the vernacular and English respectively. Arabic and English were also taught in the last two schools. Hence government policy to supersede Arabic with English did not succeed. Some boys were sent from Kayango and Mbili bush schools to Wau elementary school to learn Arabic. "In 1918 the first batch of the indigenous boys were sent from Wau to Khartoum to learn more Arabic to be able to trans-late Arabic into English and vice versa".[22] Consequent-ly Arabic teaching continued and Egyptian teachers were employed instead of the northern Sudanese who were claimed to be agents of Islamization. Arabic as the unifying language was therefore very difficult to restrict because it was principally the language of administration and trade. Thus without it the popula-tion in the bush would not be able to communicate with alien administrators. Similarly urban people could not communicate through English and consequently spoke Arabic.

When in 1920 the British authorities grouped some tribes along the main government roads, the mission-aries were able to enlist many boys for their schools. Although the Condominium government was suspicious of missionaries and had misgivings about the effectiveness of Italians teaching English to inhabitants, it steadi-ly encouraged local chiefs to send their boys to schools. If they failed to convince the chiefs, the British officials forced them against their will. Thus with government support and subsidies Catholic educa-tion constantly increased.

---

22. Interview with His Grace Archbishop Ireneo Wien Dut, op cit.

In 1921 the Verona sisters, riding donkeys and
bicycles or walking, penetrated into villages accompanied by fathers to persuade inhabitants to send their
girls to schools to learn the Gospel, hygiene, domestic
science and needlework. As a Priest approached the
inhabitants, he spoke persuasively. "Look this is a
woman, she has come from very far country to Wau and
from there to you here in the villages to teach your
women Christian religion and make them civilized".[23]
Thus despite the lack of accommodation for girls, the
sisters and fathers held classes for them under shady
trees. After the bush school, they sent them to elementary and intermediate schools to learn more religion,
needlework, hygiene domestic science, music, English
and Arabic.

The boys had technical lessons in carpentry, brick-
laying, gardening, receiving a clerical training
rather than a more literary education which the missionaries thought dangerous. They considered a boy sufficiently literate when he was able to read the word of
God.

In 1921 seven of the first batch of boys that
went to learn Arabic in Khartoum finished their studies.
They became affendia in government offices in Wau, serving as clerks, book-keepers, teachers and medical
assistants. They received salaries and were well-dressed
and tidy. This encouraged the inhabitants to send their
boys to missionary schools, a tremendous number, sons
of chiefs and headmen and many others flocked to the
schools after 1921. Even Muslims who at first had sent
their boys to the school where Arabic and Islam were
taught, moved them in 1922 to the missionaries. Muslim

23. Interview with elder Stanislaus 'Abd Allah Paysame, op cit.

boys also attended religious classes. Those who wanted
baptism and other sacrements did this after the consent
of their parents. When parents refused, however, the
boys were not baptised. "Therefore, the first Muslim
boy baptised was Mustafa, the son of the Feroge Chief
Musa Hamid who was Muslim and spoke Arabic".[24] Despite
this baptism when Mustafa returned to Raga from the
Wau school, he embraced Islam again.

Since free boarding, clothing and medical treatment were available for students who came from outlying
districts, many parents, especially chiefs, sent their
sons to the missionaries. People began to press Government and missionaries for more schools, but lack of
money and teachers made this impossible. In 1923 Kwajok
became a missionary station to evangelize the Dinka and
Luo.

In 1921 Major Wheatley, Governor of Wau persuaded
the British Government to make a grant-in-aid in order
to establish an intermediate missionary school, which
was built in 1924. Boys were taught English (from east,
south and west African textbooks), Arabic, arithmetic,
religion and gardening.

At the end of 1923, Mr Crowfoot, the Director of
Education visited Bahr al-Ghazal to acquaint himself
with the educational policy and needs of the people in
the province. In Wau area he visited various mission
schools. What he saw or heard impressed him. Consequently he recommended that the Government should participate in the responsibility to educate indigenous people
in cooperation with the missions and approve funds to
this end. This resulted in the prompt building of the
Stack memorial school in Wau in 1926 and the appointment of two resident education inspectors. The purpose

24. Ibid.

of the school was to work in close connexion with the missionaries, to educate boys for government service up to a standard equivalent to the 2nd year of Gordon College secondary course and to train teachers. The school started with three classes and a syllabus devised for the southern Sudan. It provided free education for all as well as free boarding to boys from outlying areas. The boys were taught by missionaries, lay brothers and Syrian teachers.

The opening of this school was an important landmark in the history of the province. It introduced higher education into Bahr al-Ghazal and provided for both religious and secular education on equal basis. It had, however, some draw-backs. Textbooks were difficult for the boys to understand. They contained proverbs and terminologies which were difficult to explain.

The British attempt to establish the English language and Christianity instead of Islam and Arabic was not always a success. Arabic remained the medium of communication among the lower levels of the administration and traders. This was particularly true in western district where private citizens constantly erected Qoranic schools e.g. at Raga, Kafia, Kingi, Kabalusa and Coasinga. The same happened in towns. The diehard local Muslims passively resisted the Government by deserting to the north. Sometimes they overtly resisted as in case of Isa Fartak[25] in Raga.

Islam continued to be embraced in the province by a number of citizens and Arabic remained a vehicle of communication.

---

25. He opposed Southern policy as soon as he succeeded his father towards the end of the third decade of Condominium rule. He was deposed in 1934 and exiled to Dar Fur until 1957. See Santandrea A Tribal History of Western Bahr el Ghazal, p.144.

CHRISTIAN MISSIONARY ACTIVITIES IN SUDAN
1926-1946
By
S.M. Sid Ahmed

The twenty years between 1926-1946 witnessed remarkable developments in missionary activities in the Sudan. This period was also characterised by governmental intervention in the south's affairs, through a series of steps which came to be known as 'southern policy', codified by law and adopted officially by the Government in 1930. On the other hand the same period saw the development of government-missionary cooperation, exemplified mainly by the grants-in-aid system, according to which missionary societies received fiscal aid by putting themselves under governmental jurisdiction. One of the results of this new relationship was the consolidation of missionary activities in the south. However, consolidation also meant competition between the societies, namely between the Roman Catholic Mission and the Church Missionary Society. This period of consolidation begat antagonism, awareness of the missionary presence in the south attracted the attention of the Sudanese nationalism movement which began to concern itself with what was going on in the southern Sudan. These elements genuinely tested for the first time the validity of the sphere system which had been adopted by the British authorities.

The British administration which between 1898-1920 had restricted itself to keeping law and order, collecting taxes and renaming provinces, began after the 1919 revolution in Egypt to modify its policies. The cornerstone of this change was Milner's 1920 report which said the following on Sudan, 'Having regard to its vast extent and the varied character of its inhabitants, the admin-

istration of its different parts should be left, as far
as possible, in the hands of the native authorities,
wherever they exist under British supervision'[1].

Two years later the Government prepared a memorandu
on the policy of decentralized control. Indirect rule,
which adopted local administration as a medium of gover
ment, obviously meant a revival of tribal institutions.
The culmination of this policy came with the official
declaration of southern policy on January 25 1930, when
the Civil Secretary wrote, 'The policy of the Governmen
in the Southern Sudan is to build up a series of self
contained racial or tribal units with structure and organization based, to whatever extent the requirements o
equity and good government permit, upon indigenous custc
traditional usage and beliefs'[2].

This policy necessitated the adoption of certain
steps, such as the provision of non-Arabic-speaking sta
on all administrative, clerical and technical levels,
elimination of Arab elements and control of immigrants
especially traders - from the north. British staff were
advised to familiarize themselves with tribal beliefs,
customs and languages; the use of English as a lingua
franca where communication in local vernaculars was impossible was also recommended. The restriction on Arabi
was an essential feature of this policy.

Another aspect was the discouragement of tribal
liasons between the southern Sudan and neighbouring Ara
Muslim peoples of Darfur and Kordofan. Tribes like the
Banda, Dongo, Kreish, Feruga, Nyargulgule and Togoyo wh
had always been in contact with Arabic-Islamic culture,

---

1. Central Office of Information, Basic Facts about the
   Southern Provinces, (Khartoum, 1964), p.35.

2. M.O. Beshir, The Southern Sudan: Background to Conflict (London, 1968), p.115.

were moved from their regions and rehabilitated in areas
away from the influence of northerners. This was followed by the creation of a 'no man's land' between the
southern Sudan and Bahr el Arab river in Darfur as
a barrier to interaction.

Yet the missionaries considered such a policy as
highly commendable. As early as 1904, Archdeacon Shaw of
the Christian Missionary Society said, 'Unless all these
black tribes are evangelized within the next few years
they must inevitably become Mohammadans. That danger has
now passed'[3] To Shaw, the mere presence of missionary
societies in the border areas would insulate southern
tribes from Islamic influence. So government adoption
of the southern policy aided the efforts of Christian
evangelism. Trimingham put it bluntly: '... it may be
said that, as the Uganda Mission stopped the spread of
Islam among the Baganda, so the Southern Sudan Mission,
aided by `the Southern Policy´of the Sudan Government,
are stopping Muslim penetration from sweeping around
the less impressionable Nilotes and embracing tribes
such as the Moru and Azande'.[4]

The missionary societies' contribution was not restricted to lip-service; their doings were equally remarkable. For instance, one aspect of southern policy
was to discourage northern gellaba, but the radical
solution was to develop a native class of traders, which
was a difficult task. British officials tried different
ways of achieving this, among them to establish an organization based on native administration, directed by
a committee of government officials, missionary societies and merchants and financed by the Government.[5]

3. JS. Trimingham, Christian Approach to Islam (London)
   1948).
4. Ibid, p.50.
5. M.O. Beshir, op cit, p.49.

So in terms of implementing policies, the missionary societies were reliable allies. This led of course to an era of cooperation which consolidated their position. It may be useful here to examine Christian consolidation on the continental level. The spirit of the Edinburgh Conference of 1910 was to show concern about internal affairs in the colonies which in the final analysis meant coordination with the colonial powers, for no fruitful work could be carried out unless good relations existed between missionary and administrator. If an age of cooperation was not promptly instituted after 1910, it was because of the effects of the First World War and it aftermath which checked the proposed alliance.

After the post-war return to normality the Phelps-Stokes Commission was formed. Between 1922-24 it surveyed Africa and succeeded in establishing an Advisory Committee for Education in Tropical Africa. The Committee emphasized joint consultation between the colonial powers and the missionary societies so as to create an indigenous class of Christians capable of carrying the faith before changing conditions. The basis of this attitude went back to when 'John Mott, the greatest of the ecumencial leaders, was tireless in prophesying that the rising nationalism of Asia and Africa would destroy Christianity along with western imperialism unless the faith could be early established under indigenous leadership'.[6] So, according to this concept, the Church had to share in creating future leaders to forstall any attack on Christianity and western civilization in general; the installation of an indigenous church would lessen, if not prevent, any national counterattacks.

---

6. R. Oliver, The Missionary Factor in East Africa (London, 1952), p.233.

This led finally to an alliance between the colonial administration and Christian forces, cemented by government aid and consolidation of missionary activities.

The alliance between imperial and missionary factors in education amounted to much more than an alignment of theoretical policies. In terms of finance, the annual contribution of the Government to mission schools rose during the period 1923 to 1949, from nothing to £285,000 in Tanganyika, from £10,000 to about £300,000 in Kenya. By the end of the period grants to missions were absorbing between half and two-thirds of the educational budgets of the territories, and the individual missions were receiving more money from Government in respect of their educational work than their combined receipts from home societies and from their local church members. In some denominations more than a third of the European missionaries came to be mainly supported out of government grants, while an even higher proportion received an official allowance in respect of part-time educational work. Mainly, however, the vast sums allocated to missions by governments represented the salaries of African schoolmasters and schoolmistresses, trained, employed and organized by the missions, who had became by the end of the period even more numerous and much more highly paid than the pastoral workers of the Churches.[7]

This financial support led to the expansion and consolidation of the Christian community. In East Africa for instance the growth of Christianity was remarkable. By 1938 Christians were 8% of the population of Kenya, 10% in Tanganyika, and 25% in Uganda. Figures show that Roman Catholics increased from about 300,000 in 1914 to

---

7. Ibid, pp.277-8.

over 1,000,000 in 1933 and to 1,700,000 in 1946, most o
them in Uganda. The Anglican Church, restricted by the
sphere system grew from 225,000 in 1914 to 400,000 in
1938 and to 750,000 in 1946. In Kenya the Presbyterian
Church which numbered less than 1,000 in 1914, grew to
10,000 in 1938 and 15,000 in 1947.[8]

The missionary-imperial pact showed steady progress
in the field of education especially during the two
decades 1923-1947, where government grants in the three
East African countries Tanganyika, Uganda and Kenya grew
to unprecedented levels. The immediate result of this
was the conversion of former missionary 'out-stations'
or 'bush-schools' described by the Phelps-Stokes Commission as the 'frontier of civilization' into regular
elementary schools providing three to four years of
simple education.

In the southern Sudan, the Government, aware of all
these developments, decided in 1926 to introduce the
grants-in-aid system, which gave her the right to
inspect missionary work. In 1930 'southern policy' was
officially declared and two years later the Government
felt the necessity to reform education in the southern
Sudan. In April 1932 an educational conference was held
in Juba to reassess policy and the major concern was to
satisfy the demand for parochial staff as soon as
possible.

The conference stated that measures should be taken
'to ensure that educational policy was entirely in
accord with the declared policy of the administration...
(and) not at destruction of native social institutions
or at divorcing the Southerner from his national background, but at teaching him to adapt himself and his

---

8. Ibid, p.237.

institutions to changing ideas and conditions'[9]. Thus the
stated aim of education was not detribalization of
southerners, but to produce better members of society.
During this period innumerable meetings were held between
missionary societies and government officials to attain
fuller cooperation and provide more facilities for missionaries. In 1936 C.W. Williams, then Assistant Direct-
or of Education submitted a report in which he stressed
consolidation of missionary education by increasing
fiscal aid, and suggested that grants-in-aid should be
raised from L£7,605 in 1933 to L£9,155 in 1937. Total
government subsidies between 1933-1946 were increased
by about 250% which indicates government dedication to
the aim of consolidating missionary education.

Year after year the percentage increased, especially
after the Second World War. In the provinces, for example
Upper Nile Province, aid increased by 218% and in Equatoria by 256%. This can also be attributed to the fact
that the former provinces of Bahr el Ghazal and Mongalla
were amalgamated into Equatoria[10].

Besides the Catholic Church's intense activities
needed more aid. The RCM actually received no aid till
1927 for they opposed inspection, because it might turn
into government intervention; Arther Hinsely, when
appointed Vicar Apostolic to Catholic missions in British
colonies, persuaded the RCM to cooperate.

As a result of this the establishment of schools
witnessed a remarkable spiral. Between 1927-1938 the
number of village schools increased by 310% in 1934, and

---

9. M.O. Beshir, Educational Development in the Sudan
   1898-1956 (Oxford University Press, 1969), p.119.

10. Ibid, appendix I, table X, p.204.

by 585% in 1938. Boys elementary schools showed an increased of 15% by 1934 from 1927, and 26% by 1938. Girls
elementary schools had increased by 16% in 1934 and 18%
by 1938. On the other hand the number of intermediate
schools (boys) remained constant. Trade schools increased
by about 33% in eleven years.

If we go a bit further in investigating the role of
missionary societies in the field of education, we will
find that the CMS was active in both Equatoria and Upper
Nile, while the American Presbyterians were restricted
to Upper Nile and the Roman Catholics to Equatoria
(former Bahr el Ghazal and Mongalla). The sphere system
adopted by the Government was responsible for this distribution yet the emphasis on Equatoria can be explained
by the fact that the province incorporated Bahr el Ghazal
the area most susceptible to Islamic impact. Actually it
witnessed some Islamic revival up to the end of the
Mahdist era. Mongalla on the other hand - now the second
part of Equatoria - was an area of 'pagan' tribes which
represented virgin land for the spread of the gospel.

Information and figures covering the period 1938-
1946[11] show that both RCM and CMS operated schools on
all levels of education: elementary, intermediate and
technical; against the American Presbyterians who had
no technical schools. Yet the RCM went ahead to establish teacher training schools. Concurrently, the number
of students - the better class of converts - studying
in CMS schools increased by 32% in Equatoria and by 4%
in Upper Nile Province. The American Presbyterians in
Upper Nile, increased the number of students in their
schools by 53%, a sharp rise compared to the CMS who
were bent on consolidation rather than expansion. Roman

---

11. Ibid, p.205.

Catholic students increased in Equatoria by 38% and by 84% in Upper Nile in boys' elementary education. The total increase in Equatoria and Upper Nile was 40% and 44% respectively.

The RCM was most influential as far as missionary activities were concerned, being well-equipped with personnel and financial resources. Unlike their CMS counterparts, the RCM personnel were volunteers who received no salaries, and by 1948 their staff was four times greater than the CMS.

The three types of school reflect the content of education: village or bush schools, elementary and trade; yet stress was on large numbers of bush schools, acting as mission stations to spread the gospel. The figures given above indicate clearly the intention to broaden the lower educational base. Though the RCM, concentrated on technical and industrial education the CMS, on the other hand, emphasized literary education. These attitudes were generated by the strategies of both societies as practised elsewhere in Africa and not restricted solely to Sudan.

Notably enough, although in 1926 a decision was taken making English the lingua franca, missionary schools of various types used vernaculars to teach the Bible and other religious subjects, while English was used for secular subjects. The RCM followed their previous experience in the 1840s, by using vernaculars and translations of religious subjects into vernaculars, besides teachers and churchmen tended to create a self-supporting community that lived aloof from the community at large, a logical position for a group coming from the lower classes in Italy.

Educational expansion could be regarded as one feature of consolidation of missionaries' activities.

The development of some missions was another feature.
The CMS for instance made remarkable advances, despite
limitations such as the society's concentration on
evangelism in the north, commitments elsewhere in Africa
and a difficult financial situations because of dependence on contributions. For example in 1908 the CMS was
nearly compelled to abandon its station. The headquarters
of the society in London asked Bishop Gwynne to arrange
for government supervision of mission properties. By
that time Gwynne was quite disillusioned with the CMS;
he wrote to Wingate, "... I shall tell them when I get
home that I either have a voice in the management of
the mission or I wash my hands of the whole business".[12]

This frustration, however, did not last long. Soon
Bishop Gwynne forged ahead, helping in the establishment
of Christian foundations in the Sudan, such that some
thirty-five years later, namely on 15 June 1943, the
Sudan Herald commented: "Last Sunday was a memorable
ocaasion in the history of the Supper Club when many
friends of the Bishop, servicemen and civilians gathered
on the Clergy House Lawn to listen to six speakers who
gave what might be described as sixty minutes biography
of a beloved friend and great spiritual leader". The
'friend and great spiritual leader' was Bishop Gwynne
and the occasion was the Bishops eightieth birthday.
However, the Bishop himself at that time was absent in
Lebanon for medical treatment. Among those attending
were the Governor-General of the Sudan, Huddlestone,
the Civil Secretary, D. Newbold and Bishop A.M. Gelsthorpe
The Governor-General expressed his indebtedness and
Newbold stated, "... one can't directly describe Bishop
Gwynne's influence any more than Homer could describe

---

12. G. Warburg, The Sudan Under Wingate (London, 1971), p.120

the beauty of Helen of Troy". He then read an official
letter addressed to the Bishop:

> `You have been able to make a unique contribution
> to the life and work of the Christian community
> here, because you are almost the remaining eye-
> witness among us of the progress made in the Sudan
> in the last forty-five years. The inspiration,
> understanding and loving-kindness which you, as our
> father in god, have given to all who have come into
> contact with you over this long period and through
> many vicissitudes, have been a wonderful influence
> in the life of the Sudan and will be as enduring
> a memory for us, and for those who came after us,
> as the sacrifice of Charles Gordon whose faith and
> works have been reproduced in your own life and
> teaching´.[13]

Gwynne was presented with a life-size oil portrait and
the sum of Ls.1242; the Government later contributed
Ls.1000 to his pension.

The two points to be emphasised here are that the
Government regarded Bishop Gwynne as a 'resurrection'
of Charles Gordon, who could be genuinely described as
the man who accomplished the combination of missionary
and imperialist motives and so the Government through
its Civil Secretary - re-emphasised the relationship
between missionary and imperial forces.

Furthermore, government interest in securing the
Bishop's pension indicated the extent of intervention,
from mere financial grants to private purposes- though
it is hard to differentiate between Bishop Gwynne and his
work. The Ls.1000 was a fair gesture of gratitude; yet
it is an example of the harmonious relationship between

13. Ibid.

missionaries and administrators. The career of Gwynne from the early days of 1908 to the realm of government gratitude as expressed in 1943, was a true sign of expansion and consolidation of missionary activities, at least as far as the CMS was concerned; yet this also applies to the RCM who surpassed the CMS in all respects.

From 1943 onwards, the missionary movement showed no further expansion. Escalating national upheaval, followed by the establishment of the first independent Sudanese Government, resulted in the liquidation of the grant system and direct government intervention. More importantly the umbrella that used to protect the missionary movement was withdrawn.

A report on Christian missionaries working in the southern Sudan prepared by the Ministry of the Interior in 1960 found that: the total number of missionary stations was one hundred, the total number of staff 596, including 525 expatriates and 71 Sudanese. In 1956 the commission of enquiry on the southern Sudan disturbances estimated the Christian community in the south of between 205- 230,000, was distributed as follows: 180,000-200,000 Catholics and 25,000-30,000 Protestants. Yet the total number of Christians represented less than 10% of the southern population, despite fifty-five years of freedom to prolyetize.

Out of this 230,000 Roman Catholics were in the majority, almost 90%; here the RCM like the CMS, distributed its work between the three southern provinces. Both societies, the RCM being well-backed, and CMS the government's favourite, were able to spread their shadow over the whole south. The emphasis to a large extent was on Equatoria where 45% of missionary stations were established. Two facts can explain this, one is the enormous size of Equatoria which now incorporated both

Mongalla and Bahr El Ghazal, and moreover this era coincided with the southern policy when ideas of detaching the south and making it part of East Africa were flourishing. The missionaries' contribution can't be denied for:

A large proportion of the missionary forces, however, was even in this period engaged in the opening of a new work in hitherto untouched areas, where the number of adherents gained was but a small fraction of the total Christian increase. During and after the First World War for instance, the Nilotic-speaking areas of northern Uganda were entered in force by the Catholic Verona Fathers from the Sudan and also by the CMS from the South.[14]

As early as the 1920s Bishop Gwynne found that it was nearly impossible to cope with his diocese which stretched between the Mediterranean and Uganda. By 1926 it became possible to carve a new diocese of Upper Nile-linked with Uganda - leaving the Muslim areas in Egypt and Sudan separate. Bishop Kitching was consecrated on 29 June 1926 as its first bishop.

Along with this trend of dividing geographical areas into more manageable units the Catholics divided their sphere of Nilotic-speaking people in 1932 and Equatorial Nile was carved out.[15] This concentration led to expansion and consolidation of missionary activities especially in Equatoria Province. The play between political and missionary objectives at this stage - especially those of linking the Sudan with East Africa can be illustrated by the fact that promising students and employees were sent to Uganda to receive training for higher education.

---

14. Oliver, op cit, p.237.

15. Ibid.

Equatoria through its geographical position and size could be a bridgehead for the Christian wave coming from the east coast towards the interior of the continent; its population the bulk of which were not believers in religion, could represent an asset to the Christian community or a threat.

A point to notice was the small number of Sudanese missionary staff (11%) compared with their expatriate counterparts. While the American Presbyterians trained no locals, the R.C.M. and C.M.S. had 39 and 23 respectively and the African inland Mission nine.

Nevertheless, this harmony between missionaries and administration should not be overemphasized because there were many occasions of misunderstanding and disagreement between the two. The source of antagonism could be attributed to two factors: the difference between the missionary (Christian) outlook and the administrative one. Officials adopted Lugard's gospel on native administration and tended to encourage the revival of tribal and customary practices, which in the final analysis conflicted with the objectives of the missionaries, who hoped and worked for undermining tribal structures and replacing them with a "Christian" one, maybe "national Christianity" from which sprang the concept of training Sudanese staff to carry out ecclesiastic duties. For example, the use of schools as agencies for spreading Christianity aggravated the alienation of students from their tribal roots:

the practices of giving school boys foreign Christian names was seen by some administrators as contrary to the idea of making them useful members of their tribes. The assumption of a foreign name would be a symbol of the foreignness of their religion and education and might lead to antagonism between the

tribe and the school, and the latter might be looked
upon as an enemy of tribal culture.[15]
The second reason was that the missions were part of an
external, international organ, from time to time the
missionaries resented submission to the colonial state,
thus reviving the old schism between the Church and the
State. Intervention by the Government was not always
seen in a favourable light. The RCM first opposed the
grants-in-aid system because to them inspection could
lead to government intervention in matters other than
educational. The opposition lasted till 1927 when Hinsely
succeeded in convincing the RCM to cooperate.[16]

The RCM in particular was more hostile to government
officials. It was alien in nationality and religion to
the ruling body and lack of confidence led to verbal
accusations and counter-accusations, and finally to
violation of laws. As early as February 1934 the Secretary of Education and Health, in response to complaints
raised by merchants in Mongalla accusing the RCM of
trading, circulated a letter to the governors of Mongalla,
Bahr el Ghazal, Upper Nile and Kordofan provinces in
which he made the following remarks, "Most of goods sold
and used in barter are gifts from sympathisers in Italy".
The administrative regulation stated:

The sale of clothing to natives who are not bona-
fide resident members of the Mission station would
appear to be contrary to the Administrative Regulations - 'Trading is forbidden in any form'. Barter
and payment in kind are a hindrance to ordinary economic advance - for increased circulation of money
is a crying need for the difficulty of collecting taxes.[17]

---

15. M.O. Beshir, Educational Development p.121
16. Ibid, p.68.
17. CRO Files Equatoria 1/12/51.

This was a self-explanatory letter which reveals the State's attitude. In April 1938 Parr, the Governor of Equatoria, conversed with Archbishop A. Riberi on various topics including the behaviour of missionaries. The Governor said that he had two sources of trouble: one was the use of physical force against grown students. Also since 1935: "District Commissioner, Kapoeta had been receiving a steady stream of complaints that children were being kept in the mission against their parent's will". The Governor did not miss the chance to re-emphasise his belief in the Government's wise policy regarding natives.[18]

Official criticism exceeded these matters of legal violation to speak explicitly about the defects of missionary service, which was the core of the pact between the two forces. On 9 February 1936 Williams, Assistant Director of Education, speaking in a report about education in the south, found that, "The defects of the system were the absence of trained native teachers, emphasis on religion and literary subjects, shortage of staff in C.M.S. and alien character of R.C.M. to the rulers and ruled". The CMS lacked the convenient training, the RCM failed, "to draw the best out of their boys or to imbue them with the fire, responsibility, and practical aptitude that are required of a successful teacher".[19] Eight months later, in October 1936 Cox, then the Director of Education, found that the Italians were unable to appreciate the principles and ideas of administrative policy by virtue of their nationality, social upbringing and inability to communicate well in English. Their existence in the south, therefore, was

18. CRO Files Equatoria 1/12/58
19. In Educational Development....., p.123.

a potential danger to the development and application of native administration.

The missionaries, on the other hand, were not passive; they attacked the Government and its officials as well. The RCM, rather sensitive, played a major role in the confrontation with the Government. As early as 1925, Father Stoppani, Bishop of Bahr el Ghazal, sent a letter to the Governor of the Province asking whether commissioners had changed their policy, he cited a quotation from a statement by an official who said, "It is time this Christianity of natives ceased". He then enumerated restrictions put on the RCM which included:

(a) obtaining of passes for mission teachers.

(b) All new pupils entering the mission have to get permits.

He concluded from all this that, "Now the Missions and Christian natives are openly despised in official circles and before the natives".[20] Thus missionaries viewed restrictions imposed by the medical authorities due to the sleeping sickness campaign as a constraint on their activities. The letter also revealed the bitterness felt by Bishop Stoppani who acused officials of degrading Christians.

However, in addition to these minor disputes there were of course differences due to questions of a theological nature. Here, again, the RCM were the most 'orthodox' in regard to doctrine. In the above mentioned conversation Archbishop Riberi of RCM discussed religious topics with the Governor of Equatoria, M.W. Parr. The Archbishop presented the following argument: 'Since the government, by admitting missions, allowed that the doctrines that they taught were correct so it was morally bound to enforce these doctrines; starting by

20. Ibid.

forbidding divorce. The Governor replied that he could
not "advocate for the primitive African the acceptance
of a higher moral standard about the performance of
marriage than we had in England". The Archbishop then
tackled the crucial question of polygamy, describing it
as socially and morally indefensible; yet the Government
did not use the law to enforce monogamy?[21] The Governor
answered that polygamy in Africa is a social necessity
and benefits the social system by providing for super-
fluous women, the destitute, widows etc?[22] It should be
noted that the Archbishop was ready to accept the use
of law to enforce "Christian" ideas, but the Government
insisted that its interests must receive priority.
Catholics considered their duty as being only towards
Christians, while the Government had to take into
account both Christians and non-Christians.

This equivocal relationship continued up to the out-
break of the war when it became more tense. During the
war, the Government considered the presence of Italians
in the country as a potential source of trouble. But
though it received a proposal from the Apostolic Delegate in February 1938 to replace the non-English fathers
with new London-trained ones the Civil Secretary was
slow in expelling the Italians. But the issue of security became more and more important. The work they were
doing seemed then to be irreplaceable by any other missionary with the issues of both security and expediency
in mind the Civil Secretary wrote in a letter to the
Governor of Equatoria on 12 August 1940 as follows:

1- The military authorities raised on July 17th the
question of the presence of the Italian Missions in

---

21. C.R.O. Files Equatoria 1/12/58.
22. Ibid.

three areas in your province affecting military
security. Internal insecurity west of the Nile would
be an embarrassment to military plans and may entail
withdrawal of troops from their proper defence role
east of the Nile.

2- The Major-General Commanding requested the closing down of all Mission stations in these areas, as
potential centres of Intelligence and Fifth Column
activities.[23]

Thus it was finally decided to close, "all Mission
Stations staffed by Italians on the Nile and to the East
except the intermediate school at Okaru, which is sufficiently isolated, and the Italians concentrated in one
or more places under proper supervision or guarantee".
Here again there is an echo of Wingate's equation of
stationing Italians and inspecting them. A balance
between their utility and potential had to be maintained.

The intermittent nature of these provisions was
clearly revealed when the war was over. In July 1947
C.W. Williams writing to the Civil Secretary after
a tour of the south, took a completely different attitude with regard to replacing the RCM with British
elements:

things have changed since 1939; the political factor
has been eliminated; the educational system and
methods in the Southern Sudan have been reorganized
and improved; there are some 10 Fathers and 7 Sisters
among the Verona Fathers Mission who have spent
a year in England taking the Colonial Department
Course of the Institute of Education; the latest
recruits, both Fathers and Sisters, have mostly
either spent a period of training in England or

---

23. Ibid.

have studied English under British instruction in
Italy or both before coming out to the Sudan; the
Verona Fathers Mission has willingly accepted the
proposed learning of English by Catholic School
masters.[24]

The Director of Education in this same letter to the
Civil Secretary added that it was unlikely that enough
CMS personnel would be found who would be truly English.
Also, experience with the Mill Hill Fathers was not
encouraging or comparable to the work done in evangelist-
ic and educational fields by the RCM. Furthermore, the
Director of Education could not disturb the five-year
development plan, worked out in consultation with RCM.

The importance of these arguments is that they were
put forward by a senior official, the Director of
Education, who had been the first to criticize missionary education in the south as early as 1936. This changing attitude reflects governmental dependence on the
RCM and official recognition of this development. The
best expression of this was the relaxation of restrictions in enforcing the sphere system.

On the other hand the Government's attitude towards
missions belonging to allied forces seemed a bit different during the war. In September 1940 a letter sent by
Mills, Field Superintendent of Sudan United Mission, to
a friend in Melbourne was intercepted by government
censors. The Civil Secretary, on September 30, returned
the letter with the comment that it was:

not only unduly pessimistic but even alarmist. I
should like to say at once that I fully appreciate
the factors which led you to write as you did. It
must be difficult for you at Abri or for your people

---

24. M.R.A.E. Files: Dakhlia EP/SCR/Lb-A-1.

in the Upper Nile to fit the local situation into
its proper perspective in the general war picture of
the Sudan. The shock of the tragedy at Doro, coupled
with the air raid on Malakal, must naturally have
increased your difficulties in the respect. I know
also that there has been loose talks about a likely
raid on Melut... while repeating, therefore, that
your Mission is still at liberty to evacuate whom
it will... but I can assure you that the situation
is very far from being gloomy as it no doubt appears
to you at Abri... You will also appreciate the further
most important point that the wrong impression given
to Missionaries who are in close contact with the
natives might easily be passed on to latter; perhaps
quit unconciously but with most unfortunate results.[25]

The Sudan United Mission, one of the 'conservative
evangelists', received its subsidies from international
committees in Europe, U.S.A. and Australia. Such wide
international connections necessitated the soft tone that
governed the Civil Secretary's letter. The major concern,
then, was not to reflect internal lack of confidence to
the outside world, but at the same time not to pass on
anxiety to the natives.

The main source of trouble, however, was the sphere
system both as a concept and in practice. At the time of
its inception American Presbyterians protested against
it and against the Sudan Government in putting boundaries
around the preaching of God's word.[26] The CMS were no less

25. C.R.O. Files Upper Nile 1/30/230.

26. R. Hill, 'Government and Christian Mission in the
    Anglo-Egyptian Sudan, 1899-1914' Middle Eastern Studies,
    No: 2 (January 1965), pp.113-34.

critical and the Apostolic Delegate expressed their view
in a conversation with the Civil Secretary; he described
the sphere system as restrictive and complained that
a great number of staff were unnecessarily concentrated
in certain areas.[27] Ten years later, in 1948, Archbishop
Matthews openly attacked the sphere system and called
for its abolition. He argued that it had only been practised in Germany's African colonies before 1914.[28] The RCM
had the lion's share in criticizing the sphere system
arguing that it constituted a deliberate obstacle to
their missionary work. Archbishop Hinsely, at the head
of RCM in Kenya described it as 'bad' when he was interviewed by the Secretary for Education and Health,
Matthews, in February 1930.[29] Moreover, the Vatican itself
asked for its abolition in 1935.[30]

Basically, the system was criticized both because it
bore heavily on the individual who could not always get
the spiritual comfort of his own church and because it
was not practised anywhere else. In answer to these
points the Governor of Equatoria in August 1948 pointed
out that the Sudan, unlike any other colony in Africa,
was - uniquely - ruled through a condominium treaty.[31]
He added, "the sphere has served us well and I doubt
whether we have yet outgrown the need for it. It may not
be morally right to divide the country into spheres, but

---

27. C.R.O Files Equatoria 1/12/58.

28. R.O. Collins, 'The Establishment of Christian missions
    and their rivalry in Southern Sudan', Tarikh, Vol.3,
    No. 1 (1969), p.46.

29. C.R.O. Files Bahr el-Ghazal 1/4/24.

30. C.R.O. Files Equatoria 1/12/51.

31. C.R.O. Files Upper Nile 1/29/227.

at least it has been politically expedient, it has done
no one any harm, and it has done many a lot of good".
But that is an example of obstinate officialdom. Matthews,
Secretary for Education and Health, in the conversation
with Archbishop Hinsely referred to earlier defended the
system and pointed out its merits at the early stages
and that its existence made it possible to win more converts more quickly. He added, "I was not prepared to
say that the time had yet come for their abolition in
the Sudan though I admitted that they should not per-
sist for ever.[32]

In fact the Government reaffirmed this attitude
many times through its officials. On 13 January 1926
the Private Secretary of the Governor-General wrote to
the Civil Secretary: "The Governor-General agrees that
it is understandable to alter the regulations which were
approved by Lord Cromer and circulated to the Mission
Societies by letters of the Secretary General dated
January 7th, 1905.[33] On 6 March 1933 the Secretariat for
Education and Health stated in a circulated letter that:
"It is the intention of the Government to preserve the
principle of the sphere system and His Excellency
desires the attention of the province staff drawn to
the regulations as laid down in the Administrative
Regulations Chapter XIX".[34]

Yet, on 7 February 1937, the Governor-General, in
a meeting attended by Archdeacon Shaw and Bishop Kitching of the Upper Nile bishopric re-emphasized the point
He said, "whether a Sphere System existed or not......

32. C.R.O. Files Bahr El Ghazal 1/4/24.
33. C.R.O. Files Equatoria 1/12/51.
34. Ibid.

there was no intention of a general order of abolition of the Sphere System. They could remain roughly as they exist, but any clash of interest should be settled by adjustment between the parties concerned".[35] Here the Governor-General was quoting his experience in Tanganyika. The important thing was his reference to internal arguments but its Achille's heel lay in its application, the violation of the system by the RCM presented the greater danger. The CMS, the greater rival, was in no better position in terms of finance and personnel to respond to the challenge. Moreover, it suffered internal problems - indicating the external nature of the society when the Bible Churchmen's Missionary Society in East Africa seceeded during the 1920s from the main body. So, both societies, the CMS and the Bible Churchmen's Missionary Society, though belonging to the Church of England, were now separate.[36]

The new society applied to work in Toposa area in 1932 and was granted permission to open a school at Nagie, near Kapoeta two years later. In 1938/1939 the Bible Churchmen's Missionary Society applied to open another station at Opari, but the request was viewed with disfavour because of the mission's poor record at Nagie.[37] By 1940 the society began to disintegrate when some of its staff were recalled to East Africa, and others from East Africa refused to come to Equatoria. This finally led to the withdrawal of the mission from the Sudan.

---

35. Ibid. 35.
36. M.R.A.E. Files Dakhlia MC/SC/B-A.
37. Ibid.

Yet to the CMS the main competitor and rival was
the RCM. The fragility of the sphere system became apparent by 1930. Late in 1929 R.G.C. Brook, Governor of
Bahr el Ghazal, decided to amalgamate the two districts
of Yambio and Tambura, and while investigating the problems of such amalgamation, he discovered, to his surprise,
that the RCM occupied territory belonging to CMS. An
investigation revealed that the RCM extended their work
between 1912-1926 into the territories of five chiefs:
Wando, Rikita, Bazia, Babindo and Iriwo, which was equal
to the CMS headquarters at Yambio.[38] The remarkable point
here was that neither the District Commissioners nor the
CMS knew of this and thought that the area belong to RCM;
discussions then started to readjust the sphere lines.
While CMS generously agreed to hand over all five territories except Iriwo, with other adjustments, the Catholic
prefect of Bahr el Ghazal withdrew his consent after pressure from his chiefs and instructions from Archbishop
Hinsley.[39]

The external influence here was most predominant.
More investigations of records showed that the RCM undertook this extension deliberately, for the head of RCM
was quite aware of the boundary.[40] To overcome the deadlock, MacMichael, then acting Governor-General, suggested
the retention of Iriwo's territory by the RCM against
warnings and guarantees of no further encouragement by
the Catholics. While Rev. Shaw responded to this by accusing both the Sudan Government and RCM of plotting
against the CMS. The Prefect of Bahr el Ghazal, Mgr. A.
Stoppani, put it like this:

---

38. C.R.O. Files Bahr el Ghazal 1/4/21.

39. Ibid.

40. Ibid.

We went among the people of that chief with a permit
from the local governmnnt authorities. A goodly
number of the people sought our ministrations. For
more than ten years the legality of our presence
in that country was unquestioned. In conscience we
are bound not to abandon our people who in that
district desire our religious endeavours on their
behalf. We can't accept the zone system, which is
enforced in other parts of British territory in
Africa. In school work we accept the general control
of your department; in religious matters we can't.[41]

In the end, the acting Governor-General succeeded in
settling the matter in Europe by reviving the proposal
of the CMS to give up four of the five territories to
the RCM.[42]

But this dispute led to increasing tension between
both societies. Each started by operating competing
schools and churches and police had to patrol streets at
times to keep peace during church services. The societies
proved to have little charity for each other. This raised
the issue that, "the future of the sphere system was
obviously in jeopardy if the Catholic encroachment went
unchallenged... the sphere system had failed to prevent
precisely the competition between mission societies which
Wingate and his successors had feared".[43]

The situation confronted the Government with a choice,
either to coexist with incessant disputes or to abolish
the sphere system and leave the gate open to increased
tension. In a sort of a compromise under great pressure
from Sir Stewert Symes, the Governor-General, the heads

---

41. R.C.O. Files Bahr el-Ghazal 1/4/21.
42. Collins, op. cit., p.44.
43. Ibid.

of the societies held a conference at Juba on March 4, 1935, under the auspices of the Government, where the representatives of RCM and CMS agreed to cooperate; they promised not to hinder each other's activities and to solve all disputes between them in a friendly manner. Thus the Government tried to make the missions responsible for keeping peace themselves. Collins summed up the experience as follows, "The sphere system had become a means to nationalize the violation of sphere boundaries while still permitting the Sudan Government to control the rivalry and to ensure that the mission's education activities would be contained".[44]

Yet the Government, aware of lack of good will between both sects, two months after the Juba conference started to promote a new policy, the main lines of which were:

(a) to maintain the sphere system in principle, but the gradual interaction of missionary activity on the boundaries should be worked out.

(b) that activities of one mission within the sphere of another mission might be permitted near the boundary and in response to a genuine popular local demand.

(c) activities outside the sphere should be discouraged except in response to such demand.

(d) district commissioners should observe this and act as judges.

On 8 January 1938, the Governor-General sent a note to the Secretary of Education which explained the new policy. He wrote:

The policy of Mission Spheres has been redefined. Our recognition that spheres of religious influence

---

44. Ibid, p.46.

can't be made sacrosant does not dispute their
practical advantages in some respect or that "inter-
lacement of Missions" should be affected other than
by a very gradual process. How gradual must depend
on a number of imponderable factors, material or
spiritual. Meanwhile, recognizing that "monopolistic"
treatment of the spheres is no longer practical, nor
morally defensible, shall relax prohibition of all
evangelistic development beyond the limits of existing spheres, and the intersectarian agreement of 4
March 1935 at Juba will facilitate this. We shall
nevertheless support the priority of the several
sectarian establishments each in its sphere, more
especially by preferential treatment in respect of
schools and educational, medical subsidies. The
application of this policy (no better one) will
encounter some difficulties that may be minimized
with good-will and by political intervention-frequ-
ently from district Commissioners.[45]

Besides, this new policy agreed with the ideas of
some administrators', especially in the Education Department, who, in order to execute any of their plans,
had to make a deal with each mission in its sphere and
use different languages in various fields, the result
of which would be duplication of effort and expenditure
of money for little yield. Shaw of this department,
early in 1930 thought that, "If we were going to abolish
them in near future, it would save us a vast amount of
trouble as regards rearrangements of existing boundaries
etc..i.e. the encroachment in Tambura-Yambio area".[46]
But the Government biased by the historical sanctity of

45. C.R.O. Files Equatoria 1/12/51.
46. C.R.O. Files Bahr el Ghazal 1/4/24.

the sphere system preferred natural death to incurring
responsibility for abolishing it abruptly.

Thus it is clear that between 1935-1948 each mission
worked for consolidation and expansion. The CMS increased
its staff from 30 to 46 and established a new station at
Zaraf Island. The RCM by 1948 was four times as big as
the CMS. Under the leadership of Bishop Mason the Catholics made a number of encroachments to establish stations
near Rumbek in the Dinka sphere of the CMS, who, unable
to cope with this, appealed for the British section of
the African Inland Mission to assume responsibility for
stations at Akot and Gel River to embrace the Rumbek
area, thus revealing an undeniable "national" partisan-
ship under a religious cloak. The African Inland Mission
accepted the offer.

In 1948 the RCM were granted permission to appoint
a chaplain at the government secondary school to serve
Catholic students, provided that no proselytism would be
carried out. The Catholics who intended conversion
through this chaplaincy applied in 1951 for permission
to carry out missionary work.[47] Though their application
was then rejected, through their persistence and the
failure of both CMS and the African Inland Mission to
provide convenient staff, approval was finally granted
to the RCM in 1952, although the Civil Secretary claimed
that the Government's policy was "sphere without exception", for all practical purposes the sphere system was
dead.

The sphere system had made missionary peace possible
in southern Sudan. Although denounced by the Catholics,

---

47. Collins, op cit., p. 47.

who believed that they would prevail in a land of free competition, the sphere system was also attacked by the Protestants, but attacked only in principle, since the defence of their faith depended as much on the limitation of their work as on the truth of their message. Administratively, it was a brilliant success. Wingate had wanted peace, frugality, and Christianity in the Southern Sudan - in that order.[48]

By the late 1930s the Christian presence in the southern Sudan came under attack from Islamic and Sudanese national forces. The free atmosphere in which the missions operated, though it opened the door to Christianity, had also encouraged the promotion of antagonistic elements, i.e. national and Islamic forces. It is no surprise that the newly born Sudanese nationalism concerned itself with what was going on in the South.[49] The revival of Sudanese nationalism received a new impetus by the conclusion of the Anglo-Egyptian Treaty of 1936, which permitted the return of Egyptian influence to the Sudan and aided the growing national forces at that time. The formation of the Graduate's Congress in 1937 was a landmark in the history of Sudanese nationalism.

Congress was among other things critical of the southern policy and accused the British district commissioners of working towards separating the south from the north. Its rejection of participation in the Advisory Council in 1946 was partly based on the fact that the

48. Ibid.

49. H. Abdin, 'The growth of the nationalist movement In the 'Sudan', (Unpublished Ph.D. Thesis, University of Wisconsin, 1970), pp. 68-75

council was not representative of the whole Sudan. It
went as far as ordering its members not to join the
Advisory Council. Those who did join were dismissed from
its membership.

The failure of the Advisory Council encouraged
nationalist elements to harden their opposition in the
media. Al Sudan al-jadid, a weekly paper, published from
time to time articles under the heading "What is going
on in the South". In July 1946 one of its writers called
for a unified Sudan linked with ameliorated communications, asking the political parties to give more attention to the south. It then turned to the missionary
question, accusing missionaries of connecting politics
with religion and justifying political invasion through
their evangelistic education. Success came with official
cancellation of the southern policy:

> and we whould therefore restate our Southern policy,
> and do so publicly, as follows: The policy of the
> Sudan Government regarding the Southern Sudan is to
> act upon the facts that the peoples of the Southern
> Sudan are distinctively African and negroid, but
> that geography and economics combine (so far as can
> be forseen at the present time) to render them in-
> extricably bound for future development to the
> middle-eastern arabicised Northern Sudan: and there-
> fore to ensure that they shall, by educational and
> economic development be equipped to stand up for
> themselves in the future as socially and economic-
> ally the equals of their partners of the Northern
> Sudan in the Sudan of the future.[50]

The above is an excerpt from the memorandum circulated

---

50. Beshir, The Southern Sudan, p.120.

on December 16, 1946 concelling the former southern
policy.

Along these favourable lines a conference was held
in Juba on 13 June 1947 to investigate political developments in the southern Sudan. The resolutions adopted
were, "Firstly, that the Southerners wanted a unified
Sudan; secondly, that they want to participate in the
proposed Legislative Assembly".[51] It was regarded as an
achievement under the aegis of the nationalist movement.

The second question attracting nationalists to the
south was the educational issue which caused much concern. The Graduate's congress in 1939 sent a note to
the Government on education in the south, saying:

Education in southern Sudan was mainly in hands of
missions aided by government. This, in our opinion,
is responsible for the backwardness of education in
that sphere... as the main object of Missionary
Schools is consequently low and therefore, so far,
has very little effect in the life of the Southerners. Tribes still live in such a primitive and
inhuman condition that would not be fit the twenti-
eth century.

We therefore venture to suggest that improvement of
education in the S o u t h can not be attained by
expanding and improving the present missionary
schools at the Government expense but by opening
entirely new schools on the lines of those in the
Northern Sudan. The Arabic language will provide
a suitable lingua franca as it already spoken by
most of tribesmen and will thus solve the present
difficulties expressed by the Director of Education

51. Ibid, appendix 9.

in his report for 1936.[52]

Thus the Congress outlined its attitude towards education in the South. In 1942 it was reiterated when a twelve-point memorandum called for the unification of education in both part of the country by cancelling subventions to missionary schools.[53]

Newspapers played no less important a role. Al-Sudan al-jadid published an article which claimed that the output of missionary education in the south was not in accord with the time and efforts invested, raising the issue of the Arabic language which after all is the language of Christians in the Near East. Against this overstressed issue of Arabic, the missionaries had to react. Rev. Baroni, Principal of Comboni College after surveying the history of the College wrote in the Sudan Star on 24 October, 1949: "At Wau the Mission School taught both Arabic and English from the very beginning. These days I hear some talks going on here in the North against the missionaries of the South; but the natives as well as the Muslim community, which is also strong one, and the Gallaba merchants too, have always been and are now very respectful, sympathetic and hopeful to the missionaries".

Yet the most important of these reactions was the national Islamic tide against the missionary presence. Traces of their reactions can be found in 1936. Just after the conclusion of the Anglo-Egyptian Treaty of 1936 the Grand Qadi who was an Egyptian met the Governor-General to discuss the possibility of sending an Islamic mission to the south. Not long before this

---

52. Beshir, Educational Development, appendix V.

53. K.D.D. Henderson, The Making of Modern Sudan (London, 1965), p.541.

incident when al-Sudan al-jadid published an article on "Religious Freedom and Necessity of Removing Restriction on Islam in the Southern Sudan", (25 December 1936) the pact between government and missions was severly criticized, with insistent demands to remove obstacles retarding Islamic propagation. These incidents, though appearing isolated at the time, bore the features of the new movement of Egyptian, Islamic-national complex.

The nationalist movement which boycotted the Advisory Council, received new impetus to direct its attention towards the missionary presence in the south. It started when a group of northerners appealed to the local authorities to build a mosque in Juba. The refusal attracted the attention of the nationalist movement, who grasped this opportunity and the battle of Juba mosque put into perspective the confrontation between the two main forces. The nationalist reaction to the issue was to insist on the establishment of Islamic missionary centres, starting with Juba mosque.

The Government refused at first, but the nationalist movement insisted on Juba as Equatoria was regarded as having a large non-religious population. Once permission was granted in 1946, Congress organs throughout the country mobilized and launched a subscription and almost every town and village sent its share. Egypt always contributed to philanthropic building of schools and mosques. Moreover, the Egyptian Government helped the expansion of Islam in the south by sending Sheikh Simsa'ah (of Sudanese origin), to be the Imam of the mosque. The British officials accepted reluctantly and restricted the Imam's movements to Juba area.

In 1945 the confrontation assumed wider dimensions when the Foreign Section of the Ahmedia TAriqa based in the Punjab in India, appealed to the Civil Secretary for

permission to work in the Sudan. Though they did not
mention the south directly, the Civil Secretary rejected
the request on the Grand Qadi's recommendations that,
"Ahmedia Group is adopting a creed contrary to the Islamic creed... the Sudan is an Islamic country and is
adopting a correct creed; and I don't think that the
Sudan is in need of such preachers".[54] This antagonized
the Ahmedia who sent a letter accusing the Government of
practises contrary to the declared policy of freedom of
conscience to all citizens of the empire. More important,
they argued that:

> though Sudan is a Muslem country, even Christian
> Missionaries are allowed there to do their mission-
> ary work without hindrance. It is indeed strange
> that Orthodox Muslems of Sudan are not provoked by
> the preaching of Christian Missions who reject the
> Holy Prophet of Islam, but they are provoked by the
> entry of Muslem missionaries who desire to go there
> for preaching the beauties of Islam. If a Muslem
> missionary can not enter an Islamic country for
> religious service, Christian missionaries have still
> less right to do so.[55]

Debate on this issue eventually continued for a long
time; in 1935 the Ahmedia Group asked for permission to
work in the southern Sudan only, but again their application was rejected.

These various forces: the fact that the sphere system
did not work efficiently, the development of Sudanese
nationalism with an Islamic dimension concerned about
southern affairs, the cancellation of the southern policy;
then potential external Islamic encroachment in the

---

54. M.R.A.E. Files SCO/46 B-6/2.
55. Ibid.

south exemplified by Juba mosque and the Ahmedia incident all led the Government to redefine its policy towards missionary activities in the south in 1947. The Government stated its responsibility to ensure tolerance between various creeds, it also reaffirmed its determination to establish freedom of conscience and religious teaching and to ensure that religious feeling was not aggravated by political ends. More importantly it stated that government policy towards Islamic missions was the same as towards Christian missions and could be summarized as follows: the charge of religious persecution was glaringly substantiated by the measures introduced by the 1930 'Southern Policy'... One clause, in the official document issued in 1946, embodying measures to redress the wrong done states: `Freedom of facilities for worship for all sects is indispensable, and religious discrimination such as had existed, though it may not have been admitted... must cease. A creed must prevail by administration of its own truth and not by suppression of other creeds'. It was only then that the ban was steadily lifted and other faiths, including Islam, were allowed to compete with Christian missionaries.[56]

---

56. Central Office of Information, op. cit, p.23.